Financial Reform in China

This book focuses on the importance for China to correct the present imbalance in the relationship between the financial sector and the real economy.

The book looks at China's current financial system in terms of "extractive" and "inclusive". It asserts that the financial sector is producing huge "siphonic effects" that distort the overall development of the Chinese economy. Like a giant magnet, the financial sector attracts too many innovation factors, such as talents, capital and entrepreneurship away from the real economy and inhibits the development of the latter. Hence, the book argues that China's financial system must now be thoroughly reformed to become an inclusive financial system, where finance and the rest of the economy can co-exist and develop in support of each other.

Changwen Zhao is Research Fellow and Director-General of the Research Department of Industrial Economy of the Development Research Center of the State Council (DRC), China.

Hongming Zhu is Associate Research Fellow in the Financial Research Institute, Development Research Center of the State Council (DRC), China.

Routledge Studies in the Modern World Economy

For a full list of titles in this series, please visit www.routledge.com/series/SE0432

Financial Reform in China
The Way from Extraction to Inclusion

Changwen Zhao and Hongming Zhu

LONDON AND NEW YORK

First published 2018 by Routledge

2 Park Square, Milton Park, Abingdon, Oxfordshire OX14 4RN
52 Vanderbilt Avenue, New York, NY 10017

Routledge is an imprint of the Taylor & Francis Group, an informa business

First issued in paperback 2019

British Library Cataloguing-in-Publication Data
A catalogue record for this book is available from the British Library

Library of Congress Cataloging-in-Publication Data
Names: Zhao, Changwen, 1964– author. | Zhu, Hongming, author.
Title: Financial reform in China : the way from extraction to
    inclusion / by Changwen Zhao and Hongming Zhu.
Description: Abingdon, Oxon ; New York, NY : Routledge, 2018. |
    Series: Routledge studies in the modern world economy ; 169 |
    Includes bibliographical references and index.
Identifiers: LCCN 2017008251 | ISBN 9781138736030 (hardback) |
    ISBN 9781315186139 (ebook)
Subjects: LCSH: Finance—China. | Finance—Government policy—
    China. | China—Economic policy—2000– | China—Economic
    conditions—2000–
Classification: LCC HG187.C6 Z44777 2018 | DDC
    332.0951—dc23
LC record available at https://lccn.loc.gov/2017008251

ISBN: 978-1-138-73603-0 (hbk)
ISBN: 978-0-367-37487-7 (pbk)

Typeset in Galliard
by Apex CoVantage, LLC

Contents

Figures

Tables

Preface

In order to build an analytical framework for financial reform based on coopetition, this book uses the theory of contradiction as its philosophical foundation and the theory of economic growth as the economic foundation.

This book puts forward a core concept. The Chinese financial sector is both "overdeveloped" and "underdeveloped". In the real economy, China's financial system is inefficient and "extractive". This must be transformed by financial reforms which build an efficient and inclusive financial system, where finance and the rest of the economy may co-exist and develop in harmony with each other.

The best way to realize this goal is to withdraw the "financial restraint" system (Hellmann, Murdock and Stiglitz, 1998) in order to remove interest margin protection through interest rate liberalization; lift market access control and develop multi-layer capital market and non-bank financial institutions; reform policy-oriented and commercial financial institutions to create a unified, open, competitive and orderly financial market environment; and improve regulation to ensure sound risk management while withdrawing financial restraints.

Outside the financial sector, supportive measures should be taken to eliminate government implicit guarantees for financing entities, including reform of state-owned assets and state-owned enterprises (SOEs), fiscal and taxation system reform and appropriate macro-control policies. Efforts should be made to adjust industrial policies and reform education and scientific research systems to give impetus to the development of the real economy.

We are aware that this book will cause debate, some of which may not be productive. We seek to prevent misunderstanding, and encourage readers to focus their attention on current problems in China's financial system and participate in constructive discussions on key issues for future financial reform and development in China. It is to be hoped that by exploring six questions in this preface some misunderstandings can be avoided.

What are "extraction" and "inclusiveness"?

This book is subtitled *The Way from Extraction to Inclusion*. So we first need to clarify some terms: What is "extraction"? What is an "extractive" financial system? What is meant by "inclusiveness"? And what is an "inclusive" financial system?

Unlike studies using traditional perspectives, this book looks at the relationship between finance and the real economy from the perspective of competition and cooperation and considers both as a unity of opposites. On the one hand, they are cooperative and interdependent. Finance cannot be separated from the real economy in that its growth depends on serving the real economy. The real economy cannot be divorced from finance since it needs financial support and a stable financial environment. On the other hand, they compete with and reject each other, mainly in terms of production factors, policies, profits and corporate decision making. Therefore, there are two dimensions to the development status of a country's financial sector: the "cooperative dimension" and the "competitive dimension".

"Extraction" and "inclusion" are two states of financial development operating in the competitive dimension. In an "extractive" financial system, finance is in direct competition with the real economy, posing an evident negative externality towards the growth of the real economy. In an "inclusive" financial system, competition is not apparent between the two. There is no evident negative externality.

We regard China's current financial system as "extractive" because of the severe imbalance between the financial system and the real economy. The financial sector produces an obvious "siphonic effect", and sucks many innovation factors such as talent, capital and entrepreneurship from the real economy to the fictitious sector. This can be seen as an "extractive" behaviour or exertion of an "extractive" effect on the real economy.

The terms extraction and extractive are strictly limited to the scope of economic growth. It is identical with negative externality in this book, because they both end with a negative effect on innovation and economic growth.

We set the goal for financial reforms as "inclusiveness" instead of "co-prosperity" for three reasons. First, "extraction" and "inclusiveness" are two different states in the same dimension, while "extraction" and "co-prosperity" are not. Second, "inclusiveness" emphasizes the elimination of financial negative externality, while "co-prosperity" has a broader connotation and poses more requirements under the cooperative dimension. Third, "inclusiveness" is achievable through financial reforms, while "co-prosperity" would depend more on structural reform of the real economy. To conclude, "co-prosperity" poses higher requirements than "inclusiveness".

What is financial "overdevelopment"?

"Overdevelopment" in this book does not mean that China's financial sector is well-developed and cannot possibly be better. It is "overdeveloped" compared to the status of the real economy because its high profits and high employee income have sabotaged the reasonable reward structure on which a harmonious relationship between finance and the real economy depends (Baumol, 1990). This "overdevelopment" creates a strong negative externality on the real economy.

Despite concerns over financial "overdevelopment" or negative externality, we can by no means deny the positive role of finance in supporting the real economy by facilitating payment, mobilizing savings, managing risks and providing financing services. Also, in terms of the management of financial "overdevelopment", simply limiting the growth of the financial sector is not an option. The correct way is to remove unreasonable factors in the system and mechanisms through systematic reforms.

To a certain extent, financial "overdevelopment" in China is the result of the old financial development pattern. In this case, financial reform should aim to transform the growth pattern of the financial sector.

How can there be "overdevelopment" and "underdevelopment" at the same time?

People may misunderstand or doubt the co-existence of "overdevelopment" and "underdevelopment" in the financial sector. Readers may interpret this expression in two ways when they see it for the first time.

First, "overdevelopment" and "underdevelopment" co-exist in terms of the financial structure. In other words, the banking sector is "overdeveloped" while the capital market is "underdeveloped". This is not the focus of our book, although it is one way of looking at the issue. What we discuss is their co-existence in the entire system.

Second, their co-existence from a holistic view appears self-contradictory. In fact, it is not. From the coopetition perspective, "overdevelopment" and "underdevelopment" fall into two different categories.

"Overdevelopment" refers to the financial development state in the competitive dimension between the financial system and the real economy. The other end of the spectrum is "not overdeveloped". If financial development is negatively correlated with innovation and economic growth, then the financial system has an obvious negative externality and is thus "overdeveloped"; otherwise, it is "not overdeveloped".

"Underdevelopment" refers to the financial development state under the cooperative dimension between the financial system and the real economy. The other end of the spectrum is "not underdeveloped". If the financial sector is inefficient in serving the real economy due to its high financing costs and low accessibility, then the financial system is "underdeveloped"; if the financial sector boasts high efficiency, reasonable financing costs and relatively high accessibility, then the system is "not underdeveloped".

In fact, they not only co-exist, but are also correlated. "Underdevelopment" is an essential cause of "overdevelopment", and resolving "underdevelopment" can help in addressing "overdevelopment".

"Overdevelopment" and "underdevelopment" are terms that carry different meanings in this book than elsewhere in economic discourse. That is why "overdevelopment" under the competitive dimension and "underdevelopment" under the cooperative dimension are put in quotation marks to indicate the difference.

Why should financial "overdevelopment" be re-examined?

It appears self-evident that "overdevelopment" and the "siphonic effect" of the financial sector can do harm, but this assumption merits scrutiny. For example, before the financial crisis hit the world economy, the mainstream view was, "what is good for Wall Street is good for the country".

To prove the harm of the "siphonic effect", this book makes a distinction between two links in resource distribution, "primary allocation" and "re-allocation". "Primary allocation" means that resources are distributed over the entire economic system, and in this book it refers to the distribution between the financial sector and the real economy. "Re-allocation" means that available resources are distributed among various sectors of the real economy through the financial system, for example, among enterprises with different ownership systems, different sizes, different lines of business and different innovation abilities.

The "siphonic effect" is the result of a distorted "primary allocation". If "re-allocation" is efficient enough, the "primary allocation" distortion is negligible. However, the "re-allocation" efficiency is determined by how reasonable the "primary allocation" is. This book examines two effects that the financial system produces in the "re-allocation" link: the "multiplier effect" and the "leakage effect". If the "multiplier effect" is mainly at play in "re-allocation" as a "converter" and "amplifier", then an efficient "re-allocation" could make up for a distorted "primary allocation" without dragging down the efficiency of resource distribution in the entire economic system. Unfortunately, the "multiplier effect" does not work without preconditions. As factors swarm in that the financial system can convert, a "leakage effect" would occur. Then, the distorted "primary allocation" would reduce the efficiency of resource distribution **in the entire economic system.**

Why do we say the financial sector is highly profitable?

One of the basic arguments put forward in this book is that the financial sector is highly profitable. To prove it we use six sets of data about the profit proportion and the profit margin to conduct international and domestic comparison. Even so, the argument may still cause doubts.

Some people hold that bank profits are artificially high, a fantasy resulting from the "current profits and delayed risks" which is typical in the banking sector. Others believe that the high profits of the financial sector are periodic and short-term, suggesting that they are not that high in the long run. If one looks back to the 1990s, one can find that the profitability of the banking sector did not exceed the average profit margin of all businesses and the profits were meagre. The so-called high profits are nothing but a defective, perhaps biased, conclusion derived from studies flawed because they covered only short periods of time.

Scholars reasoning from these two ideas conclude that the high profits of the banking sector are an "illusion". It is undeniable that both ideas are based on fact and can help us better understand and resolve the problem of excessively high bank profits. However, they do not pose a challenge to the basic argument in this book that the financial sector is excessively profitable.

This book looks at the high profits of the banking sector from the perspective of the allocation of innovation elements. When making decisions, individuals and enterprises are always influenced by the profit level, whether it is a short-term, temporary "illusion" or a real, long-term "fact". Therefore, "illusion" and "fact" would exert the same effect on resource allocation. There are two primary causes. First, accounting profit is the major signal for enterprise to make decisions instead of the more reasonable profit indicators which also have drawbacks. Second, it is difficult for individuals and enterprises to make decisions by considering development over a long period of time, which is seldom longer than the average lifespan of enterprises, let alone twenty years or more. Therefore, it might be too much to ask people, especially entrepreneurs, to look at bank profits from a long-term perspective.

How to interpret the banking profit growth slowdown?

Profit growth in the banking sector has slowed down. In 2014, commercial banks saw only a 9.65 percent growth of net profits. As the economy witnesses slower growth and structural adjustment, and the effect of earlier national stimulus policies settles down, it is possible that profit growth in the financial sector will drop further. So how should we approach this trend? Does it mean that China's financial system will stop being "extractive" by itself? Or does it indicate it is unnecessary to accelerate reforms so as to transform the financial system from "exclusiveness" to "inclusiveness"? The answer is no.

First, "exclusiveness" is a relative concept. Profits are distributed in a very unbalanced way between the financial sector and the real economy. As long as the financial sector has a higher profit growth rate than the real economy, it will only become more "extractive". Although the year 2014 saw a clear profit drop in the financial sector, the real economy saw an even further decline. According to the National Bureau of Statistics of China, profit growth of industrial enterprises above designated size was only 3.3 percent in 2014. Under such circumstances, the imbalance between the financial sector and the real economy has been aggravated rather than improved.

Second, even if the profit growth of the financial sector has dropped to well below that of the real economy, the financial system would only stop being "extractive" on the surface. This is where we need to make a distinction between various causes of slower financial profit growth. If it is simply driven by the economic cycle or the financial cycle, the financial system would only rid itself of the title "extraction" superficially. Once the economy starts to recover, "extraction" is expected to come back. If there are causes other than the economic cycle such as interest rate liberalization, lifting of market access control, development of a multi-layer capital market and other reform measures aimed at withdrawing "financial restraints", it is possible to remove the "extraction" once and for all.

Lastly, it is important to impede financial reforms while the financial sector manages a good profit growth rate. On the one hand, the profits can absorb some of the reform costs so as to avoid spillovers outside the financial sector. On the other hand, developing the real economy through financial reforms would help maintain financial stability. If instead of taking the initiative to make adjustments we simply wait for the profits of the financial sector to drop to a balanced level with the real economy, we would be confronted with the outbreak of a financial crisis and the subsequent expensive crisis rescue. This would be a disaster for economic growth.

This book contains nine chapters. The first four chapters focus on the principal aspect of the contradiction between the financial sector and the real economy: their competition. Chapter 1 is "From Extraction to Inclusion: A New Analytical Framework". It summarizes three views on financial centralism, financial cooperation and financial coopetition. It is argued that besides cooperation, the financial sector is also in competition with the real economy, mainly in terms of production factors, profits, preferential policies and corporate decision-making behaviours. From the perspective of financial competition and cooperation, this chapter describes China's financial system as extractive and inefficient, puts forward one-dimensional, two-dimensional and three-dimensional models of financial reforms, and explains the goals and paths of financial reforms.

Chapter 2 explores the "Extractive Financial System". First it demonstrates the co-existence of "overdevelopment" and "underdevelopment" in China's financial system, then discusses several problems which result from the "extractive" financial system: excessively high profits in the financial sector, overpaid financial workers and high financing costs for the real economy.

Chapter 3, "The Finance Curse", discusses the harm caused by an "extractive" financial system and summarizes five mechanisms which impose negative effects on economic growth: the "siphonic effect", the "erosion effect", the interest group mechanism, the corporate financial mechanism and the financial instability mechanism. In the analysis of the "siphonic effect", a distinction is made between two links of resource distribution: "primary allocation" and "re-allocation". The "multiplier effect" and the "leakage effect" in the "re-allocation" is discussed and the "siphonic effect" is considered the result of distortion in the "primary allocation".

Chapter 4 deals with "The Formation of 'Extractive' Financial Systems": why has China's financial system become "extractive"? It is believed that the cause is our financial restraint policy (mainly supported by interest margin protection and restrictions on market access and asset substitution). The preliminary conclusion is that China's "extractive" financial system first developed around 2008.

The first four chapters focus on the principal aspect of the contradiction between the financial sector and the real economy: their competition. Then Chapter 5 and Chapter 6 focus on another aspect: cooperation.

Chapter 5 examines "Insufficient Competition, Implicit Guarantee and Financial Inefficiency". It discusses why the financial sector is inefficient and suggests the cause is insufficient competition at the financial level and implicit guarantee at the non-financial level. Insufficient competition involves three levels: within the banking system, between/among banks and the capital market and between/among banks and non-bank financial institutions. Implicit guarantee is provided to industrial SOEs, local government financing vehicles and the real estate sector.

Chapter 6, "Financial Risks", discusses the status quo and the causes of risk in China's financial sector and its risk management capability under different circumstances.

If Chapters 2 to 6 diagnose the disease in China's financial system, then Chapters 7 to 9 offer a cure.

Chapter 7 explores "The Withdrawal of the Financial Restraint System: Reform within the Financial System". Specific financial reform measures are discussed from the perspective of financial competition and cooperation. Reforms include interest rate liberalization, the lifting of market access control, the development of a multi-layer capital market, further reform of financial institutions and the improvement of financial regulation.

Chapter 8 examines "The Withdrawal of Implicit Guarantee: Supportive Reforms in Other Sectors". It proceeds from consideration of implicit guarantee removal to discuss supportive reforms or polices for financial reforms, including SOE reform, fiscal and taxation system reform and social safety net construction.

Chapter 9 discusses the role of "Internet Finance" in China's financial reforms and the "exclusive-to-inclusive" transformation of our financial system.

We decided to write this book for two reasons. First, in recent years the imbalance between the finance sector and the real economy has emerged as a prominent problem for China's economic development. Second, it distills the findings from the authors' long involvement in researching financial problems and close investigation of the real economy.

This book owes a lot to discussions with our coworkers in the Development Research Center of the State Council, including Chen Daofu, Chen Ning, Wu Qing, Lei Wei, Zheng Xingchen, Zhang Liping, Tian Hui and Bo Yan. Many ideas in this book are inspired by their thoughts. We extend our heartfelt gratitude to Doctor Fang Xinghai Vice President of China Securities Regulatory Commission, and our colleagues Zhang Chenghui, Ba Shusong, Che Daofu, Liu Peilin and Zhang Yongsheng, for their constructive comments on the first draft and generous help towards the finalization of the book.

We also thank Lv Xiaolan from Haitong Futures, Li Yurong from Hengtai Securities, Doctor Liu Shijin, former Vice President of the Development Research Center of the State Council, Ben Shenglin from Zhejiang University, Professor Wang Fuzhong from the Central University of Finance and Economics, Wang Yifa from the COFCO Corporation, Yuan Qin from Chengdu Rural and Commercial Bank (CDRCB), Doctor Fan Wei from Shenwan Hongyuan Securities, Doctor Zhao Luan from the World Bank Beijing Office, Yu Ying and Li Shifeng, internees from the Financial Institution of the Development Research Center of the State Council, and Yang Qian and Wang Bin, postgraduates from the Technological and Mathematical Finance Laboratory of Sichuan University for their help with this book.

Gratitude is also extended to Wu Jinglian, Senior Research Fellow, and Liu Shi-jin, Justin Lin, Honorary President of National School of Development of Peking University, Lord Adair Turner, former chairman of Financial Services Authority and Professor Peter Nolan from the University of Cambridge, who graciously supported this book.

Finally, special thanks to Yongling Lam, Samantha Phua and Matthew Twigg, editors at Taylor & Francis, and Kate Fornadel and Renata Corbani, project managers at Apex. Without their dedication and great help, this book would not have been completed.

References

Baumol, W. J. (1990). Entrepreneurship: Productive, Unproductive, and Destructive. [J]. *Journal of Business Venturing*, Vol. 11, No. 1, pp. 3–22.

Hellmann, T., Murdock, K., and Stiglitz, S. (1998). Financial Restraint: Towards a New Paradigm. In *The Role of Government in East Asian Economic Development – Comparative Institutional Analysis*, edited by A. Masahiko, K. Hyung, and O. Masahiro. Beijing: Economic Press, April, pp. 183–235.

1   From extraction to inclusion

A new analytical framework

The law of contradiction in things, that is, the law of the unity of opposites, is the fundamental law of nature and of society and therefore also the fundamental law of thought.

– *On Contradiction* by Mao Zedong (1991a, p. 336)

An essential question

Researchers working on financial reform must answer an essential question if they use a problem-oriented methodology of reform (Wu, 2013). The question may be put in two ways:

1   When considering the whole economic system, what is the most prominent problem in the current financial system of China?
2   When considering the whole economic system, what is the essential attribute of the current financial system of China?

The answers fall into three broad categories.

Views in the first category mainly refer to financial reform targeting state-owned commercial banks since 2003 and deny the existence of major problems in the financial system. They argue marvelous achievements have been made in the previous round of financial reforms. Despite the global financial crisis, China's financial sector stayed safe and sound, with all indicators being the best in China's history and even outperforming those of other countries. When compared with advanced economies or other emerging economies, China's financial system is advantageous in that macro control is more easily applied, enabling it to focus resources on key priority areas and better ensuring financial stability. However, due to the economic slowdown and looming financial risks in recent years, fewer people support this view. Most people think that China's financial system faces severe problems that must be addressed.

According to views in the second category, efficiency is the most prominent problem in China's financial system (Wang, S., 2013). It is mainly manifested in the fact that the financial sector serves the real economy inefficiently. To be more specific, "the financial sector fails to provide timely and sufficient support for the

real economy, and there is still a big gap between the service capability and quality of the financial sector and the demand of economic and social development"
(Wen, J., 2012). More seriously, financial institutions are faring worse in service
provisions (Wang, D., 2014). These are the mainstream views today.

The third category of views attaches importance to financial stability. Pro-
ponents believe there are potential risks in the financial sector that cannot be
ignored. Therefore, they call for efforts to ensure that systemic and regional
financial risks do not develop. Such views have growing influence because China's
leverage ratio is rocketing up and as the economy enters a "new normal", hidden
risks are becoming visible.

Compared with the first category, the second and third categories are more
consistent with each other and follow the same principle of analysis. According
to this principle, financial reforms in all countries must deal with the relationship
between efficiency and stability (Wang, S., 2013). Underlying this principle are
the theories of financial co-competition discussed in this book.

The varied answers to this essential question result in different proposals for
reform. It is worth considering the answer to the question because this might
lead to successful reform of the financial sector. If we only look at the financial
system, all views discussed reflect its current status and problems from different
perspectives. However, the second category of views, which depict efficiency as
the main problem of the system, is arguably more accurate. Nevertheless, if the
whole economic system is considered, all three approaches have severe flaws. To
better explain this, we need to examine some different financial outlooks.

Three types of financial outlook

The term "financial outlook" can refer to people's basic attitude and ideas concerning the financial sector. In this book, it is defined as how people look at the
relationship between the financial sector and other economic sectors, especially
the real economy. In the last three decades of reform and opening up, two major
financial outlooks have emerged in China, financial centrism and financial cooperation. They developed at different stages of economic and financial development and in different environments.

Financial centrism and financial cooperation

Financial centrism may be summarized by Deng Xiaoping's statement during
his visit to Shanghai in early 1991: "Finance is very important, because it is the
core of the modern economy. Handling financial affairs well is the key to success in this sphere" (Deng, 1993, p. 366). Financial centrism fully recognizes
the importance of finance for economic growth and emphasizes the core role of
finance in the whole economic system. It leads to the conclusion that financial
development and economic growth are positively or even causally related. This
is empirically supported in a large amount of literature both at home and abroad
written before the outbreak of the global financial crisis in 2008. It has become

a mainstream view in the world. Take the US for example: at that time people believed that "what was good for Wall Street was good for the country" (Johnson, 2009; Stiglitz, 2011).

The discussion about the importance of finance dates back to Bagehot (1873). Later, Schumpeter (1911) highlights the important role of finance in economic development as it can evaluate and select entrepreneurs and raise funds for their innovation activities. Hicks (1967) holds that the major reason why the Industrial Revolution occurred in Britain is that the capital market development reduced liquidity risks. Dickson (1967) and Bencivenga, Smith and Starr (1996) point out that the Industrial Revolution had to wait for the financial revolution. By using data from 35 countries for the first time, Goldsmith (1969) makes a quantitative study on the relationship between financial development and economic growth and reveals their positive correlation. Likewise, King and Levine (1993a, 1993b, 1993c) also find significant positive correlation between financial development and economic growth by analyzing data from 80 countries between 1960 and 1989 and controlling for other factors affecting economic growth. Other representative works include Rajan and Zingales (1998), Levine (2005), and Hartmann et al. (2007). The influence of financial centrism was keenly felt in the recent round of financial reforms in China, which achieved great success under its guidance and promoted super-high economic growth. China's average growth rate in the first decade of the 21st century hit 10.6 percent. A craze of building financial centres swept many Chinese cities. According to a report in the *People's Daily* on July 28, 2011, at least 30 cities on mainland China proposed building financial centres of different kinds (Xiong, 2011). The financial industry was positioned as the pillar of strategic industry in many places, out of a belief in financial centrism and in the hope that the financial sector can propel development of the local economy.

The second financial outlook is based on the cooperative role of the financial sector, and highlights cooperation or interdependence between finance and the real economy. On the one hand, finance relies on the real economy. Former Premier Wen Jiabao said in his speech at the Fourth National Financial Work Conference that convened in early 2012:

> *(we should) insist that the financial sector should serve real economy. Finance is the core of modern economy. Its development finds foundation in real economy. Without real economy, finance would be like water without a source or a tree without root.*

Its development is founded in the real economy and should be achieved by enhancing its efficiency and capability to serve the real economy. On the other hand, the real economy also depends on finance. A sound and efficient financial system is a prerequisite for sustainable and healthy development of the real economy. While recognizing the importance of finance for the real economy as emphasized by finance centrism, this view also stresses the real economy's significance for the finance sector.

This line of thought leads to two inferences which are supported by many domestic and foreign studies. For example, Furceria and Mourougane (2012), Cecchetti, Kohler and Upper (2009), Boyd, Kwak and Smith (2005) and Laeven and Valencia (2012). First, financial development and economic growth are significantly and positively correlated. Second, a financial crisis or financial instability will cause substantial loss in economic output. The cooperative outlook became a dominant idea as people began to rethink and respond to the global financial crisis in 2008. It has produced so profound an impact on research into the ongoing financial reform that most reform proposals and plans are based on it, and have a view of enabling the financial sector to serve the real economy more efficiently. For example, Li (2014), Ba (2013), Xie and Zou (2013) and Wei (2013) among many.

These two outlooks, prevailing in very different periods, reflect the differing features of the times and were reasonable and appeared valid in their times. Financial centrism became dominant while the belief pertained that the financial sector was not "overdeveloped" but based on a very weak foundation. At that time, the financial sector was the limiting factor on economic development, which, if improved, would realize full economic growth potential. The outlook on cooperation between finance and the real economy took shape when the financial sector developed excessively and the global financial crisis broke out. The financial sector began to squeeze the development space for the real economy, and this ineffective expansion could not sustain healthy development of the real economy.

In comparison, the cooperative outlook is more comprehensive. It inherits and develops financial centrism and shows a deepening understanding of the relationship between finance and the real economy based on economic and financial practice in the past two decades, especially after the outbreak of the global financial crisis. Nevertheless, it has its limitations. It fails to depict all aspects of the relationship between finance and the real economy, and the resultant financial reform program designed accordingly is inevitably biased. Given that, this book proposes the third financial outlook, financial coopetition, in an attempt to accurately reflect the relation of finance and the real economy.

Financial coopetition

Financial coopetition is a theory of finance based on the method of contradiction analysis (Mao, 1991a) and comprises four core aspects.

First, it maintains that the financial sector and the real economy are in contradiction. As a unity of opposites, they cooperate and also compete with each other. On the one hand, in their partnership of interdependence, they provide the conditions of existence for each other and realize self-development by each promoting the improvement of the other. Their unity is embodied in such arguments as "The financial sector finds its foundation in real economy, without which finance would become water without sources and a tree without roots" and "Booming industries mean booming finance; and stable industries mean stable finance" (Wang, 2010). It is also manifest in the fact that financial stability is the precondition under which the financial sector can effectively serve the real economy. Without financial stability, it is futile to support the real economy. In other words, the unity of finance and the real economy is reflected in financial efficiency and financial stability.

On the other hand, finance and the real economy are rivals. They contend and reject each other, and the progress of one is impeded by the advance of the other. They are antagonistic or oppose against each other. The limitation of the argument for cooperative relationship between finance and the real economy lies in its blindness to the competition between the two.

Finance and the real economy compete in four ways. Firstly, they contend for innovation factors. As major independent economic sectors, they scramble for scarce innovation factors such as talent, capital and entrepreneurs for survival and development (Philippon, 2010). Secondly, they push for favourable policies. As part of different interest groups, they exert influence on decision-making bodies so that the government may implement polices benefiting themselves but perhaps impeding the development of others. Thirdly, they vie for profits. Since interest derives from profits (Schumpeter, 1911), the financing cost of the real economy reflects the relative position of the two sectors in profit distribution. Fourthly, the financial system may exert influence on non-financial enterprises, so that non-financial enterprises make decisions good for the whole financial sector but not for the enterprise itself. Mukunda (2014) takes the case of the Boeing Company as an example. It seems that the company, under pressure from the financial market, made decisions leading to excessive outsourcing and reduction of R&D spending. This enhanced the company's short-term financial performance but perhaps dampened its development in the long run. Clayton Christensen, Professor at the Business School of Harvard University and an innovation expert, maintained that CEOs are responsible to shareholders. Under pressure from Wall Street, they should reach the profit target; however, innovation, in most cases, brings meagre profits at the primary stage but large profits in the long term. It is noteworthy that competition between different financial systems and the real economy is not necessarily reflected in all these four aspects.

The second core aspect of the financial coopetition outlook holds that the contradiction between finance and the real economy has principal and secondary aspects. The scramble for profits in the real sector may dominate the relationship between finance and the real economy in a particular period if the financial sector exerts too much improper influence on policymaking and non-financial enterprises. The principal aspect of the contradiction is the competition between the two and the unity is the secondary aspect. Otherwise, the two sectors depend on each other, no matter the capability of finance in serving the real economy and the magnitude of financial risks. Unity is the principal aspect of the contradiction and competition the secondary aspect.

The financial sector has made outstanding progress after the previous round of fruitful financial reforms. This is manifested in rapid expansion of its size, significant improvement of assets quality, high average profits and profit margins and average remuneration far above the average level of the real sector. All these achievements have drastically changed the compensation structure of the whole economy (Baumol, 1990), making the financial sector outperform in attracting various factors and competing with other industries. Meanwhile, due to reasons related to the financial system and structure, the financial sector also gains the upper hand in profit distribution of the real sector. Obviously, competition is the principal aspect of the contradiction between finance and the real economy. To be specific, with "overdevelopment", the financial sector absorbs too many resources, channels such production factors as talent, capita and entrepreneurship and even the innovation factor from the real sector to the fictitious sector and chokes the development of the real sector. The low efficiency of the financial sector in serving the real sector, although a prominent problem, is only the secondary aspect of the contradiction.

Third, the coopetition outlook argues that the principal and secondary aspects may switch, as economic and financial environments change. By looking back at the evolution in the relationship between finance and the real economy in the past two decades, we find that before and shortly after the previous round of financial reforms kick-started cooperation between finance and the real sector remained the principal aspect. This was specifically embodied as the ineptitude of finance to support and serve the development of the real sector. Competition between the two was the secondary aspect before 2008 after which it became dominant.

It should be noted that the principal aspect may switch from competition, as it is now, to cooperation if financial risks accumulate excessively or systematic risks break out. On the one hand, excessive risk accumulation and financial instability will mute the fundamental function of the financial system, and make it harder for the real economy to get access to basic financial services. As a result, cooperation will become the principal aspect of the contradiction. On the other hand, in the case of financial instability, the profits, average remuneration and attractiveness of the financial sector will drastically decline, restraining and even reversing the flow of various factors from the real sector to the fictitious sector. Naturally, competition will become the secondary aspect. Cooperation will become the principal aspect again if the new round of financial reforms can solve the "overdevelopment" problem of the financial sector. Finally, the financial coopetition outlook insists that the nature of the financial system "is determined mainly by the principal aspect of a contradiction, the aspect which has gained the dominant position" (Mao, 1991a, p. 322).

The financial coopetition outlook stresses the unity of opposition between finance and the real economy dialectically and comprehensively. The line of reasons according to this outlook leads to a result that the relationship between finance and the real economy is not simply linear but forms an inverted "U" shape. In other words, the financial sector should develop moderately at the optimal value or in the optimal range. In the optimal range, the financial sector has the status of "not being overdeveloped" before it exceeds the optimal range. In that case, cooperation is the principal aspect of the contradiction, and the financial development and economic growth are positively correlated. Beyond the optimal range, the financial sector is overdeveloped. The principal aspect of the contradiction switches to competition, and financial development and economic growth are negatively correlated. This inference is increasingly supported by the latest literature in the post-crisis era.

Although a few studies focused on the non-monotonic relationship between financial development and economic development before the outbreak of the global financial crisis, they failed to reveal the negative correlation between financial and economic development when financial development went beyond a certain limit. For example, Deidda and Fattouh (2002) use the threshold regress model to explore the relationship between financial depth and economic growth, and find positive but not significant correlation between the two in the case of low financial depth and significant and positive correlation in countries with a high level of financial or economic development. Rioja and Valev (2004) divide all regions into three categories to study how financial development is correlated with economic development. It finds that financial development and economic growth are in no significant correlation in regions with poor financial development, are in strong positive correlation in areas with medium financial development and are in significant but weak positive correlation in regions with high financial development level. After the global financial crisis, the International Monetary Fund and the International Settlement Bank made important breakthroughs in relevant research. For example, Arcand, Berkes and Panizza (2012) find that finance begins to exert negative influence on economic growth when the proportion of private sector credit in the GDP exceeds 100 percent. Almost at the same time, Cecchetti and Kharroubi (2012) reach a similar conclusion and argue that reevaluation of the finance-growth relationship in the modern economic system is urgently needed. They discover the inverted "U" relationship between financial development and economic growth, in which finance impedes economic growth if its development exceeds a certain range, and find that a fast growing financial sector is harmful for the aggregate economic output in developed countries. They explain the negative effects of overdeveloped finance on economic growth as caused by scramble for scarce resources by financial and non-financial sectors. Christensen and Shaxson (2013) propose the concept of a finance curse. According to this notion, the growth of the financial sector, if it exceeds a certain limit, brings harm in many ways to the country; for example, it may lower economic growth in the long-run, increase inequality and mute genuine productivity and entrepreneurship.

The financial system under the financial coopetition outlook: an "extractive" financial system

Now we can answer the basic question proposed at the beginning of this chapter according to the financial coopetition outlook as follows.

1   As far as the whole economic system is concerned, the most prominent problem in China's financial system now is the excessive strength or

"overdevelopment" of the financial sector, which leads to the inappropriate flow of many innovation factors into the financial sector and infringes the profits of the real sector on the other to further reinforce the extraction of innovation factors by the financial sector.

2   As far as the whole economic system is concerned, China's financial system now is extractive by nature and is an extractive financial system.

"Extraction" is widely seen in China's economic and social system. In this book, "extraction" is a purely economic term to describe a negative externality that should not be ignored. In the economic and social spheres, a sector is extractive if its size or profits are disproportionally high and too many innovation factors are attracted to flow into this sector, leading to a significant decline of resource allocation efficiency across the whole economy. In line with this definition, the following three sectors, besides the financial sector, are obviously extractive too.

First, the real estate sector is extractive in a way similar to the negative externality of asset bubbles. For one thing, the real estate sector is so booming that it brings excess return to investment in this sector, which distorts the compensation structure of the whole society and gathers too many innovation factors (mainly capital and entrepreneurship). For example, a great number of enterprises in the real sector switch to involvement in the real estate business. Some enterprises invest in the real sector mainly to gain the added value of land where the project is constructed, or the added value of land provided by local government as the consideration to the project investment, rather than for profits from the real sector. That is also an important reason and mechanism causing excess capacity of the real economy. For the other, the booming real estate sector pushes up enterprises' business cost (rent and even labor cost), to further squeeze the living space of enterprises in the real sector. According to analysis of changes in urban industry competitiveness, rocketing property prices usually precede competitiveness decline of the real sector, for example this was the case in Hong Kong and Tokyo. Nevertheless, as real estate industry development returns back to normal, its extraction effect is weakening.

Second, the public sector is extractive. Too many talented people swarm to the public sector, as indicated by the "public servant frenzy". As the winner of Nobel Prize for Economics Edmund S. Phelps (2013) puts it, the public sector absorbs too many outstanding fresh-graduates; however, China's private businesses need these highly skilled people, and start-ups need them to create innovation projects. Luckily, since the 18th CPC National Congress was convened, especially the Third and Fourth Plenary Session of the 18th CPC Central Committee were held, China has been comprehensively deepening reform, promoting law-based governance and in an all-round way, and normalizing the combat against corruption. Thanks to all these efforts, the public sector is less attractive to talents and thus significantly less extractive. According to Liu (2014), the "national examination fever" (the national civil servant recruitment examination) has been cooled down. A total of 1.409 million applicants passed the qualification review in 2015,

115,000 less than the previous year, and the admission rate dropped from 77:1 in the previous year to 64:1. The extraction of the public sector will fizzle out, as a lasting mechanism is established so that officials neither want to be nor dare to be corrupt and could not be so even if they wished it, and the market plays a bigger role in resource allocation.

Third, large SOEs are extractive. SOEs referred to in the following two reports include state-holding financial institutions. Large SOEs, especially monopolistic central SOEs and local SOEs, also extract highly skilled people and financial resources. According to the *Report on Employment Quality of Peking University Graduates in 2013*, 38.89 percent of master's graduates from the Peking University get employed in SOEs, much higher than the proportion employed in private business, joint venture and other types of businesses. As indicated in the *Report on Employment Quality of Tsinghua University Graduates in 2013*, 43.8 percent of all graduates from Tsinghua University in 2013 found a job in SOEs, far above the share of other types of employers. However, as the fight against corruption and SOEs reforms proceed, the extraction of SOEs will be reduced and finally fade away.

Financial reform: the one-dimensional model

According to the financial coopetition outlook, finance and the real economy, in contradiction to each other, constitute a unity of opposites, as they compete and cooperate with each other. Competition dominates the contradiction in the present, as the financial system is extractive. The task of the financial reform is to focus on competition between finance and the real economy to eliminate extraction by the financial system. To this end, we start from establishing a one-dimensional model exploring "extraction" and "inclusiveness".

In this model, the financial systems are classified into two categories: extractive systems and inclusive systems. The financial system is extractive when the "overdevelopment" of the financial sector leads to strong negative externality and is at the expense of the real economy. It is inclusive if moderate development of the financial sector generates low negative externality and brings forth harmony, capability and shared prosperity of the financial sector and the real sector.

It is noteworthy that "exclusiveness" and "inclusiveness" cannot cover all aspects of the competition between finance and the real economy. "Inclusiveness" means the two sides are in harmony while competing with each other, and "extraction" describes the situation in which the financial sector gains the upper hand in the competition. Theoretically, there is another case in which the real sector is at an advantage or the financial sector is at a disadvantage. This case is not considered in this book, because China has moved on from situation and it is impossible for it to re-emerge after the previous round of financial reforms.

In the one-dimensional model, the aim of financial reform is to balance the financial sector and the real economy, rather than deal with problems in the financial system. The most pressing problem now is that overdevelopment of the financial sector squeezes space for the real sector; therefore, the target of China's financial reform is to establish an inclusive financial system. In Figure 1.1 the path of reform is from left to right: the extractive financial system transforms into an inclusive one. In the extractive financial system, the priority for financial reform or financial development is to do no harm to the real economy, rather than to serve it.

According to the financial coopetition outlook, the one-dimensional model focuses on the principal aspect of the contradiction between finance and the real economy, and broadly points out the reform target and a path to achieve it. However, it misses the secondary aspect of the contradiction, and fails to articulate adequately the reform target and path. Therefore, we should add a new dimension to the model to reflect the secondary aspect of the finance-real-economy contradiction.

Before we construct the two-dimension model, we should examine the one-dimensional model using the financial cooperation outlook (Figure 1.2), which underlies the majority of financial reform schemes. Unlike the financial coopetition model, in the one-dimension model the financial cooperation outlook deals with the cooperation between finance and the real economy. Current financial reform schemes focus on financial efficiency, or the efficiency of the financial sector in serving the real sector. Using the criteria of financial efficiency, financial systems are divided into two groups: high-efficiency and low-efficiency. "It has been proved both practically and theoretically that market-based resource allocation is

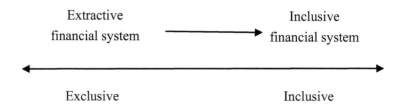

Figure 1.1 The one-dimensional model under the financial coopetition outlook

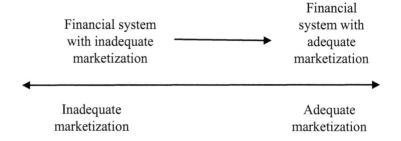

Figure 1.2 The one-dimensional model according to the financial cooperation outlook

the most efficient" (Xi, 2013). The decision adopted in the Third Plenary Session of the 18th CPC Central Committee also proposes to let the market play a decisive role in resource allocation; therefore, the dimension of financial efficiency can be replaced with the dimension of marketization. Strictly speaking, the marketization dimension is not identical with financial efficiency. Transformation of the financial efficiency dimension into the marketization dimension makes it easier to introduce a more concrete reform or policy meaning. In other words, high-efficiency financial systems usually feature a high marketization level, while low-efficiency ones are poor in marketization. According to this model, financial reform should focus on enhancing marketization of the financial system to realize adequate modernization.

Financial reform: the two-dimensional model

Compared with the one-dimensional model, the two-dimensional model according to the financial coopetition outlook includes a new dimension to reflect the cooperation between finance and the real economy. The new dimension is used to further classify financial systems into four different types, and point out a more detailed and clearer target and a path to change the extractive financial system into an inclusive system.

Four types of financial systems

"Exclusiveness-Inclusion" and marketization can constitute a matrix which classifies financial systems into four types: an extractive financial system with inadequate marketization, an extractive system with adequate marketization, an inclusive system with inadequate marketization and an inclusive system with adequate marketization (Figure 1.3).

The first is the extractive financial system with inadequate marketization at the left-hand bottom in Figure 1.3. Featuring inadequate marketization, insufficient competition and lower efficiency of the financial sector in serving the real sector, these financial systems, due to inadequate marketization and many other reasons, overdevelop in relation to real economy, generate negative spillovers on the development of the real economy.

The second is the extractive financial system with adequate marketization at the right-hand bottom of the figure. On the one hand, such financial systems boast adequate marketization, sufficient competition and high financial efficiency. On the other hand, due to excessive marketization or the absence of financial regulation, the financial sector disproportionally expands and causes severe negative externality to the real sector. Examples in this category include the US and British financial systems from the 1980s to the eve of the global financial crisis and the US financial system in the 1920s.

These two categories are both extractive, as they produce a "crowd-out" effect and huge negative externality. However, they are extractive for different reasons. The extractive financial system with inadequate marketization is extractive

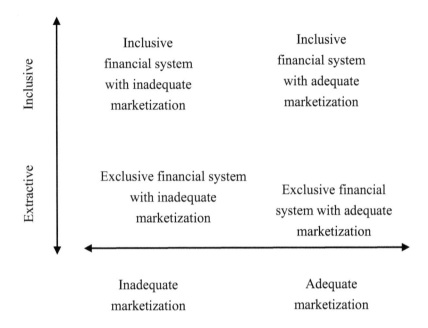

Figure 1.3 Classification of financial systems in the two-dimensional model according to the financial coopetition outlook

because of inadequate marketization, but the extractive financial system with adequate marketization is extractive because the financial sector is oversized due to excessive marketization and lack of regulation. Comparatively, the latter is more efficient in serving the real sector.

The third category is the inclusive financial system with inadequate marketization at the left-hand top of the figure. This category is in harmony with the real economic sector, thanks to its moderate development and low negative externality. However, it fails to serve the real sector efficiently due to inadequate marketization and poor development of the financial sector. The financial system after the US Great Depression and before financial liberalization in the 1980s is of this kind.

The fourth category is the inclusive financial system with adequate marketization at the right-hand top of the figure. Such a financial system is theoretically superior. From the perspective of contradiction analysis, the extractive financial system with adequate marketization is a unity of opposites, in which finance and real economy are in perfect harmony. However, the unity of opposites is conditional, temporary and relative. Therefore, the extractive financial system with absolute and adequate marketization is not in constant stability, but only theoretically superior.

The inclusive financial system with adequate marketization is the goal of China's financial reform. Under such a system, the financial sector develops moderately and in harmony with the real economy, and its development does not impede economic growth as little negative externality is generated. The financial sector can serve the real sector efficiently and facilitate economic growth. The present German financial system is an example of this category. The US *Dodd-Frank Wall Street Reform and Consumer Protection Act* is designed to transform the country's extractive financial system with adequate marketization into an inclusive one while maintaining adequate marketization.

The third and fourth category are both inclusive. They produce low negative externality to the real economy, and under such systems, financial development does not impede economic growth. The difference between them lies in the higher efficiency of the fourth category in serving the real economy. But they are the same by nature according to the notion that finance is the servant of industry.

Since the principal and secondary aspect of the finance-real-economy contradiction can switch, the aforementioned four types of financial systems can mutually transform. Given the nature of self-expansion of currency and finance (Chen, D., 2008; Xia and Chen, 2011), the financial system is naturally inclined to turn from inclusion to "extraction". It should be noticed that marketization catalyzes the transformation from an inclusive financial system to an exclusive one in many advanced economies including the US. However, that does not mean China cannot resort to marketization to transform the extractive financial system to an inclusive one. Instead, given the special feature of China's extractive financial system, further marketization is inevitable for the transformation of its financial system.

The reform path for the "exclusive-to-inclusive" transformation

In the two-dimensional model under the financial coopetition outlook, financial reform should solve two major problems: competition and cooperation. From the perspective of resource allocation, the competition issue can be solved by proper and rational primary resource allocation between finance and the real economy, while the cooperation can be achieved through resource re-allocation, so that financial resources are reasonably allocated to sectors of the real economy. According to the financial coopetition outlook, resource allocation consists of two phases: primary and secondary distribution. The first distribution means the allocation of factors among finance and the real economy, and the secondary distribution refers to allocation of resources among sectors of real economy through the financial system. Please refer to Chapter 3 for a more detailed discussion.

As shown in Figure 1.4, what we have at present is the extractive financial system with inadequate marketization at the left-hand bottom, while the goal of the reform is the inclusive financial system with adequate marketization at the right-hand top of the figure. The matrix shows three paths to reach the goal.

First, we can start from the reform for marketization and then transform the extractive system to an inclusive one, as indicated as the two legs of the right-hand triangle at the right-hand bottom in Figure 1.4. The reform following this path proceeds from the secondary aspect of the finance-real-economy contradiction

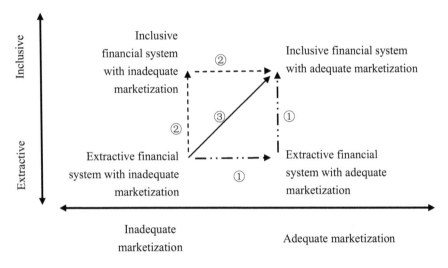

Figure 1.4 Financial reform paths in the two-dimensional model based on the financial coopetition outlook

and focuses on problems inside the financial system, to improve the financial
efficiency by enhancing marketization and competition of the financial system.
Then, the reform will take into account the whole economy to address the principal aspect of the contradiction. To this end, the reform will properly handle the
relation between finance and the real economy and reduce the negative externality generated by financial overdevelopment.

   A great number of financial reform proposals pay inadequate attention to
the negative externality of finance; instead, they merely emphasize the importance of enhancing financial efficiency. These proposals follow the path in
the two-dimensional model based on the financial coopetition outlook. However, these proposals do not yield reform design. In other words, they fail to take
into consideration the "extractive-to-inclusive" transformation after the reform
for marketization. Perfectly matching the orientation for marketization, this path
is widely recognized and helps to enhance financial resource allocation efficiency.
However, they have obvious potential deficiencies. They fail to solve prominent
problems in the current financial system: instead, they worsen the imbalance
between finance and the real economy. After inadequate marketization is realized, too many social resources will be absorbed by the financial sector in the
primary distribution, which may possibly further reduce the resource allocation
efficiency of the whole economic system. If only marketization is considered, the
financial system might be more extractive and produce more negative spillover
effects. According to the financial coopetition outlook, this reform path may do
more harm than good, since it fails to capture the essence of the contradiction to
solve its principal aspect.

The second reform path is to transform the extractive system into an inclusive one before the reform for marketization, as indicated by the two legs of the right triangle at the left top of Figure 1.4. Taking stock of the principal aspect of the finance-real-economy contradiction, reform following this path focuses on reducing the negative spillover effects of finance by dampening competition, and curbs various factors from flowing into the financial sector from the real sector. After the exclusive-to-inclusive transformation, the principal aspect of the contradiction will switch from competition to cooperation, and low efficiency in serving the real sector will become the prominent problem of the financial system, which can be solved by enhancing marketization. The advantage of this path lies in its capability to prevent various factors from flowing into the fictitious sector from the real sector and solving pressing problems in the financial system. However, it fails to solve the problem of low financial efficiency because it improves inclusion without advancing marketization reform. In addition, the establishment of the extractive financial system in China owes a lot to inadequate marketization manifested in interest margin protection and access restriction. Therefore, it is infeasible to transform the extractive financial system into an inclusive one without promoting marketization. The extractive-to-inclusive transformation, even if realized through non-market-based tools (mandatory low-interest-rate loans, tax increase and limits on pay), is at the expense of efficiency and is unsustainable. According to the financial coopetition outlook, this path, although capturing the essence of the contradiction and emphasizing the principal aspect of the contradiction, fails to take the secondary aspect of the contradiction into consideration. Therefore, it is a sub-optimal choice but better than the first.

The third path is to simultaneously promote the extractive-to-inclusive transformation and the marketization, as shown by the diagonal line in the square in Figure 1.4. This path can be subcategorized into three types, depending on whether marketization or transformation dominates the reform.

Firstly, this sub-category of the third path makes simultaneous efforts on marketization and transformation with marketization being the principal focus. This is the upgraded edition of the first reform path. From the perspective of the financial coopetition outlook, disadvantages outweigh advantages if we take this path. This is because it fails to address the principal aspect of the contradiction, although it pays a certain attention to the establishment of the inclusive financial system as the goal of the reform.

Secondly, this sub-category of the third path makes equal and simultaneous efforts on marketization and transformation. According to the financial coopetition outlook, this path does not distinguish the principal and secondary aspects of the contradiction, grasping all at one time. Therefore, this one is not theoretically optimal.

Thirdly, this sub-category of the third path makes simultaneous efforts on transformation and marketization with priority given to transformation while supportive significance is given to marketization. From the perspective of the financial coopetition outlook, this path is the best choice theoretically as the upgraded edition of the second reform path. For one thing, priority is given transformation in order to address the principal aspect of the contradiction, which means to reduce the negative externality of finance first and curb the flow of various factors from the real economy to the fictitious sector. While highlighting its focus on the principal aspect of the contradiction, this path also considers the secondary aspect. Besides, given how China's extractive financial system was established and marketization reinforces inclusion, the "two-point" path with clear focus appears to be more meaningful practically and in terms of the policy.

The "dominant" and "secondary" roles should be further clarified. In this book these roles differ more qualitatively than quantitatively. Qualitative differences mean that transformation and marketization play a different role as "goal" and "tool" to reach that goal. The target is dominant and the tool is secondary, just like the relation between the target and the arrow as discussed by Mao (1991b, p. 799).

The secondary role of marketization means marketization is the tool rather than the target. Marketization is not advisable or at least should be taken seriously if marketization makes the financial system even more extractive. Marketization can bring forth better inclusiveness as long as it reaches to a certain level, but may not go further to be one hundred percent, since it is not true that the higher the level of the marketization the better, given financial risks and many other factors. Whether and how much an economic sector should be marketized depends on whether marketization can enhance inclusion and realize sustainable inclusion. Against the backdrop of the financial crisis, a shrinking financial sector cannot bring forth real inclusion. Inclusion at the expense of financial robustness is temporary and unsustainable.

Compared with the one-dimensional model, the two-dimensional model considers not only the principal aspect of the finance-real-economy contradiction but also its secondary aspect. It addresses secondary issues. The two-dimensional model more precisely categorizes financial systems and articulates more clearly the goal and path of the reform. However, it only considers the financial efficiency, one dimension of the secondary aspect of the contradiction, but turns a blind eye to financial stability. Therefore, we can add financial stability to the model and build a three-dimensional model.

We start from looking closely at the two-dimensional model based on the financial cooperation outlook, which describes the financial system from the perspective of the marketization level and financial stability (Figure 1.5). In this model, financial systems fall into four categories: firstly, a robust financial system with inadequate marketization; secondly, a robust financial system with adequate marketization; thirdly, a fragile financial system with inadequate marketization, and fourthly, a fragile financial system with adequate marketization. Establishing a robust financial system with adequate marketization is the goal of the reform. Transforming the robust financial system with inadequate marketization is the path to reach it, as in the path ① in Figure 1.5. Financial reform should make progress while balancing financial efficiency improvement and financial stability maintenance. It should keep the financial system from degrading into a fragile

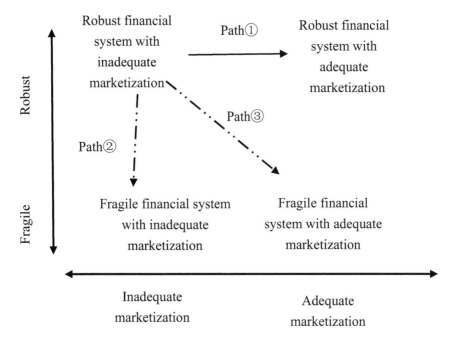

Figure 1.5 Financial reform under the two-dimensional model based on the financial cooperation outlook

financial system with inadequate marketization (path ②) and avoid the trap of the fragile financial system with adequate marketization (path ③).

Financial reform: the three-dimensional model

According to the financial coopetition outlook, the financial system should be described in three dimensions, first "exclusiveness-inclusion", second financial efficiency or marketization and third financial stability. The first dimension reflects the competition with and rejection of each other by finance and the real economy, while the other two dimensions deal with cooperation and interdependence between the two. Particularly, financial efficiency reveals the dependence of finance on the real economy, which means the financial sector should base itself on serving the real economy, and financial stability addresses the dependence of the real economy on finance.

The three-dimensional model based on the financial coopetition outlook adds financial stability which is not included in the two-dimensional model. The two-dimensional model assumes financial stability and does not consider financial risks the major problem for the financial system. Currently, although financial risks have accumulated to a level that cannot be neglected, the implicit assumption of financial stability makes sense. Financial risk accumulation is still under control and the financial system is highly risk resistant. Therefore, inclusion and financial efficiency enhancement are more important priorities in financial reform.

Financial stability is added to establish a three-dimensional model for two reasons. First, the principal aspect of the contradiction may switch as economic and financial environments change. Despite extraction as the nature of China's financial system at present, the principal aspect of the contradiction will switch from competition between finance and the real economy to cooperation between the two, if financial risks keep mounting up to such a degree as to harm financial stability. As a result, the financial system will fail to provide a stable financial environment for the development of the real economy. Therefore, the financial system becomes unstable rather than extractive, and the major target of financial reform is changed to improving financial stability. In that case the paths shown in Figure 1.4 are incomplete. Secondly, risks should be managed during financial reform and basic financial stability should be guaranteed.

We would like to discuss how the three dimensions are related to each other before expounding on the three-dimensional model. Besides the principal and secondary aspects of the contradiction between finance and the real economy, there are some special features of China's financial system to be considered. Low financial efficiency or poor marketization is an important reason for the extraction of China's financial system. The extractive financial system is unstable by nature as it erodes the foundation for the development of the real economy. Financial efficiency and financial stability are substitutes for each other, a relationship which we are all familiar with.

To make the model simple and clear, we establish a new model consisting of two phases as indicated in Figure 1.6 and Figure 1.4, rather than one consisting of "extraction-inclusion", marketization and financial stability. When financial stability becomes the principal aspect of the contradiction, the financial reform should focus on maintaining financial stability, so an unstable system can become stable (Figure 1.6). After this stage is completed, the principal aspect of the contradiction switches back to competition between finance and the real economy, and the financial system becomes extractive by nature again. Then the financial reform should follow the path as indicated in Figure 1.4, and focus on reducing negative externality caused by financial overdevelopment, to ultimately finish the exclusive-to-inclusive transformation.

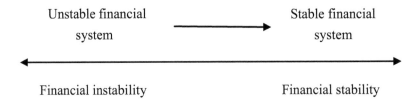

Figure 1.6 Financial system categorization under the dimension of financial stability

Here now we have all financial reforms respectively consisting of one dimension, two dimensions and three dimensions. To be clear, the one-dimensional model is to establish the basic goal and direction of the reform; the two-dimensional model is to articulate the path of the financial reform while making the goal clearer; and the three-dimensional model is to reveal the importance of financial stability for advancing reform and to elaborate on the reform path. Theoretically, the three-dimensional model is consummate. However, given the complexity of the three-dimensional model and because financial stability is not the most pressing problem now, the two-dimensional model should be the basic model used to analyze financial reform in this book.

Questions left for further discussion

Will "extraction" naturally disappear?

Some argue that "extraction" of financial overdevelopment or the financial system will naturally go away, and the market can spontaneously correct such imbalance or deviation. For example, Sylla (2011) holds that:

> *The excessive financialization will be solved naturally. As business is slack and profits go lean, banks and intermediary institutions downsize themselves. Wall Street provides fewer and fewer jobs, and graduates from business schools and colleges gradually flow to sectors other than the financial sector. Therefore, the market is rectifying excessive financialization by itself.*

Ideas like that of Sylla (2011) make sense. After all, the US underwent a similar process during these years. Besides, such ideas are basically in line with changes of post-crisis human resource allocation in all countries. Does that mean we should let financial overdevelopment and extraction be? Surely not. Indeed, Sylla and scholars sharing his ideas neglect two important interlinked problems.

First, under what conditions will the market kick-start to rectify excessive financialization? Despite the severe financialization in China, the self rectification mechanism of the market remains dormant. Likewise, that mechanism in the US failed to become effective before the outbreak of the financial crisis, although excessive financialization triggered the crisis.

Second, what is the cost of letting excessive financialization be solved naturally?

It is hard to activate the spontaneous rectification mechanism before a financial crisis. The outbreak of the financial crisis is the precondition to excessive financialization being solved naturally. For example, the market started to rectify excessive financialization only after the country suffered from the worst financial crisis since the Great Depression. Given the high cost of triggering a financial crisis and the huge economic and social losses thus caused, we cannot wait and let the market spontaneously take time to solve excessive financialization and the siphonic effect of finance.

Is the financial crisis an option?

A review of global financial history reveals a recurring phenomenon. The profit of the financial sector and its share in the total profit of all businesses significantly dropped after the financial crisis, which changed the imbalance between finance and the real economy. Given that, is the financial crisis an alternative path to transform the extractive financial system into an inclusive one? Generally, the answer is no. As defined in *The New Palgrave Dictionary of Economics* and interpreted by Kindleberger (1992), the financial crisis refers to a sharp, brief, ultracyclical deterioration of all or most of a group of financial indicators: short-term interest rates, asset (stock, real estate, land) prices, commercial insolvencies and failures of financial institutions. Once a financial crisis breaks out, the financial system stops performing its basic functions, bringing severe damage to the real economy and even threatening social stability. According to a study organized by the International Monetary Fund, the banking crisis which occurred between 1970 and 2011 caused average losses as high as 23 percent of the GDP (Laeven and Valencia, 2012). Obviously, a financial crisis does more harm than the negative externality of the extractive financial system. Since we have to choose the lesser of two evils, when financial risks threaten a financial crisis, the top priority of financial reform is to maintain financial stability in order to address the principal aspect of the contradiction.

A financial crisis only brings temporary and spurious transformation from the extractive financial crisis to an inclusive one. The root of the extractive financial system cannot be eradicated without radical financial reform. The inclusive financial system established during the financial system is temporary and unsustainable due to lack of practical basis. The financial system begins to extract again because the old factors start to be effective again when the crisis passes. Therefore, we need the inclusive financial crisis, but we need more an environment in which such a system can be sustained.

Financial crisis and financial reform come hand in hand. The financial crisis catalyzes consensus on the reform and facilitates the execution of reform actions. A sweeping financial crisis is always accompanied by a radical financial reform which reshapes the relation between finance and the real economy. For example, after the 1929–1933 financial crisis, the Roosevelt administration launched a complete financial reform, thanks to which the US financial system maintained inclusiveness for the next half-century. The US started another round of radical financial reform after the global financial crisis of 2008. The reform, if successful, will transform the US extractive financial system into an inclusive one. According to Palley (2007), both discussion and action concerning US financial reform are limited to "stability" and prevention of another financial crisis from happening. The reforms lack deeper exploration, for example, how to make finance serve the real economy, rather than the real economy serving the finance sector.

Whether or not the financial crisis is an alternative path depends on the scale of the financial crisis, the difficulty in carrying out the financial reform and resilience of the economic and financial systems. It is an alternative path if the financial crisis only brings partial rather than systematic effects. Financial reform will stagnate because it's restricted by vested interests, and the economy and finance will be resilient enough. Otherwise, we should try all out to avoid a financial crisis.

Once a financial crisis breaks out, "never want a serious crisis to go to waste", which is a famous comment on the outbreak of the financial crisis in November 2008 by Rahm Emanuel, former Whitehouse Chief of Staff to President Obama (Emanuel, 2008). Instead, it should be capitalized on to reach consensus on launching a radical financial reform and eliminating institutional deficiencies in the extractive financial system.

Can the "extractive-inclusive" dimension be integrated with the marketization dimension?

A key reason underlying the establishment of China's extractive financial system is inadequate marketization of the financial system. Then can the "extractive-inclusive" dimension be included in the marketization dimension? In other words, can inclusion come from inside marketization? If yes, the exclusive-to-inclusive transformation and marketization are simply repetition. As a result, the aforementioned two-dimensional model based on the financial coopetition outlook has no real meaning for financial reform.

We think the answer to this question is no. Firstly, marketization is not the only path for the transformation of an extractive system into an inclusive one. Indeed, there are reasons other than marketization for the extraction of the financial system. Therefore, in the financial reform, other means should be employed to transform the financial system besides marketization.

Secondly, marketization does not necessarily bring forth inclusion; instead, it might be counterproductive. On the one hand, interest rate liberalization, uplifting restrictions on market access, developing the multi-layer capital market and other actions of the reform for marketization reinforce competition in the financial system and help reduce the relative profits of the financial sector. On the other hand, as affected by marketization, self expansion of finance is likely to lead to a kind of financial system featuring high profit and with little relevance to the real economy. There are a great number of highly extractive financial systems with adequate marketization, such as those in the US and Britain before the global financial crisis. Since the 1980s, these two financial systems have been increasingly extractive, as they are increasingly market-based.

Thirdly, with the absence of the "extractive-inclusive" dimension, the rational process of marketization might be blocked. At present, interest rate liberalization and uplifting restrictions on market access are slower than expected. An important reason for that is the concern about financial efficiency and stability. People worry that interest rate liberalization may increase the financing cost of the real economy and impose more pressure on commercial banks; and uplifting control on market access may lead to excessive competition and harm financial stability. Without the "extractive-inclusive" dimension, the financial reform only considers the balance between financial stability and efficiency. However, if this dimension is added to the model, a different conclusion might be reached. Interest rate liberalization may enhance the financing cost of the real economy and impose negative influence on resource allocation efficiency, and the primary allocation might be more efficient because the liberalization reduces extraction of the financial system. In general, the interest rate should be further liberalized, since that helps to make resource allocation more efficient across the economic system. Besides, looser control over market access may threaten a financial crisis, but it can make the financial system more robust by reducing its extraction. Given its positive effect on building a robust financial system, market access control should be uplifted further.

Fourthly, lacking the "extractive-inclusive" dimension may lead to excessive marketization. To what degree is that marketization rational? As the global financial crisis taught us, it is not the case that the higher the marketization, the better. An alternative criterion is whether marketization affects financial stability and results in hysteresis. In this case, the "extractive-inclusive" dimension can be an alternative option, especially for China's financial reform. Marketization does not necessarily go further when the reform reaches the goal of inclusion.

Finally, the "extractive-inclusive" dimension cannot be integrated with the marketization dimension because of their difference as the goal and the tool of financial reform. Despite the importance of marketization, it is only a tool to realize the goal of inclusion. It is neither the only tool nor the goal itself.

References

Arcand, J., Berkes, E. and Panizza, U. (2012). *Too Much Finance?* [R]. IMF Working Paper, June.

Ba, S. (2013). Thoughts and Focus of Financial Reform Deepening [N]. *China Economic Times*, September 3.

Bagehot, W. (1873). *Lombard Street: A Description of the Money Market* [M]. New York: Scribner, Armstrong & Co.

Baumol, W. (1990). Entrepreneurship: Productive, Unproductive, and Destructive [J]. *Journal of Business Venturing*, Vol. 11, No. 1, pp. 3–22.

Bencivenga, V., Smith, B. and Starr, R. (1996). Equity Markets, Transactions Costs, and Capital Accumulation: An Illustration [J]. *The World Bank Economic Review*, Vol. 10, No. 2, pp. 241–265.

Boyd, J., Kwak, S. and Smith, B. (2005). The Real Output Losses Associated With Modern Banking Crises [J]. *Journal of Money, Credit, and Banking*, Vol. 37, No. 6, pp. 977–999.

Cecchetti, S. and Kharroubi, E. (2012). *Reassessing the Impact of Finance on Growth* [R]. BIS Working Paper No. 381, July.

Cecchetti, S., Kohler, M. and Upper, C. (2009). *Financial Crises and Economic Activity* [R]. NBER Working Paper 15379.

Chen, D. (2008). Root and Effect of US Subprime Mortgage Crisis and Inspiration to China – An Interview With Chen Daofu From Financial Institution of Development Research Center of the State Council [N]. *DRCnet*, September 26.

Christensen, J. and Shaxson, N. (2013). *The Finance Curse: Exploring the Possible Impacts of Hosting an Oversized Financial Centre* [M]. Kent: Commonwealth Publishing, May.

Deidda, L. and Fattouh, B. (2002). Non-Linearity Between Finance and Growth [J]. *Economics Letters*, Vol. 74, No. 3, pp. 339–345.

Deng, X. (1993). *Selected Works of Deng Xiaoping* (Vol. III) [M]. Beijing: People's Publishing House, October.

Dickson, P. G. M. (1967). *The Financial Revolution in England* [M]. London: Macmillan.

Emanuel, R. (2008). Rahm Emanuel: Don't Waste a 'Serious Crisis'. *Wall Street Journal*, November 21.

Furceria, D. and Mourougane, A. (2012). The Effect of Financial Crises on Potential Output: New Empirical Evidence From OECD Countries [J]. *Journal of Macroeconomics*, Vol. 34, No. 3, pp. 822–832.

Goldsmith, R. W. (1969). *Financial Structure and Development* [M]. New Haven, CT: Yale University Press.

Hartmann, P., Heider, F., Papaioannou, E. and Lo Duca, M. (2007). *The Role of Financial Markets and Innovation in Productivity and Growth in Europe [R]*. ECB Occasional Paper No. 72.

Hicks, J. (1967). *A Theory of Economic History* [M]. Oxford: Clarendon Press.

Jiabao, W. (2012). Excerpt of Wen Jiabao's Speech on the National Financial World Conference [N]. *People's Daily*, January 30.

Johnson, S. (2009). The Quiet Coup [N]. *The Atlantic*, May 1.

Kindleberger, C. P. (1992). Financial Crises, entry in the *New Palgrave Dictionary of Money and Finance* [K]. London: MacMillan.

King, R. and Levine, R. (1993a). Financial Intermediation and Economic Development. In *Financial Intermediation in the Construction of Europe* [A], edited by C. Mayer and X. Vives. London: Centre for Economic Policy Research, pp. 156–189.

King, R. and Levine, R. (1993b). Finance and Growth: Schumpeter Might Be Right [J]. *The Quarterly Journal of Economics*, Vol. 108, No. 3, pp. 717–737.

King, R. and Levine, R. (1993c). Finance, Entrepreneurship and Growth: Theory and Evidence [J]. *Journal of Monetary Economics*, Vol. 32, No. 3, pp. 513–542.

Laeven, L. and Valencia, F. (2012). *Systemic Banking Crises Database: An Update* [R]. IMF Working Paper WP/12/163, June.

Levine, R. (2005). Finance and Growth: Theory and Evidence [J]. *Handbook of Economic Growth*, Vol. 1, pp. 865–934.

Li, Y. (2014). Finance Reforms in the Deep Water Zone [J]. *China Finance*, Vol. 19, pp. 68–70.

Liu, S. (2014). The National Civil Servant Recruitment Examination has been cooled down but Still is Hot [N], *People's Daily Overseas Edition*, Vol. 64, No. 1, Nov. 4, 2014.

Mao, Z. (1991a). *Selected Works of Mao Zedong* (Vol. I) [M]. Beijing: People's Publishing House, pp. 299–340.

Mao, Z. (1991b). *Selected Works of Mao Zedong* (Vol. III) [M]. Beijing: People's Publishing House, pp. 795–803.

Mukunda, G. (2014). The Price of Wall Street's Power [J]. *Harvard Business Review*, June.

Palley, T. (2007). *Financialization: What It Is and Why It Matters* [R]. Economics Working Paper Archive wp525, Levy Economics Institute.

Phelps, E. (2013). Interview With Nobel Laureate Edmund S. Phelps by Zhang Weiying, Why Do Chinese Enterprises Always Fail in Innovation? [N]. *Boao Review*, September 12.

Philippon, T. (2010). Financiers versus Engineers: Should the Financial Sector Be Taxed or Subsidized? [J]. *American Economic Journal: Macroeconomics*, Vol. 2, No. 3, pp. 158–182.

Rajan, R. and Zingales, L. (1998). Financial Dependence and Growth [J]. *American Economic Review*, Vol. 88, pp. 559–586.

Rioja, F. and Valev, N. (2004). Does One Size Fit All? A Reexamination of the Finance and Growth Relationship [J]. *Journal of Development Economics*, Vol. 74, No. 2, pp. 429–447.

Schumpeter, J. (1911). *A Theory of Economic Development* [M]. Cambridge, MA: Harvard University Press.

Stiglitz, J. (2011). *Freefall: America, Free Markets, and the Sinking of the World Economy* [M]. Beijing: China Machine Press, January.

Sylla, R. (2011). Excessive Financialization Disappears by Its Own [N]. *21st Century Economic Report*, October 22.

Wang, D. (2014). *Address at Tsinghua PBOCSF Global Finance Forum* [N]. http://finance.sina.com.cn, May 10.

Wang, Q. (2010). Wang Qishan Emphasizes on Maintaining Stable and Robust Financial Operation [N]. *China Securities Journal*, July 9.

Wang, S. (2013). Thoughts on China's Financial Reform [J]. *The Banker*, Vol. 5, pp. 1–2.

Wei, S. (2013). Focus of China's Further Financial Reform In *Comparative Studies* (Vol. 64) [A]. Edited by Wu Jinglian, I. Beijing: China Citic Press.

Wu, J. (2013). Reform Plan Designed through Problem-Oriented Approach [N]. *Securities Times*, January 11.

Xi, J. (2013). *Explanations on the Decision of the Central Committee of the Communist Party of China on Some Major Issues Concerning Comprehensively Continuing the Reform*, quoted from *Supporting Reading Material of the Decision of the Central Committee of the Communist Party of China on Some Major Issues Concerning Comprehensively Continuing the Reform* [M]. Beijing: People's Publishing House, November 2013.

Xia, B. and Chen, D. (2011). *China Financial Strategy 2020* [M]. Beijing: People's Publishing House, January.

Xie, P. and Zou, C. (2013). *Thought on China's Financial Reform* [M]. Beijing: China Financial Publishing House, April.

Xiong, J. (2011). Do We Need 30 "Financial Centers"? [N]. *People's Daily*, July 28.

2 The "extractive" financial system

Not even a blade of grass grows under a big tree.

– A Chinese proverb

China's financial system is extractive and features imbalance between finance and the real economy. In such a system, financial overdevelopment is mainly manifested in the overly high employees' pay and profit margin of the financial sector. Financial overdevelopment pushes various innovation factors to flow from the real sector to the fictitious economy and enter the non-productive financial sector, resulting in lower resource allocation efficiency in the economic system. The term "extractive financial system" naturally reminds people of the predatory lending found in the financial system, which means financial institutions sign misleading loan contracts with disadvantaged entities in need of financing. Predatory lending is typically represented by loans from US financial institutions to secondary lenders before the outbreak of the subprime mortgage crisis. In China, the mutually or jointly guaranteed lending is also predatory. However, the extractive financial system discussed in this book is not like this predatory lending. It is safe to say that "extraction" is the negative externality (Viner, 1932) of financial overdevelopment. Unlike those in advanced economies such as the US and Britain, China's extractive financial system features the high financing costs of the real economy and the low efficiency of finance in serving the real sector.

China's financial sector: "underdeveloped" or "overdeveloped"?

Is China's financial system "underdeveloped" or "overdeveloped"? The answer to this important question determines whether the idea in this book makes sense. Before answering it is necessary to discuss how financial development should be observed.

Three perspectives from which to observe financial development

Financial development can be observed in two dimensions or three perspectives. The first dimension is based on the government-market relationship and in line with the theory of financial deepening. We can divide the status of financial development into three types, according to the role of the government (top-down) and market (bottom-up), including financial repression, financial restraint and financial liberalization. Among them, financial repression and financial liberalization are defined in traditional financial development theory (Shaw, 1973; McKinnon, 1973). Financial repression refers to a situation in which the government intervenes in the market too much, while financial liberalization means the market mechanism plays a decisive role. Financial restraint is a concept proposed by Hellmann, Murdock and Stiglitz (1998) to describe the developmental relation between financial repression and financial liberalization by drawing on lessons learned from financial liberalization and the experience of governments involved in working out the East Asian Miracle. According to this analysis, the government only plays a role in providing incentives to financial institutions to participate in financial deepening. Since China's financial sector has deviated from typical financial repression and China has expressly determined to implement reforms for marketization, few analyze China's financial reform from this angle, although it is still used in the analysis of financial development status.

The second dimension is based on the relationship between finance and economic growth or between finance and the real economy. The second dimension is examined in this book. This dimension is subdivided into two perspectives.

The first is the efficiency or function of the financial sector. Currently, China's financial development is analyzed mostly from this angle. As far as financial efficiency is concerned, it is widely believed that finance serves the real economy with low efficiency or is underdeveloped. We will not use this perspective because it is used by a superfluity of studies.

The second perspective is the size or the negative externality of finance, which emerges when people rethink the global financial crisis. According to this point of view, the financial sector should be kept in a reasonable range in terms of its size. It is not true that the bigger the better or the deeper the better. However, if we intend to analyze from this perspective, we have to determine whether the financial sector overdevelops in the first place: this is a hard nut to crack for the whole world. Nobel Prize-winning economist Robert Shiller writes in this book *Finance and the Good Society* (2012, pp. 17–18) that:

> *To some critics, the current percentage of financial activity in the economy as a whole seems too high, and the upward trend is cause for concern. But how are we to know whether it really is too high or whether the trend is in fact warranted by our advancing economy? What standard do we have?*

Although consensus is seldom reached on the standard, studies in recent years have made a useful attempt to formulate some quantitative standards. Arcand and others working with the International Monetary Fund conducted an empirical study using the data of over 100 advanced and developing economies during 1960 to 2010 (Arcand, Berkes and Panizza, 2012). According to this research, if financial development is measured by the proportion of private sector credit in the GDP, finance is positively correlated with economic growth when the proportion is 100 percent and negatively correlated when the proportion is higher than 100 percent. Cecchetti and others working in the International Settlement Bank made a similar empirical study based on the data of 50 advanced and emerging economies between 1980 and 2010, and reached a similar conclusion (Cecchetti and Kharroubi, 2012). Law and Singh (2014) analyze data from 87 developed and developing countries, and find that the correlation between finance and economic growth is changed when the proportion of private sector credit in the GDP reaches 88 percent. If the proportion of the credit granted by banks to the private sector is used as a measurement, the turning point is close to 90 percent; and if the finance and economic growth correlation is measured by the proportion of employees the financial sector in total employees, the turning point is 3.9 percent.

According to this criterion, most countries hit by the global financial crisis, such as the US, Britain, Ireland, Iceland, Portugal and Spain, were in a state of financial overdevelopment. Deeply influenced by the notion that "finance is the core of modern economy" and given the fact that China has never been hit by a financial crisis and has an underdeveloped financial sector, few discussions and studies of financial reform in China adopt this perspective.

Typical manifestation of financial underdevelopment

The assumption of financial underdevelopment has become a prerequisite to discussion about China's financial reform. It will be analyzed in detail in Chapter 5, therefore only a few characteristics of financial overdevelopment are provided here.

First, most small and medium-sized enterprises encounter the difficulty of hard and costly financing which has caused social concern. Second, banks rely too much on collateral for risk control, and suffer from poor credit technologies and a low proportion of unsecured loans. Third, many necessary basic products and markets are lacking in the financial system: for example, markets of options, interest swap, foreign currency futures and many other hedging products and derivatives severely stagnate in development. Fourth, the proportion of market capitalization and outstanding bonds is far lower than that of advanced economies.

Nevertheless, this book will provide an explanation starkly different from mainstream ideas. Underdevelopment and overdevelopment are both features of China's financial system, with overdevelopment being the dominant. We expect readers' doubts about three aspects.

"Overdeveloped" vs. "not overdeveloped", "undeveloped" vs. "not underdeveloped"

First, as opposites of each other, how can "overdevelopment" and "underdevelopment" co-exist from a holistic point of view? It is easy to demonstrate the co-existence of "overdevelopment" and "underdevelopment" from a non-holistic view, for example, from the perspective of the internal layout of the financial sector or the financial structure. Compared with major economies, whether with the market or banks playing a dominant role, we can undoubtedly conclude the over-developed banking system can co-exist with an underdeveloped capital market. In terms of the structure of financial products or financial innovation categories, China's financial system also features overdevelopment and underdevelopment. On the one hand, financial innovation is excessive, as it aims at institutional arbitrage (Li, 2013) and cannot facilitate the development of the real sector, such as extending the trade chain, increasing opacity and enhancing trade cost; on the other hand, financial innovation is inadequate because of the lack of financial products which help to improve the financial efficiency and basic financial derivatives.

According to the financial cooperation outlook, "overdeveloped" and "underdeveloped" describe the relation between finance and the real economy from different perspectives. Being "overdeveloped" refers to a state of financial development by considering the competition between finance and the real economy, and its opposite is being "not overdeveloped". Such a classification is inspired by the Two Factor Theory or Motivator-Hygiene Theory proposed by US psychologist Fredrick Herzberg (1966). This theory of work motivation distinguishes "satisfied" vs. "not satisfied" and "dissatisfied" vs. "not dissatisfied".

The financial system is "overdeveloped" if it is negatively correlated with innovation and economic growth, it produces strong negative externality and imposes a "crowd out" effect on the real economy; otherwise it is "not overdeveloped".

Being "underdeveloped" refers to a state of financial development from the perspective of the cooperation between finance and the real economy. More precisely, it is concerned with financial efficiency. The classification of financial development status in the sense of financial stability is similar in the sense of competition, namely "over-innovated" and "not over-innovated". It is "not over-innovated" if financial regulation is basically in harmony with financial innovation; otherwise, it is "over-innovated" if the two are not coordinated, and there are pervasive financial innovations for institutional arbitrage (Li, 2013). Being "underdeveloped" is the opposite of the "not underdeveloped" status. The financial system is underdeveloped in the case of low efficiency in serving the real economy, the continuously high financing cost of the real sector and poor financial accessibility; otherwise, the financial system is not "underdeveloped".

Therefore, according to the financial coopetition perspective, the "overdeveloped" and "underdeveloped" status are not necessarily opposite to each other, and poor financial efficiency and strong negative externality of the financial sector can co-exist. People always follow their habit of thinking and speaking to regard the two descriptions as opposites to each other. It is counterintuitive to think they co-exist with each other.

"Overdeveloped" financial sector of China

Question 2: Why is China's financial system viewed as being "overdeveloped"?

Although many financial professionals proclaim that "the real economy is gradually shrinking, while finance grows stronger" (Wang, 2014), the idea that

China's financial system is "overdeveloped" is counterintuitive for most people. Therefore, the top priority of this chapter is to demonstrate the "overdevelopment" of China's financial system.

China's financial system is a typical example of "overdevelopment" according to the quantitative standard aforementioned, since the proportion of private sector credit to that of credit provided by banks to the private sector in the GDP (Figure 2.1) is far above the threshold value provided in the previous discussion.

Despite that, we forego the quantitative standard provided by empirical studies as the basis for our demonstration in this book. First, as a big country with 1.37 billion people and a catch-up economy whose economic aggregate amounts to USD11.18 trillion, China is too unique to be measured by a general standard. Second, according to the aforementioned quantitative standard, China's financial sector was "overdeveloped" as early as 1998, which is hardly convincing. Finally, all such studies have deficiencies; for example, they fail to exclude the effects of the economic development stage on the economic growth rate.

Then is there any evidence of financial "overdevelopment"? The main grounds for this argument in this book is the severe imbalance of the remuneration structure in the financial sector and the real sector. In terms of capital and entrepreneurship, overdevelopment is manifested in the overly high profit rate of the financial sector, or the imbalance of profit structure; regarding talent as an innovation factor, it is embodied in the fact that the income of employees in the financial sector, or the excessive income disparity of employees in the two sectors. We use the profit proportion to measure the relationship between finance and the real economy. On the contrary, many other studies of financial overdevelopment or financialization mainly use the proportion of financial employees or

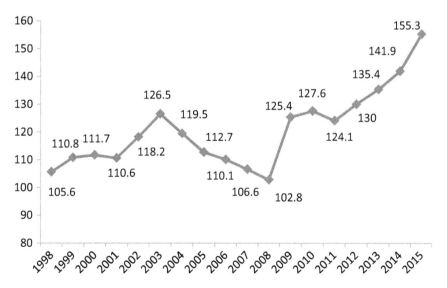

Figure 2.1 China domestic credit to private sector (% of GDP)
Source: World Bank.

that of added value of the financial sector as a measurement. As classified by Krippner (2005), profit proportion is an accumulation-centred view, while the financial overdevelopment is an activity-based view. Krippner (2005) adopts the accumulation-centred view to analyze US financialization; in other words, measured by the profit proportion of the financial sector, financialization is defined as that more and more profits are from the financial sector, rather than trade and goods production. According to his study, such a definition is more inclusive and proper than other definitions: when most profits are generated by financial activities, it is expected that the corporate financial mechanism reflects the rule of the whole financial market; entities once obtaining the strategic position in profit earning will get political and economic power; besides, financial innovation and financial flow are expected to rise, which will impede the activities of the real sector. Such an explanation is also the reason why we use the profit proportion of the financial sector to measure the extraction of the financial system. If the profits of the financial sector account for too big a part in the total profits of all businesses, we can expect other mechanisms to influence the development of the real sector, such as the siphonic effect, the interest group mechanism and the corporate finance mechanism (see Chapter 3 for details).

Since the reward structure (Baumol, 1990) determines allocation of capital and talent, the severe imbalance in the reward structure between the financial and real sector has pushed such factors as entrepreneurship, talent and capital to flow from the real economy to the fictitious economy, generating significant negative externality to the real economy. In addition, financial "overdevelopment" also finds expression in the overly high financing cost of the real economy. All these aspects will be discussed in detail later.

Besides evidence found in the aforementioned three aspects, China's financial overdevelopment is also proven by the proportion of added value of its financial sector in the GDP. In 2015, the added value of the financial sector accounted for as high as 8.4 percent of China's GDP, higher than that of the US (7.1 percent in 2014) and the UK (7.2 percent in 2015), which are famous for developed financial sectors and far above that of Japan (4.4 percent in 2014) and Germany (4.1 percent in 2015), known for their booming manufacturing industry (Figure 2.2).

Overdevelopment as a prominent feature of China's financial sector

Question 3: China's current financial system mainly features "overdevelopment" rather than "underdevelopment", why?

According to the financial coopetition view, the finance-real-economy contradiction contains a principal aspect and a secondary aspect. Therefore, "overdevelopment" and "underdevelopment", if they co-exist, must differ in terms of significance, with either being the dominant. Then which one is dominant? It depends. We think "overdevelopment" is dominant for two reasons.

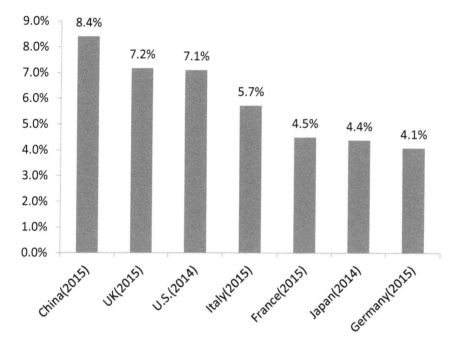

Figure 2.2 The proportion of added value of the financial sector in the GDP: international comparison

Source: National Bureau of Statistics of the PRC, OECD.

First, financial "overdevelopment" coincides with economic downturn. Second, the correlation between the two can be theoretically explained. The analysis framework used by Baumol (1990) reveals the mechanism through which financial "overdevelopment" imposes negative effects on the economy. To be specific, a good number of factors of production are absorbed by such non-productive sectors like finance, thus reducing the overall efficiency of resource allocation. Please refer to Chapter 3 for how financial overdevelopment negatively affects innovation and economic growth.

Excessively profitable financial sector

The "extractive" nature of China's financial system is reflected in the overly high profits of the financial sector, which is hard to deny. China's financial system is a typical bank-oriented one, since the banking sector plays a dominant role in the financial system in terms of the size of assets and profits. For example, at the end of 2012, the assets of financial institutions in China's banking system amounted to RMB13.36 trillion, roughly accounting for 91.3 percent of total assets in the financial sector; while insurance companies, securities firms and funds accounted for less than 10 percent, with assets totalling RMB12.67 trillion. In 2012, the net profits of financial institutions in the banking system amounted to RMB1.51 trillion, taking more than 90 percent of all profits of the financial sector.

Therefore, when data about the profits of the whole financial sector is hardly scarce, we analyze data of the banking system to show severe imbalance between finance and the real economy. We start from introducing two publicly expressed and influential opinions before the dry and boring data.

Hong Qi, President of China Minsheng Bank, said at the Global Entrepreneur Summit convened at the end of 2011 that:

> *We all clearly see fabulous figures of the banking industry in these years. Especially this year when all business lacked funds and faced great pressure to survive and grow, the banking sector outperformed all other industries with huge profits and low ratio of non-performing loans. We sometimes feel guilty for such a sharp contrast, and feel too embarrassed to release the overly high figure of our profits.*

> (Hong, 2011)

Former Premier Wen Jiabao said at a symposium of entrepreneurs during his inspection in Guangxi and Fujian in early April 2012:

> *About financial cost, I would like to be frank here, it is too easy for banks to earn profits.*

> (Xiao and Zhang, 2012)

The two statements sparked off a debate over "windfall profits" of banks at the end of 2011 and the beginning of 2012. However, the debate fizzled out in 2013 and is seldom discussed by scholars on the financial reform and the public from then on.

Nevertheless, there are others who deny the high profitability of the banking sector. Given that, we provide six groups of data about the profit proportion and the profit rate, to further demonstrate the grim truth of severe profit disproportion between finance and the real economy.

Profit proportion: listed banks vs. all listed companies

The profit proportion data of listed banks is frequently cited. Since 2006, this proportion has been rocketing and profit disproportion between the banking sector and non-banking sector has sharply deteriorated (Figure 2.3). In 2011, 16 listed banks earned net profits totalling RMB882.5 billion, accounting for 43.64 percent of total net profits made by all A-share listed companies, testifying Mr. Hong's words about overly high profits of banks.

Bank profits went up even further in 2012 when the total net profits of 16 listed banks increased by 17.35 percent to RMB1.04 trillion, compared to that

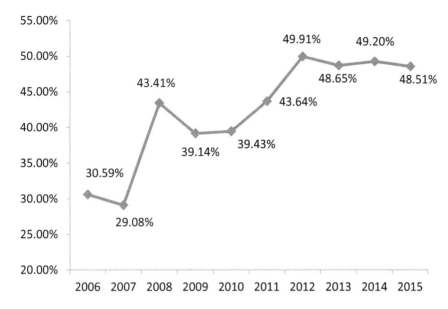

Figure 2.3 The profit proportion of listed banks to A-share listed companies
Source: Wind database.

of all listed companies which edged up by 0.89 percent to RMB2.07 trillion. We should notice that this growth rate of 0.89 percent is also contributed to by new listed non-banking companies. At the end of 2012, the number of A-share listed companies reached 2,387, 153 more than in 2011. None of the 153 new listed companies is in the banking sector. The profit proportion of listed banks grew by 6.27 percentage points on a year-on-year basis to 49.91 percent. The banks' profits were higher in 2012 than the "overly high" level in 2011. Disappointingly, the profit disproportion between the banking sector and the non-banking sector was not effectively curbed. The profit proportion of listed banks stood at 48.65 percent, 49.20 percent and 48.51 percent respectively in 2013, 2014 and 2015 (Figure 2.3).

However, the profit proportion of listed banks is a deficient indicator which simply divides the whole economic system into banking and non-banking sectors. Since the banking sector is much more concentrated than the non-banking sector, listed-company-based sampling leads to severe selection bias. For example, at the end of 2012, the total assets and net profits of 16 listed companies respectively amounted to RMB85.90 trillion and RMB1.04 trillion, accounting for 63.30 percent and 68.57 percent respectively of total assets and net profits of the banking sector. In 2012, industrial companies above the designated size saw their profits total RMB5.56 trillion and the total net profits stood roughly at RMB4.17 trillion with the income tax deducted. Listed companies in the non-banking sector, if all counted as industrial companies, only accounted for 25.04 percent of all industrial companies above the designated size in terms of net profits. In other words, listed banks can represent the banking sector well but listed companies cannot completely and accurately reflect the situation of the non-banking sector. Given that, the profit proportion of listed banks at a specific point in time cannot lead us to properly judge the profit relationship between the banking sector and the real sector. However, we are sure about the severe profit imbalance between finance and the real economy based on the vertical comparison of listed companies' profit proportion.

The profit proportion: financial institutions vs. all businesses

To eliminate selection bias, we use the profit proportion of financial institutions to all businesses as an indicator sampling from all enterprises. Due to lack of data about total profits for the financial sector and all businesses, we cannot work out the value of this indicator directly. Instead, we evaluate it according to business income tax data by proposing some hypotheses. The calculation method has two deficiencies. First, the total profit estimated according to business income tax is actually the taxable income, which may differ from the pre-tax accounting profit. Second, since business income tax should be paid within 15 days after the end of the month or quarter, the estimate may fail to reflect all profits of December or the fourth quarter of the year.

> Hypothesis 1: The financial sector, industrial companies and the non-financial sector are subject to an equal average income tax rate.
> Hypothesis 2: All businesses earn profits.
> Hypothesis 3: The financial sector and the non-financial sector are subject to relatively equal severity of taxation.

Each of them, if seen separately, seems not in line with the real condition in one way or another. For hypothesis 1, despite the basis rate of business income tax being 25 percent, the average tax rate for the financial sector might be higher than in the non-financial sector due to tax collection administration efficiency and tax preference (for example, eligible small enterprises with meagre profits, key state-supported high-tech enterprises and eligible enterprises in western development regions pay their income tax at the rate of 20 percent, 15 percent and 15 percent respectively). Therefore, Hypothesis 1 leads to an overestimate of the financial sector profits.

Regarding Hypothesis 2, the losses of financial companies running under deficits account for a very small proportion of total profits of the financial sector, but this proportion is too big to be neglected in the non-financial sector. For example, in year 2015, 13.16 percent of industrial companies above the designated size suffered from losses which accounted for 14.24 percent of the total profits of industrial companies (Figure 2.4). Therefore, Hypothesis 2 may result in an overestimate of the total net profits of businesses. For instance, in an economy with

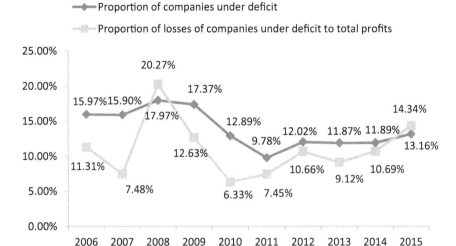

Figure 2.4 Loss of industrial companies above the designated size

Source: National Bureau of Statistics of the PRC.

only two companies, one with pre-tax profits of RMB10 billion and the other losing RMB10 billion, business income tax of RMB2.5 billion is paid if the tax rate is 25 percent. In this case, according to Hypothesis 2, the total profits of all companies should be RMB10 billion, which, however, is zero. The assumption about losses would be theoretically more reasonable. Nevertheless, we cannot obtain data of the total losses of all businesses and cannot work out a credible estimation.

As for Hypothesis 3, Xiao (2011) points out that IT application represented by the Golden Tax Project enhances the tax collection administration efficiency; Lou (2013) holds that the budget system based on balance between income and expenditure may lead to "pro-cyclicality" of tax collection administration. To be specific, when the economy booms, the tax collection administration efficiency is low; otherwise, it is high. Since the financial sector is relatively well regulated and has strong bargaining power with the government, the tax collection administration has been reinforced in recent years in the non-financial sector, leading to an underestimate of its profits.

Combination of the three hypotheses leads to a different conclusion. Although the first and third hypothesis result in a relative overestimate of the financial sector's profits, the second hypothesis may cause a relative overestimate of the non-financial sector's profits. The two errors can offset each other to some degree. Considering data accessibility and other factors, we think the three hypotheses are reasonable in general.

As shown in Table 2.1, the profit of the financial sector accounted for 30.57 percent of that of all businesses in 2014, and the profit ratio between the financial

Table 2.1 The profit proportion: financial institutions vs. all businesses

	(Unit: RMB100 million)				
	2011	2012	2013	2014	2015
Income tax of financial institutions	4,022	5,491	6,276	7,529	8,572
Income tax of industrial companies	7,162	7,349	7,422	7,837	7,425
Income tax of all businesses	16,770	19,654	22,416	24,632	27,125
Financial institutions vs. All businesses	23.98%	27.94%	28.00%	30.57%	31.60%
Financial companies vs Non-Financial companies	31.54%	38.77%	38.89%	44.02%	46.20%
Financial companies vs. Industrial companies	56.16%	74.72%	84.56%	96.07%	115.45%

Source: Ministry of Finance, calculation by authors.

and non-financial sector reached 44.02 percent. Mukunda (2014) claims that the US financial sector is experiencing overdevelopment; however, the profit ratio between the financial and non-financial sector was just 38 percent in 2013.

Considering that the real sector is identical with the industry, we pay special attention to the profit relationship between the financial sector and the industry. According to the calculation result, the profit disproportion between the financial sector and industry deteriorated startlingly. In 2011, the net profit of the financial sector was about 56.16 percent of the profit of industry. The figure soared to 84.56 percent in 2013 and even to 115.45 percent in 2015. Nevertheless, data about the total profits of industrial companies above the designated size released by the National Bureau of Statistics may lead to a different conclusion.

We also calculate the ratio of bank profits to all businesses' profits, as shown in Table 2.2. Between 2008 and 2014, banks' share in the total profits saw a year-on-year increase and reached 26.09 percent in 2014, 9.54 percentage points more than in 2008.

The profit proportion of Chinese banks listed in Fortune Global 500

The third group of data is the profit proportion of Chinese banks in the Fortune Global 500. In 2013, 86 enterprises based in mainland China were included in the Fortune Global 500 (Global 500), including nine commercial banks. Their net profit in 2012 totalled USD256.4 billion, with 57.27 percent or USD146.8 billion contributed by the nine commercial banks (Figure 2.5).

Is this figure high? To what degree is it high? We can answer these questions through vertical historical comparison and horizontal international comparison.

Historical comparison reveals a significant increase of profit proportion of banks based in mainland China in the Global 500 in general. The evolution of this figure has undergone two phases. In the first phase in and before 2008, the

Table 2.2 The proportion of banks' profit

	2008	2009	2010	2011	2012	2013	2014	2015
Income tax of all businesses	11,176	11,537	12,844	16,770	19,654	22,416	24,632	27,125
Total net profit of all businesses	33,527	34,611	38,531	50,309	58,962	67,248	73,896	81,375
Net profit of banks[1]	5,549.10	6,385.50	8,582.90	11,919.90	14,290	16,384.90	19,277.40	19,738.10
Proportion of banks' net profit	16.55%	18.45%	22.28%	23.69%	24.24%	24.36%	26.09%	24.26%

Note: Total net profit of all businesses = business tax income/tax rate-business tax.

It should be noted that banks (depository institutions) and financial institutions in the banking sector are not identical. Besides banks, financial institutions in the banking sector include such non-banking financial institutions as the trust. Data about banks' net profit are from annual reports of China Banking Regulatory Commission (CBRC) in corresponding years. We get the value of banks' net profit by deducting the net profit of non-banking financial institutions from the net profit of financial institutions regulated by the CBRC.

Source: China Banking Regulatory Commission, Ministry of Finance, calculation by authors.

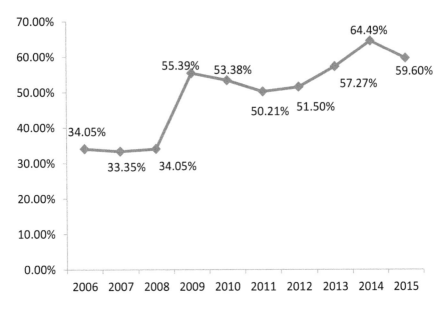

Figure 2.5 The profit proportion of banks in companies based in the mainland of
China among Fortune Global 500

Note: The ranking of Fortune Global 500 is based on the financial data of the previous year.
Source: Fortune Global 500.

figure stood at about 34 percent, a comparatively low level. In the second phase
in and after 2009, it exceeded 50 percent, a quite high level. Besides, it increased
by a large margin compared with the previous two years, indicating the profit
disproportion between the banking sector and the real sector worsened.

According to international comparison, China's banking sector takes too
large a proportion of total profits of all businesses. In 2013, 132 US companies
were included in the Global 500, with the net profit totalling USD567.5 billion. Among them were eight commercial banks, of which the net profit was
only USD67.5 billion, or 11.89 percent of the total, 45.38 percentage points
lower than that of their Chinese counterparts. As per the horizontal comparison
with economies other than the mainland of China, 45 banks in these economies ranked among the Global 500 in 2013. Their profit of USD186 billion
accounted for 14.47 percent of the total profit of 415 Global 500 companies
in economies other than mainland China, 42.80 percentage points more than
their Chinese counterparts. As indicated by the horizontal comparison among
banks, 54 banks in the world were added to the Global 500 list in 2013. Their
total profit stood at USD319.9 billion, with 45.89 percent contributed by nine
Chinese banks. Despite the incomparability caused by differences in the financial
structure and the financial cycle, the huge disparity as just discussed makes it safe
to say that the profit of China's banking system is too high.

Shen (2014) compares the proportion of banks' profit to the GDP in major economies (Table 2.3), and finds that the proportion in China was too high and reached 2.9 percent in 2012, far above that in other major economies in the same period and above their peak after 1970.

We should recognize that the international comparison has limits and situations in different countries may not be completely comparable. On the one hand, financial structures vary a lot in different countries. For example, compared with banks in market-dominated economies (like the US economy), banks, if they play a dominant role in the economy (as in the Chinese economy) have much higher profits. On the other hand, incomparability is also caused by differences in the financial cycle of different countries. For instance, in 2013, when China's financial sector was in an upswing, all banks earned fat profits. In Europe trapped by the debt crisis, a good number of banks suffered huge losses during the financial downturn; and many US banks were trying to restore profitability, since the whole economy was recovering.

Return on equity: listed banks vs. non-bank listed companies

The fourth group of data is about the return on equity (ROE) of banks and non-bank companies among A-share listed companies. The ROE and the return on assets (ROA) are the most important indicators to measure the profit rate of a company. They differ from each other, since the former takes into consideration the company's leverage ratio while the latter does not. Given the remarkable difference in the leverage ratio between the banking sector and the non-banking sector, the ROA is not advisable to compare the profit rate of the banking and non-banking sectors.

In 2013, the ROE of listed banks and non-bank listed companies reached 20.21 percent and 10.14 percent respectively, with a difference of 10.07 percentage points. Is that a big difference? To what degree should we should call it big? It seems to be a big difference, since one is about twice the other. It is also a big one as suggested by the historical comparison. During the period of 2007–2013, the listed banks' ROE has maintained an upward trend since 2007, while that of

Table 2.3 International comparison in terms of the proportion of banks' profit in the GDP

	2012	Peak after 1970	Peak year
China	2.90%	2.90%	2012
US	0.70%	1.00%	2006
Japan	0.50%	0.80%	2005
Germany	0.80%	1.10%	2004

Source: CEIC, Morgan Stanley Research, quoted from PPT presentation entitled "Global Economic and Financial Situation: Hints for China's Macro-prudential Regulation" by Shen Liantao.

listed non-bank companies has been declining. In the past two years the ROE of the banking sector has declined sharply, the difference of ROE between the banking sector and the non-banking sector still remains huge (Figure 2.6).

Some scholars may have different ideas about the banks' excessively high profits, an ROE-based conclusion. Instead, they hold that industrial companies much outperform banks in terms of profit making if the ROA is considered. For example, Yang Kaisheng (2014a, 2013, 2012) compares the profit rate of banks and industrial companies above the designated size. By using data of listed banks and those about industrial companies above the designated size released by the National Bureau of Statistics of the PRC, Yang Kaisheng (2013) concludes that the average ROA of listed banks stood at 1.23 percent while that of industrial companies reached 7.39 percent in 2013. However, as a more important indicator for capital or stockholders, the ROE should prevail in the case of inconsistency or deviation between the two indicators.

International comparison of the banking sector's yields

The sixth group of data is about the profit margin of the 1,000 largest banks in the world. Among the top 1,000 banks selected by the British magazine *The Banker* in 2013, Chinese banks accounted for 13 percent of all assets of these banks, but 30 percent in terms of the profit. That means the profit rate of Chinese banks was 2.31 times the average level of the international banking industry.

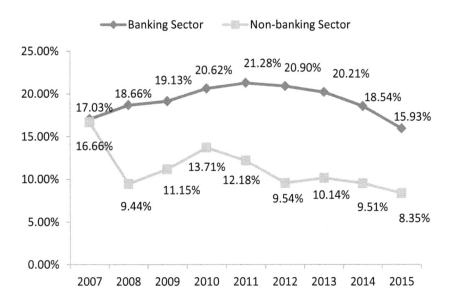

Figure 2.6 ROE of listed companies: banking sector vs. non-banking sector

Source: Wind database.

The sixth group of data tells the ROE of the banking sector in different countries. As shown in Figure 2.7, the ROE of China's banking sector is significantly higher than that of major economies like the US and Germany and also far above the average level of the upper middle-income and high-income economies.

Two doubts about the overly high profit of the banking sector

The historical comparison and international comparison based on the aforementioned five groups of data show the high profit of the financial sector from the perspectives of the profit proportion and the profit rate. However, there are still some doubts. Besides those based on data, for example, Yang (2012, 2013, 2014a), another two ideas are typical.

Some argue that the high profit of banks is only an accounting phenomenon. For instance, in an article named "Inflate Banking Profits Fail to Cover Lagged Credit Loss" (Xu, 2012), Liao Qiang holds that "underlying the high ROA is the time lag of credit losses". Similarly, Wu Weijun (2012) maintains that "the credit cost accounting is limited, as it only records credit cost incurred, but fails to reflect expected credit cost of the economic cycle". Niu (2013) shares the same idea that the banks' profits look high because the risks lag behind the profit for the period. To summarize, people may regard the high profit of the banking sector as a false phenomenon and attribute it to the unreasonable accounting

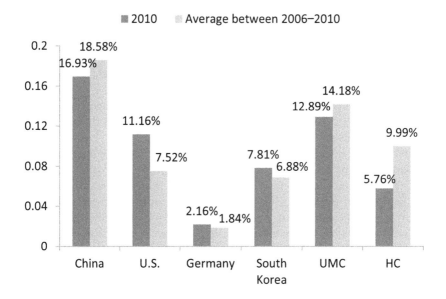

Figure 2.7 ROE international comparison of the banking sector

Note: UMC means upper middle-income economies, and HC indicates high-income economies.

Source: IMF.

principles to some degree; therefore, they argue that banks do not deserve too much criticism and blame.

Some others think the profit of the financial sector is cyclically and temporarily high in a certain stage, rather than lastingly high in the long run. In other words, the conclusion that the banking sector has high profits is a deficient and one-sided one, because the analysis behind it is based on a too short period of time. Zhou (2012) points that the profit of the banking sector is highly cyclical. In the article mentioned in previous paragraph, Xiang (2012) claims that "in the long run, banks do not earn high or windfall profits"; Niu (2013) shares the same idea and said in 2013 at The Bund Global Financial Summit that:

> *China has never undergone a complete economic cycle. Banks made huge profits in the past decades. According to rough calculation, their accumulated profits amounted to RMB3 trillion in the past ten years; particularly, they exceeded RMB1 trillion in the past two years. However, things are different if we look back in twenty years. Banks earned no profit between 1992 and 2002; instead, their non-performing loans reached RMB3 trillion. Therefore, banks' profit rate has been under the average level as far as past two decades are concerned.*

The aforementioned two theories hold the high profit of the banking sector to be an "illusion" or a "false phenomenon". Undeniably, they both tell the truth and can help us to develop a comprehensive understanding of the high profit problem in the banking sector and work out an effective solution. However, such ideas do not impose severe challenges to our proportion about the extractive financial system. Given the habit of decision making, the high profit, whether inflated or temporary as different scholars put it, has almost the same effect on decision making by individuals and enterprises as the real and lasting high profit does. Such illusions impose effects on resource allocation just as real factors.

1   Enterprises rely mainly on the accounting profit rather than the seemingly more reasonable profit indicators when making decisions: these indicators have deficiencies.
2   Neither enterprises nor individuals can make decisions for a period longer than a few decades and usually shorter than the lifespan of the enterprise, let alone an economic cycle. According to information from the Enterprise Registration Bureau and the Economic Information Center of the State Administration of Industry and Commerce of the PRC (2013), by the end of 2012, almost half of all enterprise had been running for less than five years; a special investigation group of the Central Committee of China National Democratic Construction Association (2010) reveals that the average lifespan of small and medium-sized enterprises is only 3.7 years in China and 8.2 years even in the US. It is too demanding for people, especially entrepreneurs, to take a long-term perspective as far as banks' profits are concerned.

Therefore, the two opposite ideas demonstrate the extractive character of the present financial system rather than deny the proposition about the banks' high profits. In the long run, the financial system based on temporary and inflated profits is more extractive and generates more negative externality.

The excessively high income of financial employees

The "extractive" financial system also features the excessively high income of financial employees, which is associated with the overly high profits of the financial sector. To demonstrate this, we provide three groups of data.

Per capita remuneration of urban employees: financial institutions vs. all employers

We compare the per capita remuneration of urban employees working for financial institutions and those working for all urban employers through sampling. In the past decade the average remuneration for urban financial employees was significantly enhanced compared with that for all urban employees: in 2013, it was 1.94 times higher (Figure 2.8).

Along with the upward trend of the average remuneration for financial employees, the financial sector in 2009 replaced information transmission, computer

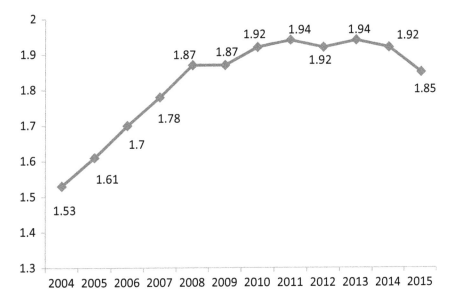

Figure 2.8 Average remuneration of urban employees: financial institutions/all employers

Source: National Bureau of Statistics of the PRC.

service and software and the high-tech industry, to have the highest average remuneration for its employees. About half of all financial employees are those working with insurance companies and with a comparatively low income. If only employees in the banking sector and the securities sector are considered, their average remuneration is much higher than their counterparts in information transmission, computer service and software industries (Figure 2.9).

Per capita income: listed banks vs. non-bank listed companies

The second group of data is about the per capita income of listed banks and non-bank listed companies. In both absolute or relative numbers, the gap of per capita income between listed banks and non-bank listed companies widened in recent years. In 2012, the per capita income of listed banks was RMB261,800. This figure is RMB152,200 higher than that of non-bank listed companies, a disparity RMB58,900 larger than in 2008. Besides, it is 2.39 times the per capita income of non-bank listed companies. In 2008 the per capita income of listed banks was 2.11 times that of non-bank listed companies in 2008 and in 2009 it rose to 2.15 (Figure 2.10).

The comparison is from 2008 due to data accessibility. For example, data about the number of employees in the Agricultural Bank of China at the beginning of 2007 (or at the end of 2006) is absent, so it is hard to calculate the per capita remuneration in 2007. Samples selected from listed banks are unrepresentative if we look back further.

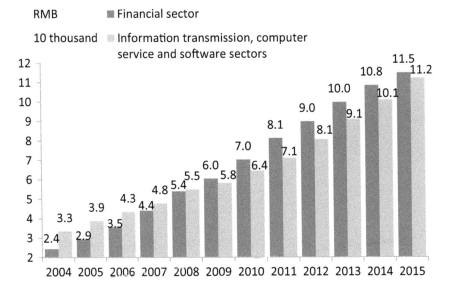

Figure 2.9 Average remuneration of urban employees in different industries

Source: National Bureau of Statistics of the PRC.

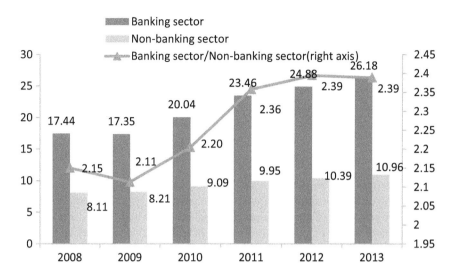

Figure 2.10 Average annual remuneration of listed companies: banking industry vs. non-banking industry (Unit: RMB10,000)

Source: Wind database.

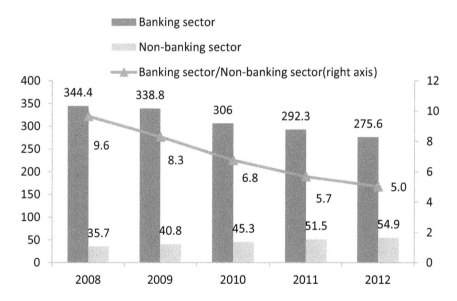

Figure 2.11 Average annual remuneration of the top three executives in listed companies: banking sector vs. non-banking sector (Unit: RMB10,000)

Source: Wind database.

The per capita income of executives: listed banks vs. non-bank listed companies

The third group of data is the average annual remuneration of the top three executives in listed banks and non-bank listed companies. The gap between listed banks and non-bank listed companies became narrow in terms of the absolute and relative number although the average disparity is still large. In 2012, the average annual remuneration of the top three executives in listed banks stood at RMB2.756 million, 5.02 times that in non-bank listed banks (Figure 2.11).

High financing cost for real economy

The excessively high financing costs of the real sector are an important manifestation of the extraction of the financial system. According to the financial coopetition outlook, finance and the real economy compete with each other in four aspects, particularly for the real economy's profits after tax and before interest. Too costly financing for the real economy means, to some degree, finance gains an upper hand in the competition.

We should also notice that costly financing for the real economy also reflects low financial efficiency. How can we distinguish the extraction of the financial system from low efficiency? Generally speaking, if the high financial cost is due to technical reasons of the financial system, such as poor infrastructure and lack of risk control techniques, it is a manifestation of low financial efficiency. Otherwise, it reflects the extraction of the financial system, if dominance of the financial sector leads to an unreasonably high price for financial services and co-existence of high financing cost of real economy and high profits of finance.

This book regards the high financing cost of the real economy to be a manifestation of the extraction of the financial system for three reasons. First, the high financing cost of the real economy is accompanied by handsome profits and a high profit rate for the banking sector. That means the banking sector gains at the expense of the real economy. High financing costs mainly reflect the superiority of financial institutions over the real economy.

Second, low financial efficiency, which is also a cause of high financing costs, is caused by the superiority of financial institutions. Therefore, high financing costs reflect the extraction of the financial system. That is the case in China.

Third, costly financing makes the financing system even more "extractive". It brings more profits to the financial sector and directly lowers the profits of the real sector. This trade-off worsens the profit disproportion between finance and the real economy and leads to an imbalance of the reward structure in these two sectors. Consequently, the real economy is disadvantaged in contending for innovation factors which increasingly flow to the financial sector.

The costly financing of the real economy will be further discussed in Chapter 5.

References

Arcand, J-L., Berkes, E. and Panizza, U. (2012). *Too Much Finance?* [R]. IMF Working Paper, June.

Baumol, W. J. (1990). Entrepreneurship: Productive, Unproductive, and Destructive [J]. *Journal of Business Venturing*, Vol. 11, No. 1, pp. 3–22.

Cecchetti, S. G. and Kharroubi, E. (2012). *Reassessing the Impact of Finance on Growth* [R]. BIS Working Paper No. 381, July.

Enterprise Registration Bureau and Economic Information Center of the State Administration of Industry and Commerce of the PRC (2013). Breaking "Bottleneck" and "Dangerous Period" to Embrace the Critical Stage – Analysis Report on the Lifetime of Domestic Enterprises in China [J]. *China Development Observations*, Vol. 9, pp. 28–32.

Hellmann, T., Murdock, K. and Stiglitz, S. (1998). Financial Restraint: Towards a New Paradigm. In *The Role of Government in East Asian Economic Development – Comparative Institutional Analysis* [A], edited by A. Masahiko, K. Hyung and O. Masahiro. Economic Press China, April, pp. 183–235.

Herzberg, F. (1966). *Work and the Nature of Man* [M]. Cleveland: World Publishing.

Hong, Q. (2011). CMBC President: Banking Industry's Profit Too High to Release [N]. *China Economic Net*, December 2.

Krippner, G. (2005). The Financialization of the American Economy [J]. *Socio-Economic Review*, (3). pp. 173–208.

Law, S. and Singh, N. (2014). Does Too Much Finance Harm Economic Growth? [J]. *Journal of Banking & Finance*, Vol. 41(C), pp. 36–44.

Li, J. (2013). Financial Reform: From Conception to Action [N]. *Caixin.com*, September 27.

Lou, J. (2013). *Establishing the Modern Fiscal System*. In *Supporting Reading Material About Decision of the Central Committee of the Communist Party of China on Some Major Issues Concerning Comprehensively Continuing the Reform* [A], edited by the Writing Group of Supporting Reading Material About Decision of the Central Committee of the Communist Party of China on Some Major Issues Concerning Comprehensively Continuing the Reform. Beijing: People's Publishing House, November.

McKinnon, R. I. (1973). *Money and Capital in Economic Development* [M]. Washington, DC: Brookings Institute.

Mukunda, G. (2014). The Price of Wall Street's Power [J]. *Harvard Business Review*, June. pp. 70–78.

Niu, X. (2013). Weak Risk Control in Internet Finance [N]. *www.finance. sina.com. cn*, June 2.

Qiang (2012). Inflate Banking Profits Fail to Cover Lagged Credit Loss [N]. *China Business News*, April 26.

Shaw, E. (1973). *Financial Deepening in Economic Development* [M]. New York: Oxford University Press.

Shen, L. (2014). *Global Economic and Financial Situation: Hints for China's Macro-Prudential Regulation* [Z].

Shiller, R. (2012). Translated by S. Yu. *Finance and the Good Society* [M]. Beijing: China Citic Press.

Special Investigation Group of the Central Committee of China National Democratic Construction Association (2010). *Investigation of and Suggestions for Transformation and Innovation of SMEs in the Post-Crisis Era* [R], December.

Viner, J. (1932). Cost Curves and Supply Curves [J]. *Journal of Economics*, Vol. 3, No. 1, pp. 23–46.

Wang, D. (2014). Address at Tsinghua PBOCSF Global Finance Forum [N]. *http://finance.sina.com.cn*, May 10.

Weijun, Wu (2012). Inflate Banking Profits Fail to Cover Lagged Credit Loss [N]. *China Business News*, April 26.

Xiang (2012). Inflate Banking Profits Fail to Cover Lagged Credit Loss [N]. *China Business News*, April 26.

Xiao, J. (2011). Reform and Innovation of Tax Collection and Administration System – Interview With Xiao Jie, Minister of the State Administration of Taxation [N]. *Study Times*, August 29.

Xiao, Z. and Zhang, H. (2012). Wen Jiabao: Domestic Banks Easily Earn Profits [N]. *www.cnr.cn*, April.3.

Xu, Y. (2012), Inflate Banking Profits Fail to Cover Lagged Credit Loss [N], *China Business News*, April 26.

Yang, K. (2012). Comparatively Low Profit Margin of China's Banking Sector: A Comprehensive Interpretation Is Need. *China Economic Net*, March 5.

Yang, K. (2013). A Tentative Opinion on Banks Funded by Private Capital [J]. *Century Weekly*, Vol. 48, pp. 62–63.

Yang, K. (2014). Misunderstandings to Be Clarified about China's Banking Sector [N]. *www.caixin.com*, June 2.

Zhou, X. (2012). Zhou Xiaochuan: China's Banking Sector Have Handsome Profits But Far From Windfall Profits [N]. *Xinhuanet*, March 12.

3 The "finance curse"

We are throwing more and more of our resources, including the cream of our youth, into financial activities remote from the production of goods and services, into activities that generate high private rewards disproportionate to their social productivity.

– [US] James Tobin (1984, p. 14)

In this chapter, we will discuss the harm caused by the "extractive" financial system, or the so-called "Financial Curse". Some scholars discuss the positive effect of the overly high profits of the financial system. For example, Lu Lei (2012) says:

Whether we like it or not, the banking sector will continue to earn fat profits. Only in this way, can economic hard landing and financial instability be avoided, and can the economic development model, structural adjustment and steady growth be realized through financial resource allocation.

As with the "Resource Curse" (Auty, 1993; Sachs and Warners, 2001) or the "Dutch Disease", the "Finance Curse" was first proposed by Christensen and Shaxson (2013) to describe the negative effect of an oversized financial centre and financial sector on the whole economy. It refers in this book to the phenomenon that financial development not only fails to promote innovation and economic growth but becomes a "curse" which blocks them.

The term "Finance Curse" refers to the negative correlation between financial development and economic growth. We define five mechanisms through which the "Finance Curse" functions: the "siphonic effect", the "erosion effect", the interest group, corporate finance and financial instability. The first four mechanisms reflect the competition between finance and the real economy. The fifth results from the combined effects of the first four.

The mystery of China's economic growth

Economic growth and its engine lie in the core of economics. Nobel Laureate Robert Lucas (1988, p. 5) once said: "Once one starts to think about them (economic growth problems), it is hard to think about anything else". That is especially true for Chinese economists. On the one hand, China has undergone a miracle of economic growth since the reform and opening up were launched, but its growth has been slowing down in recent years. The mystery of China's economic growth puzzles people in two ways: the secret of the Chinese miracle and the secret of China's slowdown.

China has made its mark in the history of the world economy with its outstanding achievements in reform and opening up. Many economists at home and abroad explain this miracle from different perspectives. A typical idea represented by those using the model proposed by Baumol (1990) attributes the economic takeoff mainly to a higher allocation efficiency caused by the reallocation of resources or factors of production. Wu Jinglian (2008) proposes two reasons for the rapid economic growth in China. Reform provides numerous possibilities for capable entrepreneurs to start productive activities; and, it enhances the reward for such activities. As a result, entrepreneurs are devoted to production activities, bringing forth the boom of private entrepreneurship and the prosperity of the private sector. Zhang (2012) points out that the biggest change resulting from the reform and opening up is the flow of entrepreneurs from government departments and the agricultural sector to commerce and industry, which promotes the optimization of resource allocation and of productive innovation. Baumol (1990) proposes that the allocation of such factors of innovation as entrepreneurs will have great influence on economic growth.

China's economic development slowed down to a medium or medium high growth rate (Liu, 2013) which became the "new normal". Although economists dispute whether China can maintain the average growth rate of about 8 percent as it has done in the past two decades, they all agree about the slowdown of China's potential growth and only differ in terms of the degree of decline. China's potential growth slowdown is explained from both the supply and demand sides in many studies. The supply-side explanation is represented by Cai (2012) which attributes the slowdown to changes in the demographic structure and the labor supply-demand relationship, or the disappearance of the demographic dividend. Wang, Zhang and He (2009) and others provide more reasons from the supply side, such as the decline of the savings rate and capital formation and less space for total factor productivity improvement.

Explanations based on the demand side are represented by Liu (2013), who argues that under given technical conditions and budgets, the boundary constraint of demand will lead to excess capacity (which perhaps lasts for a long time as reflected by the whole history of industrialization and urbanization) despite supply adequacy and thus reduce the economic growth rate.

The economic slowdown can also be interpreted from the financial perspective. It may be caused by the lower efficiency of the financial sector in serving the real economy or the decline of the financial resource allocation efficiency.

To some degree, it is a simple and direct explanation with a certain rationality. However, according to the financial coopetition outlook, finance exerts influence on the real economy through other mechanisms than can be explained by the Baumol (1990) model. The re-allocation of entrepreneurs from government departments and the agricultural sector to commerce and industry, as described by Zhang (2012) is not reversed. Financial "overdevelopment" or reinforced "extraction" of the financial system, the reward of non-productive activities such as finance, is enhanced much more than in the real sector, allocation of entrepreneurs inside the commercial and industrial sector is changed, with more flowing into the financial sector instead of the real economy, leading to deterioration of resource allocation structure and decline of productive innovation capacity and performance. Allocation of talent, capital and other factors is changed in a similar way.

Is low financial efficiency or the financial "extraction" dominant? According to the financial cooperation outlook and the financial centralism perspective, the dominant mechanism is the low efficiency of financial resource allocation; on the contrary, the financial coopetition outlook foregrounds the deterioration of innovation factor allocation between finance and the real economy. We analyze the fall of Britain for a further demonstration.

A lesson from the fall of Britain

The fall of Britain is a thought-provoking case in modern world economic history. Britain underwent a severe economic downfall when compared with its heyday in the mid-19th century and in the period shortly after World War II. As recorded by the eminent British diplomat Sir Nicholas Henderson (1987), between 1954 and 1977, Britain's GDP increased by 75 percent in total and France and Germany saw a rise of 197 percent and 210 percent respectively; besides, the per capita GDP of France and Germany was only 93 percent of that of Britain in 1954, and the ratio grew to 141 percent and 146 percent respectively in 1977.

Britain's economic downfall was mainly manifested by the decline of the real economy or industry, which is testified by data provided by Henderson (1987). Among the total export value of manufactured goods of OECD countries, Britain, France and Germany accounted for 18.9 percent, 7.2 percent and 12.2 percent respectively in 1954, and the ratios became 8.5 percent, 8.9 percent and 18.8 percent respectively in 1977. That means the key to understanding the fall of Britain is to determine why its real economy declined.

Britain used to be a world financial centre with a highly advanced financial sector. Its financial system had high efficiency in terms of the turnover rate in the stock market and the interest margin and the proportion of the operating cost in the total assets in the banking system (Levine, 2002). Therefore, the fall of Britain's real economy equals the downfall of a real economy with high efficiency of financial resource allocation.

From the perspective of resource allocation, the basic reason for the downfall of Britain's real economy is that the best talents were not allocated to the real economy.

> *We have a different attitude towards a career in industry. In the federal republic – as indeed in Germany since the time of Bismarck – industry has tended to attract the best people, whereas in the United Kingdom those leaving school and university seem less prepared to make a career in industry than to join a merchant bank in the City of London or one of the public services. It is partly a question of tradition and prestige but also one of finance. According to the latest figures, the average salary of a middle-grade manager, adjusted for taxes and differences in cost of living, is nearly twice as high in France and Germany as in the United Kingdom.*
>
> (Henderson, 1987, p. 69)

Why did Britain's real economy attract so few of the best people? As Henderson says, it is partly a question of tradition and prestige but also one of finance. Tradition and prestige count because of culture, which means the culture of suspicion of material and technical development and the decline of the industrial spirit (Wiener, 2013). It is a question of finance because of the income disparity between financial employees and their counterparts in the real economy. The root of this disparity is the imbalance between finance and the real economy, or the "overdevelopment" of the financial sector.

Based on the aforementioned analysis, we can establish a logical chain demonstrating the positive feedback between the "overdevelopment" of the financial sector and the fall of Britain's real economy (Figure 3.1).

Notably, besides the relationship indicated in Figure 3.1, financial "overdevelopment" and the fall of the real economy in Britain correlate with each other in another way. Financial overdevelopment spawned a great stratum of financiers, which then become a powerful group of vested interests inside the economic system, imposing considerable influence on Britain's policies. Due to significant inconsistency in interests between financiers and the real economy, the development of the latter was impeded by unfair policies. For example, a powerful stratum

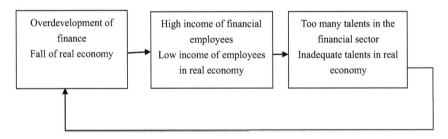

Figure 3.1 Rationale for the relation between financial overdevelopment and the fall of the real economy in Britain

of financers favoured policies leading to interest rate overvaluation, which did no good to the export-oriented manufacturing industry in Britain (Chang, Andreoni and Kuan, 2013; Mukunda, 2014).

The "siphonic effect": a major mechanism of the "finance curse"

Two links in resource allocation: primary allocation and re-allocation

Resource allocation is an important function of the financial system and is regarded by Levine (2005) as the leading function among the functions of the financial system. Levine (2005) describes the functions of the financial system, including information supply and capital allocation (resource allocation), monitoring investments and exerting corporate governance after providing finance, facilitating the trading, diversification and management of risk, mobilizing and pooling savings, and easing the exchange of goods and services. Many studies observing the financial coopetition outlook regard improving the resource allocation function of the financial system as the objective for reforms (Li, 2014; Xie and Zou, 2013; Ba, 2013). We agree that financial reform should aim at enhancing resource allocation efficiency. However, under the "extractive" financial system, resource allocation efficiency cannot be enhanced by improving the efficiency of the financial system in serving the real economy.

Based on this analysis of the mystery of China's economic takeoff and the fall of Britain, we think it is necessary to distinguish two types of resource allocation respectively based on the financial cooperation outlook and the financial coopetition outlook. The two types of resource allocation have significantly different connotations, since the underlying financial outlooks have essential differences as far as the competition between finance and the real economy is concerned.

According to the financial cooperation outlook, resource allocation, from the perspective of the financial system, means the financial system can allocate its disposable resources to different sectors of the real economy. In this case, the low efficiency of finance in serving the real economy indicates that the financial system fails to allocate financial resources to more profitable or efficient sectors in the real economy. Such low efficiency is mainly reflected in the fact that financial resources, mainly banks' credit, concentrate in low-efficiency sectors: instead, market-based sectors with outstanding performance and medium-size and small-size enterprises lack financial support (Ba, 2013).

According to the financial coopetition outlook, resource allocation, taking stock of the whole economic system, refers to not just allocation of resources in the financial system among different sectors of the real economy, but also refers to allocation of such factors of production and innovation like talents, capital and entrepreneurs, between finance and the real economy. If resource allocation based on the financial cooperation outlook is resource allocation in the narrow sense, then that based on the financial coopetition outlook is resource allocation in the broad sense.

For better understanding, resource allocation based on the financial competition outlook is divided theoretically in two parts: primary allocation and re-allocation. Primary allocation means the distribution of resources in the whole economic system and refers to resource distribution between finance and the real economy. Re-allocation means that the financial system can distribute its disposable resources among different sectors of the real economy. For example, financial resources can be allocated among enterprises with different ownership, different sizes, in different industries and with different innovation capacities.

To conclude, resource allocation based on the financial coopetition outlook includes primary allocation and re-allocation: but resource allocation based on the financial cooperation outlook only refers to re-allocation.

Re-allocation: multiplier effect or leakage effect?

From the perspective of financial allocation, the financial coopetition outlook differs from the financial cooperation outlook since it considers the primary allocation of resources. Whether it is necessary to consider primary allocation depends on the role of finance in the primary allocation. What effect does finance produce, a "multiplier effect" or a "leakage effect"? Which one is dominant?

Finance might produce the "multiplier effect" in re-allocation. Outstanding talents flowing to the financial sector in the primary allocation can apply their capability to sectors in the real economy by using finance as a "converter" and even an "amplifier". The most typical example is venture capital. A good number of capable entrepreneurs with rich experience in management and starting up businesses and profound industrial background are devoted to venture capital. They might be re-allocated to the real economy by serving as directors or executives of the invested company who assist or lead the development of the company. Their rich experiences can provide a great deal of value-added service to innovative enterprises, especially fledgling businesses. Besides, venture capitalists can work with many invested companies and provide value-added services to more than one company at a time or over their career.

In terms of capital allocation, capital distributed to the financial system in the primary allocation can enhance the overall capability of the financial sector in providing services to the real economy. Besides, with such capital, the financial sector can play a better role in mobilizing savings. For example, the capital strength of the banking sector can be reinforced if capital flows in. Under the restriction of the capital adequacy ratio, capital increase indicates more deposits and further financial deepening. In addition, when access control is relaxed, capital swarming brings forth fiercer competition, which propels financial service suppliers to enhance their service efficiency. Notably, only when not being overdeveloped, can finance produce the "multiplier effect"; otherwise, the "leakage effect" is spawned.

Finance may produce the "leakage effect" in allocating talents. For example, the venture capital sector attracts too many talents who lie idle, since there are not sufficient enterprises in real economy for investment. Besides, a large number of talents get involved in non-productive innovation activities in banks and other companies in the financing sector, indicating innovation talents are not fully used.

The same effect may also exist in terms of capital allocation. For example, as too much capital flows to banks, some may lie idle and circulate only inside the financial system if the real economy has limited demand or fails to provide benefits as expected by the financial sector. The leakage effect leads to two results. The first is the empty operation of funds, which is occurring now in China. The second is excessive expansion of proprietary trading desks, which was the case in the US before the financial crisis swept the world.

If the "leakage effect" is not the major way through which the financial sector plays its role in resource re-allocation, or the financial sector is not overdeveloped, it is of no practical use to distinguish primary allocation from re-allocation. That is because the financial sector can re-allocate excessive factors, which are distributed to the financial sector in the primary allocation, to the real economy through the "multiplier effect".

On the contrary, if the financial sector affects the resource re-allocation mainly through the "leakage effect" or it is "overdeveloped", it is very necessary to divide resource allocation into primary allocation and re-allocation. The aforementioned analysis of the "multiplier effect" or the "leakage effect" of the financial system does not consider the differences in financial structure. For example, non-traditional financial sectors, such as venture capital, angel investment and buyout funds, produce a more prominent "multiplier effect" in allocating talents and financial resources. In general, the "multiplier effect" of the banking system is reflected mainly in its role in financial resource allocation but hardly at all in talents allocation. If the banking system provides guidance, management training and other value-added services besides loans, it produces the "multiplier effect" in talents allocation. The "leakage effect" of the banking system is felt in terms of allocation of both talents and capital; on the contrary, non-traditional finance like venture capital, angel investment and buyout funds can produce little effect. The "finance curse" is attributed to the "leakage effect" of finance in re-allocation which is materialized under such mechanisms as the "siphonic effect", the "erosion effect", interest groups and corporate finance.

To further elaborate on primary allocation and re-allocation as well as the "multiplier effect" and the "leakage effect" during re-allocation, we would like to use the metaphor of a reservoir beside a river as an example. A reservoir is constructed to irrigate downstream farmland more efficiently by using limited water resources. In primary allocation, water is partially reserved in the reservoir and partially remains in the river. In re-allocation, some water in the reservoir is distributed to the downstream river course and some remains in the reservoir. When the reservoir is not "overdeveloped", for example, no fish farms, tourism facilities (like amusement parks) or power plants are constructed, the reservoir has a "multiplier effect" on irrigation in the downstream river course. In other words, it can facilitate irrigation by adjusting the water resource. However, when the reservoir is overdeveloped or businesses are started on the reservoir, it may produce a "leakage effect" on downstream irrigation in the case of a conflict of interest between the reservoir and downstream agriculture. To maintain operation of businesses built on the reservoir, the reservoir will retain too much water regardless of the downstream irrigation demand. What is worse, if businesses on the reservoir bring more benefits, they may attract more workers from the downstream irrigation sector, leading to decline of the downstream agriculture.

Distortion in primary allocation: the "siphonic effect"

People gather together or disperse for benefits. Allocation of outstanding talents including entrepreneurs is deeply affected by the reward structure of the economy (Baumol, 1990; Murphy, Shleifer and Vishny 1991; Acemoglu, 1995). Against the backdrop of excessively high profits in the financial sector and the overly high income of financial employees and under-the-market mechanisms featuring profit-rate-guided capital allocation and reward-based career selection, the financial sector is like a gigantic magnetic field, to which plenty of innovation factors or scarce resources including entrepreneurship, capital and talents flood in, leading to excessive resource allocation to this non-productive sector. In other words, due to over-prosperity of the financial sector, factors of production flow from the real economy to the fictitious economy in a primary allocation of resources, and too much is allocated to the financial sector. In this case, it is inevitable that the production and innovation sectors receive insufficient innovation factors, leading to a systematic resource mismatch, reduction of the driving force and capability of innovation, lower resource allocation efficiency and decline of potential economic growth.

Some scholars disagree. For example, Nicholas Oulton (2000) denies that allocation of resources to the financial sector and other sectors in which the productivity is slowly enhanced will lead to productivity growth slowdown for the whole economy. For one thing, despite its slow growth of productivity, the financial sector contributes more, instead of less, to economic growth, whether in Britain or the US, due to changes in the economic structure. For the other, the total factor productivity growth rate of the financial sector might be underestimated, while that of the manufacturing industry might be overestimated. Philippon (2010) argues that the transfer of the best people into the financial sector might not be beneficial to the whole of society, since such talents may create more social benefits if they are in other sectors. According to Kneer (2013), the flow of highly skilled workers from real sectors to the banking industry leads to lower labor productivity, especially for industries relying on highly skilled workers.

Due to the "siphonic" effect in the "extractive" financial system, too many factors of innovation are allocated to non-productive innovation sectors, leading to lower efficiency of resource allocation and innovation in the entire economic system and erosion of potential economic growth. A causal sequence forms: "prosperity of the financial sector leads to decline of the real economy which results in economic growth slowdown". This is true in Britain and in today's China, and is also true in the US and other economies with "extractive" financial systems.

The "siphonic effect" in China

The "siphonic effect" of China's "extractive" financial system is very prominent and is manifested in three aspects according to innovation factors extracted by the financial system.

From the "real sector" to the "fictitious sector"

A typical manifestation is the allocation of excessive entrepreneur resources to the financial sector. A report on the *Economic Information Daily* in 2011 (Wang and Huang, 2011) quoted a rhetorical question proposed by the proprietor of a medium-size enterprise (SME): "I'm exhausted to run the business just to maintain a profit rate at about 5 percent, accounting for only a trivial part of usurious loan interest. If you were me, what would you do?" Under the "extractive" financial system, a large number of SME owners are in this dilemma and many of them decide to invest their money in the fictitious sector rather than in production. On the Tsinghua PBOCSF Global Finance Forum 2014, Wang (2014) said: "Many people are not interested in real sectors any more; instead, they spend profits earned from real sectors on usury". Chen (2014b, p. 9) also points out that:

> *enterprises withdraw from the real sector and get involved in financial activities (such as small loans, guarantee, impawn and P2P).*
> *In addition, they make use of their cash flow for operating activities and to enhance their financial leverage to help adjust capital surplus and deficiency. For example, entrusted loans, trust loans and private lending drastically increase.*

Playing a role in integrating talents, techniques, capital and other factors of innovation, promoting innovation and optimizing the production function, entrepreneurs are scarce resources; therefore, allocation of too many entrepreneurs to the financial sectors is the most severe harm brought forth by the "siphonic effect".

The "craze for finance" in the job market and the college entrance examination

The second is the excessive talents allocation to the financial sector, typically reflected by the craze for finance in the job market and in speciality selection by college freshmen. The competitively high reward makes the financial sector very attractive to talents and generates a craze for finance. According to the *Report on Employment Quality of Tsinghua University Graduates in 2014*, among master's graduates from Tsinghua University who signed the tripartite employment contract in 2014, 22.4 percent got employment in the financial sector, seven percentage points higher than that of the information transmission, software and information technology service industries which is second only to the financial sector in terms of absorbing master's graduates. Graduates may get employed, pursue further study or remain unemployed.

According to the *Report on Employment Quality of Peking University Graduates in 2014*, the financial sector provided jobs to as many as 29.9 percent of master's graduates from the Peking University who signed the tripartite contract, 7.05 percentage points higher than the IT/internet/communication/electronics industry, the second most popular target among these graduates. However, in the national employment structure in 2013, financial employees only accounted for 2.97 percent of the total urban employees. As shown by the *Investigation Report on Employment of Overseas Returnees* released by the EIC Education for four years in a row, the financial sector has been the top target of returnees, and the proportion of overseas returnees employed in the financial sector exceeded 20 percent from 2010 to 2012.

Under the influence of an employment-oriented education outlook (Shi, 2014), the competition for finance in the college entrance exam is a natural result of the finance frenzy in the job market. On the one hand, candidates for the entrance exam or their parents pay high attention to the financial sector. According to the ranking of attractive specialities released on the website www.edu.sina.com.cn, finance tops the total 598 specialities by capturing attention from 2,916,893 people (Table 3.1).

The finance departments in these colleges are highly competitive. From 2010 to 2012, 17 universities and colleges in the "985 Program" allowed their finance departments and relevant specialities to recruit high school science students independently. These schools include Tsinghua University, Renmin University of China, Beijing University of Aeronautics and Astronautics, Beijing Normal University, Minzu University of China, Nankai University, Tianjin University, East China Normal University, Xiamen University, Wuhan University, Huazhong University of Science and Technology, Sichuan University, Chongqing University, Hunan University, Northeastern University, Jilin University and Ocean University of China. Relevant specialities refer to those with "finance" in their name. Comparing the average admission rate for finance and that of other specialities, we find high competition rates in the entrance exam for finance (Figure 3.2 and Figure 3.3). In 2012, the admission rate of candidates who selected finance as their first choice in the college entrance exam was 17.685 percent and 20.41 percent of candidates passed the admission criteria of the exam, and these rates for other specialities was as high as 48.25 percent and 59.40 percent respectively.

The preference for finance for college entrants exerts a more far-reaching influence on talents allocation than that in the job market. It means the "siphonic effect" has extended to the deeper talent structure or education structure, leading to a mismatch not only in current but also future talent allocation. There is a time lag in the elimination of the "siphonic effect" of the financial sector and to correct the mismatch in talents allocation, which lasts at least four years or as far as the duration of higher learning.

Excessive talent allocation may cause severe problems for the whole of society. Baumol (1990) and Murphy, Shleifer and Vishny (1991) all point out that the

Table 3.1 Ranking of specialities in terms of attractiveness

Rank	Speciality	Category	Attractiveness (measured by the number of people paying attention to the speciality)
1	Finance	Economics	2916893
2	Civil engineering	Engineering	2480224
3	International economics and trade	Economics	2377221
4	Mechanical design and manufacturing and its automation	Engineering	2148936
5	Accounting	Management science	1994517
6	Economics	Economics	1901665
7	Electrical engineering and automation	Engineering	1885464
8	Clinical medicine	Medical science	1557084
9	Law	Law	1481936
10	English	Literature	1458323
11	Electronic information engineering	Engineering	1045797
12	Business administration	Management Science	1033652
13	Computer science and technology	Engineering	1021240
14	Communication engineering	Engineering	957891
15	Automation	Engineering	919772
16	Architecture	Engineering	817597
17	Information and computing science	Science	710153
18	Financial management	Management science	688921
19	Marketing	Management science	664317
20	Information management and information system	Management science	653272

Source: edu.sina.com.cn (on January 8, 2015).

excessive allocation of talents to the financial sector does no good to the whole economy, because these talents would bring more social benefits if they were in other sectors. Professor Shi Yigong (2014), academician from the Chinese Academy of Social Sciences, says:

> *Where do 70–80 percent top scorers in the entrance exam to Tsinghua University go? They are in Tsinghua University School of Economics and Management. Even my best student and the one I want to cultivate most told me, boss, I want to work in a financial institution. I'm not denying the possibility of innovation in finance; however, if all elites in the country wanted to get involved in finance, there would be a big problem to this country.*

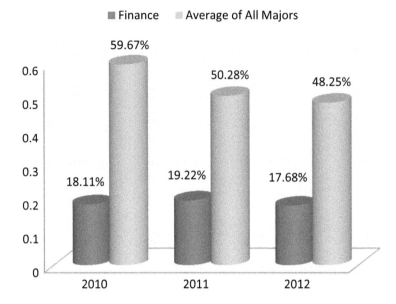

Figure 3.2 Finance competition rate: admission rate of candidates with finance as their first choice

Source: Statistics about admission score of ordinary colleges and universities for candidates in Beijing (2010–2012).

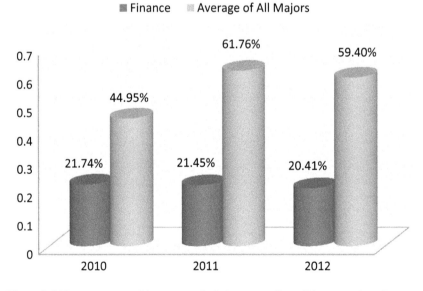

Figure 3.3 Finance competition rate: admission rate of candidates passing the entry level

Source: Statistics about admission score of ordinary colleges and universities for candidates in Beijing (2010–2012).

The integration of industry and finance, informal financial bubbles and the internet finance frenzy

The third is the excessive capital allocation to the financial sector, which is primarily manifested as the preference for an industry and finance combination. Take the combination of central SOEs as an example. By the end of 2011, 117 central SOEs funded by the State-Owned Assets Supervision and Administration Commission of the State Council of China (SASAC) operate normally and take finance as a non-main business; 68.38 percent have been involved in a combination of industry and finance to different degrees (Zhao and Zhu, 2012). In addition, the rise of private banks, the internet finance frenzy and private finance bubbles also show the great attractiveness of the financial sector to capital. In particular, the internet finance frenzy and private finance bubbles are a direct expression of capital swarming to the financial sector under the bank access restriction.

Other mechanisms for the "finance curse"

Besides the "siphonic effect", the "extractive" financial system impedes innovation and economic growth through four channels or mechanisms.

The interest group mechanism

First, the "overdevelopment" of the financial sector inevitably generates a financial interest group with great lobbying power. Notably, we need to distinguish an interest group from a vested interest (group). In this book, the interest group is a neutral term defined as the "individual or organization trying to exert influence on public policies for the same purpose". A vested interest (group) refers in a derogatory sense to stakeholders who enjoy benefits that they should not have or at least should not continue to enjoy under the current irrational institutions or policy arrangements and may try to impede reforms designed to establish a rational structure.

The interest group reflects the competition between finance and the real economy in terms of policy. The financial interest group, once formed, may impose pressure on the government in all possible aspects, so that the government maintains or formulates policies favourable to the financial sector. There is an inconsistency of interest between different sectors in most cases. From the perspective of the contradiction theory, the financial sector and the real economy may be in interest confliction, and pro-finance policies may do harm to the real economy. The most typical example for this is Britain's financial policies. The strong pound policy, while good for the financial sector, exerts obvious negative effects on the real economy (Chang, Andreoni and Kuan, 2013; Mukunda, 2014). Another example is in the US. We see the influence of Wall Street in excessively relaxed regulation before the outbreak of the global financial crisis or in the repeated delay of the Volcker Rule in the post-crisis period.

The financial sector of an advanced economy influences the government or its policies through three channels: "revolving door", ideology advocacy and campaign contribution (Johnson, 2009). The "revolving door" refers to the two-way channel through which financial employees flow to government departments and government officials go to work in the financial sector. Through the "revolving door", former government officials who get employed in the financial sector can capitalize their personal connections to influence government officials and policies; on the other hand, government officials who used to be financial employees can inject their ideology of finance into the government. Ideological advocacy, different from but associated with the "revolving door", makes financial centralism become mainstream in government departments and even in the entire society. In the three decades before the global financial crisis, financial centralism has become a consensus along with the popularity of market fundamentalism. For example, it was a fundamental belief at that time in the US that "what was good for Wall Street was good for the country" (Johnson, 2009; Stiglitz, 2011).

The erosion effect

Secondly, China's "extractive" financial system causes damage through the "erosion effect" which reflects the competition between finance and the real economy in term of distribution of real economy profits. Some argue that the erosion effect of China's financial system is also manifested in low yields on deposits, leading to deterioration of the income distribution structure between the household sector and the corporate sector and dampening of consumption growth. This erosion effect is not in the domain of this book.

Interest comes from profits and is the tax levied from profits (Shumpeter, 1911). When the financial sector has the upper hand, the financial system can take advantage of its bargaining power to obtain profits which should be distributed to the corporate sector to balance finance and the real economy. In this way, development sustainability of the real economy declines due to profit erosion. A typical manifestation of the "erosion effect" of China's financial system is the overly high financing cost of the real economy, which directly causes difficulties for the real economy. The overly high financing cost in the real economy is explored in Chapter 2 and Chapter 5.

Corporate finance

Thirdly, the separation of ownership and managerial power makes the use of proxy a major problem in corporate governance. To solve this problem, the capital market provides an important mechanism for corporate governance. For one thing, capital-market-based control over the company increases the takeover risk and restricts senior executives of the company. For the other, the capital market can reflect the market capitalization of the company in real time and facilitate the performance appraisal of the management, linking management reward to company performance and thus provide incentives for executives. Through these two channels, the capital market can play a positive role in improving corporate governance (Jensen and Murphy, 1990).

However, this governance mechanism has deficiencies. Hostile takeover based on the right of control and the reward incentive linked to the company's performance in the capital market lead to rushed decisions by the management (Crotty, 2005; Lazonick and O'Sullivan, 2000). As a result, some scholars began to pay attention to the impediment of capital market to innovation, although comparison of literature related to the financial system shows that the capital market is more effective in promoting innovation (Allen and Gale, 2002). Mukunda (2014) points out that under the pressure of short-term outstanding performance in the capital market, management pays too much attention to temporary financial performance, which impedes innovation. Kay (2013) holds that the capital market is not a channel for financing; instead, it is a way of spending the company's money.

There are two connected reasons for this. The first is the expansion of the capital market. For example, the market capitalization of the US-listed companies accounted for 53.1 percent of the country's GDP in 1988, and the figure reached 137.8 percent in 2007 (Table 3.2). The second reason is the prevalence of the belief in shareholders' value maximization or shareholder primacy. Shareholder primacy became a dominant principle for corporate governance in the 1980s, which is attributed to the rise of institutional investors (Lazonick and O'Sullivan, 2000) and the expansion of the capital market in terms of its size and influence.

Financial instability

Fourthly, the financial instability mechanism means the erosion of financial stability imposes negative effects on innovation and economic growth. The "extractive" financial system is unstable by nature. On the one hand, the excessively large size of the financial system may reflect by itself risk increasing or the flow of credit to low-efficiency sectors (Cœuré, 2014), entailing instability. On the other hand, due to the "siphonic effect", the "erosion effect", the effect of interest groups and governance, the foundation for sustainable development of the real economy is severely damaged, leading to the decline of the hedge finance proportion and the increase of speculative finance and the Ponzi finance proportion in the financing structure, which may bring about financial instability (Minsky, 2010).

Table 3.2 Capital market size in typical countries: proportion of listed companies' market capitalization in GDP (%)

Year	US	Britain	Canada	South Korea	Australia	Malaysia
1988	53.1	86.6	47.8	56.7	58.5	66.1
2007	137.8	130.2	152.1	100.1	150	168.3

Source: World Bank.

The "extractive" financial system as a global phenomenon

Excessive financialization and the "extractive" financial system

Financialization means the financial market, financial institutions and elites in the financial sector exert increasing effect on economic policies and achievements (Palley, 2007; Epstein, 2005), which is directly manifested by the swelling size of the financial sector. Financialization is a worldwide trend in two to three decades before the outbreak of the global financial crisis in 2008.

From the perspective of the proportion of credit from the financial sector in the GPD, in the three decades before the global financial crisis, the financial sector in major economies other than France and Brazil expanded (Table 3.3).

From the perspective of the ratio of added value of the financial sector to the GDP, most advanced economies, especially Britain but not Germany and France, underwent a process of expansion of the financial sector in the decade before the global financial crisis (Figure 3.4).

The outbreak of the global financial crisis caused a wave of reflection on financialization. A great deal of literature finds a negative effect because of overfinancialization or excessive expansion of the financial sector on entrepreneurship, innovation and economic growth (Assa, 2012; Kedrosky and Stangler, 2011). According to the financial coopetition outlook, over financialization leads to an "extractive" financial system. Before the global financial crisis, the US and Britain had typical "extractive" financial systems.

Types of "extractive" financial systems

The "extractive" financial system generally features financial "overdevelopment". Considering differences between types of "extractive" financial systems, we analyze extractive systems in two dimensions.

The first dimension is financial efficiency. "Extractive" financial systems are divided into high-efficiency and low-efficiency systems. The high-efficiency type features adequate marketization and is typical of advanced economies like the pre-crisis financial systems in the US and Britain. In such systems, the financing cost of the real economy is not so high that it directly hurts the real economy, and the expansion and overly high profits of the financial sector are mainly attributed to the huge trading sector derived from inside the financial sector, or the hedge

Table 3.3 Proportion of domestic credit of the private sector to GDP in major economies (%)

Year	US	China	Japan	Germany	France	Britain	Brazil	Italy	India	Average
1980	94.2	53.1	129.4	73.9	99	26.1	42.5	52.8	20.2	65.69
2007	206.3	107.5	181.3	101.8	102.4	177.7	47.9	97.1	44.8	118.53

Source: World Bank.

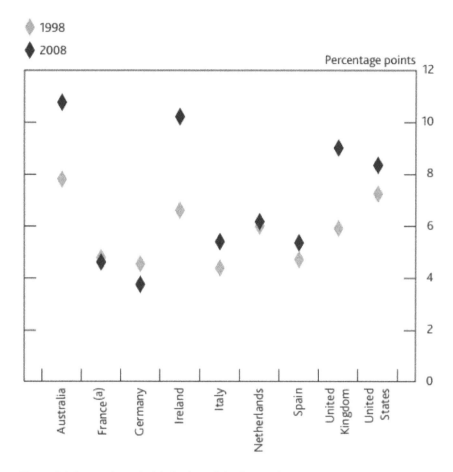

Figure 3.4 Proportion of added value of the financial sector in GDP

(a) Data for France are for the years 1999 and 2008.

Source: Stephen Burgess (2011).

finance of risk aversion and arbitrage with the real economy and financial products as the underlying assets (Yu, 2013).

Low-efficiency financial systems, found mostly in developing countries, may feature adequate or inadequate marketization, represented by the current financial system in China. The overly high profits and employees' income in the financial sector is at the price of excessively high financing cost to the real economy. Damage to the real economy is the precondition for excessive expansion of the financial sector in China.

The financial system is gauged by its efficiency for three reasons. The first is to reaffirm a notion that "overdevelopment" of financial systems, whether they are high-efficiency or low-efficiency systems, leads to "extractive" financial systems.

The financial system of China where the financial sector is not developed and even "underdeveloped" is "extractive"; so was the pre-crisis financial system of the US where finance is highly advanced. "Overdeveloped" and "underdeveloped" finance are not mutually exclusive. "Overdeveloped" is the opposite of "not over-developed", based on the competition between finance and real economy; on the other hand, "underdeveloped" is the opposite of "not underdeveloped", according to the cooperation between finance and the real economy. Therefore, the two kinds of status can co-exist. Please see Chapter 2 for details.

Secondly, mechanisms underlying the "finance curse" are different for the two types of "extractive" financial systems. Through the "siphonic effect" and the interest group effect, a low-efficiency "extractive" financial system produces negative spillover on the real economy through the erosion effect. Thirdly, the two types of systems are formed for different reasons and differ from each other in terms of government mechanisms. The low-efficiency "extractive" financial systems take shape possibly because of inadequate marketization; therefore, promoting marketization is an important option to reform such systems. High-efficiency systems are attributed to excessive marketization, and tighter regulation is a major way to reform them.

The second dimension is "market domination-bank domination". "Extractive" financial systems can be market-dominated or bank-dominated according to the disparity of relative importance of the capital market and the banking industry. In the market-dominated "extractive" financial system, the capital market is relatively important, while the banking system plays a secondary role. The US financial system is a typical representative of this type. In bank-dominated systems, the banking sector plays a leading role, while the capital market is less important. China's financial system is typical of this kind.

This dimension is introduced for three reasons. First, to reaffirm a notion that "overdevelopment" of the financial system, whether market-dominated or bank-dominated, leads to its degradation to an "extractive" system. Bank-dominated financial systems in China and Japan are "extractive", as are the market-dominated systems in the US and Britain. According to the financial coopetition outlook, market-dominated and bank-dominated systems are not necessarily better than each other.

Second, different mechanisms underlie the "finance curse" in the two types of systems. Through the "siphonic effect" and the interest group effect, market-dominated systems produce negative spillover into the real economy through corporate finance, or by encouraging short-sighted or temporary behaviours by companies.

Third, causes and governance mechanisms of the two types are different. Market-dominated systems take shape because of the prevalence of shareholders' belief in value maximization and temporary investment in the capital market, etcetera. Focusing more on the interests of other stakeholders and improving the investor structure are important measures to improve this type of "extractive" financial system.

For these two dimensions, "extractive" financial systems are divided into four types: low-efficiency market-dominated systems, low-efficiency bank-dominated

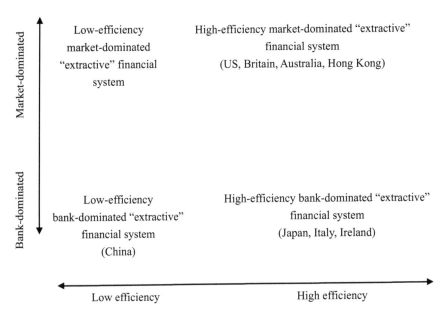

Figure 3.5 Classification of "extractive" financial systems

systems, high-efficiency market-dominated systems, and high-efficiency bank-dominated systems (Figure 3.5). It is almost certain that the financial systems of the US, Britain, Australia and Hong Kong before the global financial crisis were high-efficiency and market-dominated "extractive" systems; on the contrary, Japan's financial system and those in Italy and Ireland before the European debt crisis were high-efficiency bank-dominated systems; and China's financial system after 2008 was a low-efficiency bank-dominated "extractive" financial system.

The "extractive" financial system in the US

A drastically expanding financial sector

Much literature finds drastic expansion of the US financial sector (Greenwood and Scharfstein, 2013; Shiller, 2012; Krippner, 2005, 2012; Johnson, 2009; Philippon, 2008). Since 1940, the relative size of the financial sector has generally kept increasing, and this upward momentum has been even more evident from 1980.

The proportion of output of the financial sector of the US expressed in GDP has been as high as about 8 percent in 2006, while it was only slightly above 4 percent in 1970 (Figure 3.6). According to Mukunda (2014), the profit ratio between the US financial sector and non-financial sector was 24 percent in 1970, which hiked to 37 percent in 2013 and soared to 60 percent in 2003.

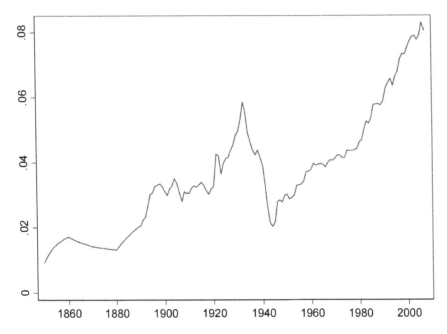

Figure 3.6 GDP share of US financial industry

Source: Philippon (2008).

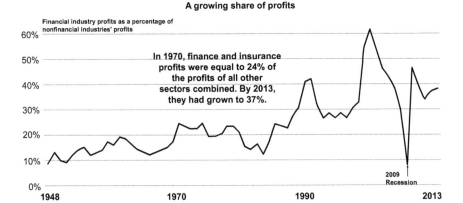

Figure 3.7 Profit ratio: financial sector vs. non-financial sector in the US

Source: Mukunda (2014).

Talents swarming to the financial sector

The swelling financial sector changed the reward structure in the US economy and brought excess income to financial employees. According to Philippon and Reshef (2012), before 1940 and after 1985, financial employees earned even more income. This disparity still existed with the human capital factor deducted (educational background of employees), and reached 50 percent in 2006. The excess income of executives in the financial sector became more evident, and was 250 percent of executives' income in other sectors in 2006, with the human capital factor deducted. This parity was as high as 200 percent even if the unemployment risk factor is deducted too. Johnson (2009) reaches a similar conclusion. Between 1948 and 1982, the average remuneration of financial employees was 99 percent–108 percent of the average remuneration of the entire US private sector, but began to rocket in 1980 and soared to 181 percent in 2007.

The reward structure determines the allocation of human capital including entrepreneurship (Baumol, 1990; Murphy, Shleifer and Vishny, 1991; Acemoglu, 1995). In the US a good number of outstanding talents flooded into the financial sector attracted by excessive salaries. Tobin (1984, p. 14) noted this phenomenon as early as 1984:

> *We are throwing more and more of our resources, including the cream of our youth, into financial activities remote from the production of goods and services, into activities that generate high private rewards disproportionate to their social productivity.*

Goldin and Katz (2008) compare the career development of alumni admitted to Harvard University in different periods and find a similar trend. Among male alumni entering and graduating from Harvard University between 1969 and 1972, 5 percent of them were employed in the financial sector 15 years after graduation. Among those in the period from 1989 to 1992, this proportion drastically increased to 15 percent; for their female counterparts, this figure rocketed from 12 percent to 23 percent.

Philippon and Reshef (2012) find that while financial employees earn more income, their relative educational attainment is also enhanced (Figure 3.8). As a result of too many talents flowing to the financial sector, entrepreneurship declines. Kedrosky and Stangler (2011) find a drop in the new business formation rate in the US and attribute it to the expansion of the financial sector and the high income of financial employees.

Too many talents are allocated to the financial sector and get involved in nonproductive, even rent-seeking activities instead of innovative or productive activities thus reducing the resource allocation efficiency in the US economy. Murphy, Shleifer and Vishny (1991) write that the flow of the best people into sectors like finance is an important reason for the low growth rate of US productivity.

The price of Wall Street power

The expansion of the financial sector reinforces the financial systems and magnifies the influence of the capital market on the real economy. According to an article "The Price of Wall Street's Power" (Mukunda, 2014) published in the *Harvard Business Review* in June 2014, the capital market improperly affects the company's decision making; in addition, businessmen succumb to attractive

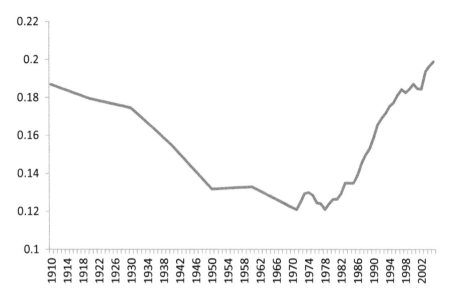

Figure 3.8 The relative educational attainment of financial employees

Note: The relative educational attainment refers to the educational attainment disparity between financial employees and their counterparts in non-agricultural sector (except for the financial sector). Educational attainment is expressed as the proportion of employees receiving education higher than (not including) high school in the industry concerned.

short-term performance on the capital market, and pay too much attention to temporary financial performance rather than innovation with strategic significance, which is harmful for the company's development in the long run.

The delayed implementation of the "Volcker Rule"

The expanding financial sector has more influence on the government. A typical example is the postponed implementation of the Volcker Rule. The Volcker Rule is stipulated in Section 619 in the *Dodd-Frank Wall Street Reform and Consumer Protection Act*, and is an important part of US financial regulation reform in the post-crisis era. The Volcker Rule has three aspects: first, prohibiting banks from engaging in proprietary trading; second, prohibiting ownership or investment in a hedge fund or private equity fund; and third, limiting the liabilities that the largest banks can hold. The first prohibition was postponed till June 21, 2014, instead of July 21, 2012 as scheduled, and again to July 21, 2015.

Repeated delay of the "Volcker Rule" reflects the strong lobbying power of the financial sector, which was severely criticized by former Fed Chairman Paul Volcker (2014):

> *It's striking, that the world's leading investment bankers, noted for their cleverness and agility in advising clients on how to restructure companies and even*

industries however complicated, apparently can't manage the orderly reorgani-
zation of their own activities in more than five years. . . .

Or, do I understand that lobbying is eternal, and by 2017 or beyond, the
expectation can be fostered that the law itself can be changed?

Mukunda (2014, p. 72) states that:

From 1998 through 2013 the finance, insurance, and real estate industries
spent almost $6 billion on lobbying; the only sector to spend more was health care.
In the wake of the 2008 crisis, the financial sector actually intensified its pres-
sure on the government. Look at the 2013–2014 election cycle: As of March 2014
finance, insurance, and real estate had spent almost $485 million on lobbying –
more than any other industry – and donated almost $149 million to the cam-
paigns of federal candidates, nearly three times as much as health care had
donated.

A further question: is a financial centre compatible with an innovation centre?

For most people, the answer to this question is evident. After all, Deng Xiaoping said (Deng, 1993, p. 366): "Finance is very important, because it is the core
of the modern economy. Handling financial affairs well is the key to success
in this sphere". Schumpeter's (1911) innovation theory also points out that
the function of bankers is to identify and screen entrepreneurs with potential
and provide them with capital support. Likewise, classic financial development
theories also argue for the positive correlation or even causality between financial development and economic growth. Since the enhancement of total factor productivity driven by technical innovation is the powerhouse of sustained
economic growth, an inference of financial development theories is that finance
is good for technical innovation. Therefore, compared with the non-financial
centre, the financial centre, which gathers financial institutions, financial factors and financial talents or financers and where financial innovation occurs
frequently, boasts a higher entrepreneur screening efficiency and capability of
providing more capital support; therefore, it can promote productive innovation and become an innovation centre. Apparently, a financial centre is theoretically compatible with an innovation centre. However, the reality is completely
different.

By comparing the distribution of financial centres and innovation centres in
major economies, one may find that usually they are not in the same place. The
most important financial centre is generally not the most important innovation
centre. For example, New York is the financial centre of the US, while the heart
of innovation is Silicon Valley; London is the core of finance in Britain, while
Cambridge has the most innovative ideas; Tokyo is the powerhouse for the financial sector of Japan, while for innovation it is Tsukuba; Frankfurt serves as the
financial centre in Germany, but Munich is the innovation centre; and in India,
Mumbai is the financial centre, and Bangalore the innovation centre.

China's financial centre is in Shanghai and its innovation centre in Shenzhen. At the industrial level, the added value of strategic emerging industries in Shanghai increased by 7 percent to stand at RMB299.75 billion in 2013, a rate lower than the growth rate of the added value of the financial sector and that of Shanghai's GDP. It accounted for 13.9 percent of Shanghai's GDP. Also in 2013, the added value of strategic emerging industries in Shenzhen grew by 20.5 percent to RMB500.250 billion, 10.0 percentage points higher than Shenzhen's GDP growth rate and 6.3 percentage points above that of the added value of the financial sector, and it accounted for 34.5 percent of Shenzhen's GDP. At the enterprise level, few innovation enterprises with world influence are established in Shanghai, although a number of higher learning institutions and research institutions are concentrated in this city; on the contrary, a great number of innovation enterprises emerge in Shenzhen where colleges, universities and research institutions such as Huawei, Tencent, ZTE and BYD are scarce.

Then why are innovation and financial centres not compatible? We find inspiration in industry cluster theory. Among all such theories, the new industrial district theory is a representative and influential theory. According to this theory, the major factor that determines whether an economy, a district or an enterprise can develop high-tech industry and how well they can perform in developing such an industry is not the amount and quality of material capital. Instead, it is determined by social factors such as economic organizations, structure and cultural tradition which can help to tap the potential of human capital.

Based on this theory, we provide a hypothetical explanation of the incompatibility of the financial centre and the innovation centre. The financial sector and high-tech industry need significantly different economic organizational structures and cultures and other social environment factors to tap the potential of their human capital. As the agglomeration of the financial sector is enhanced, the central status of finance is consolidated and the regional influence of finance is increased, so the cultural atmosphere is changed accordingly: this does not cater to the development of innovation enterprises or the high-tech industry any more. An apparent example is that financial employees dress and behave formally, while their counterparts in the high-tech industry follow a casual and relaxed style.

We are also inspired by financialization theories. Financialization refers to the increasing significance of the financial system in economic operations, manifested as an increase in indicators, such as the proportion of the financial sector in the GDP, the profit ratio between the financial sector and all businesses and the proportion of financial employees among all employees. After the outbreak of the global financial crisis, more and more studies focus on the negative effect of financialization on innovation and economic growth. The negative effect is attributed to the aforementioned mechanisms, which cause the incompatibility of the financial and innovation centres. The "erosion effect" is not evident for financial centres, thanks to their high level of financial development and high financial efficiency.

The first is the "siphonic effect". The increasing profit (rate) and employees' income make the financial sector a giant "magnetic field" which absorbs too many innovation factors, such as talents, capital and entrepreneurship. In China for example, in 2013, 25.6 percent of master's graduates from Peking University were employed in the financial sector, and 18.8 percent of graduates from sciences departments of Tsinghua University went to the financial sector, while in 2012, financial employees only accounted for 3.46 percent of all employees in the country. In this case, high-tech industry stagnated due to lack of innovation factors which were excessively absorbed by the financial sector.

The second is the corporate finance mechanism. Affected by the financial market, companies pay too much attention to short-term financial income and invest insufficiently in innovation. This reduces short-term financial income but has a long-run strategic value. In "The Price of Wall Street's Power" (Mukunda, 2014), the Boeing Company was criticized for its overspending and the battery fire on the Boeing 787 because the company, affected by Wall Street, relied too much on outsourcing due to overemphasis on the ROE. It abandoned the former engineering-driven culture and cut necessary R&D spending. Under such a circumstance, innovation-based enterprises can hardly develop themselves because the driving force for innovation is eroded.

The third is the effect of interest groups. The excessive strength of finance provides enough motivation and capability for the financial sector to lobby policy makers to formulate pro-finance policies. Britain is a typical example. Under the influence of the powerful stratum of financers, Britain has implemented the Strong Pound Policy which was favourable to the financial sector for a long time. However, sterling over valuation has impeded the development of the manufacturing industry and as a result the real economy of Britain declined compared with Germany and France. In this case, high-tech industry may fail to prosper due to the unfavourable policy environment.

Then is it true that a financial centre is always incompatible with an innovation centre? Definitely no. Among the aforementioned examples, Silicon Valley and Shenzhen are innovation centres and financial centres as well. Silicon Valley is the venture capital centre in the US, while Shenzhen also ranks among financial centres in China, boasting an active venture capital and mainboard, an SME board and a Growth Enterprise Market. Why are Silicon Valley and Shenzhen major innovation centres? We try to explain in the following ways.

First, it might be because of the size difference of financial centres. Neither Silicon Valley nor Shenzhen is the most important financial centre in their country. Their financial sectors are far from being "overdeveloped". They have remarkably higher employees' income than that in the high-tech industry and impose an evident "siphonic effect" on innovation factors but it is not strong enough to exert influence on local governments so that they formulate policies encouraging the development of finance but dampening that of the high-tech industries.

The other explanation is the heterogeneity of financial centres. In other words, financial centres are different from each other. Silicon Valley and Shenzhen are essentially different from New York and Shanghai, because Silicon Valley and Shenzhen are technical finance centres with particularly active venture capital, while New York and Shanghai represent traditional financial centres. Technical finance is innovation-friendly and affects innovation in a way completely opposite to the mechanism elaborated on by the new industrial district theory and the financialization theory.

First, the venture capital centre needs a free and easy cultural atmosphere and the organizational structure of venture capital institutions is flatter than traditional financial institutions, which is consistent with the requirements of high-tech industry clusters.

Secondly, though absorbing a great deal of capital and talents, venture capital will re-allocate them into innovation-oriented enterprises. What is more, it may exert the "multiplier effect"; for example, venture capitalists may often be sent to work in different innovation-oriented enterprises.

Thirdly, as the long-term strategic investor, venture capital has a risk-benefit structure which is more in line with that of innovation-oriented enterprises, and thus helps to eliminate the short-term behaviours of such enterprises.

Finally, the interests of venture capital and innovation-oriented enterprise are similar. If venture capital can affect government policies, it will push the government to formulate policies favourable to high-tech industries or innovation-oriented enterprises.

References

Acemoglu, D. (1995). Reward Structures and the Allocation of Talent [J]. *European Economic Review*, Vol. 39, No. 1, pp. 17–33.

Allen, F. and Gale, D. (2002). *Comparing Financial Systems* [M]. Beijing: China Remin University Press, June.

Assa, J. (2012). Financialization and Its Consequences: The OECD Experience [J]. *Finance Research*, Vol. 1, pp. 35–39.

Auty, R. (1993). *Sustaining Development in Mineral Economics: The Resource Curse Thesis*. London: Routledge.

Ba, S. (2013). Thoughts and Focus of Financial Reform Deepening [N]. *China Economic Times*, September 3.

Baumol, W. (1990). Entrepreneurship: Productive, Unproductive, and Destructive [J]. *Journal of Business Venturing*, Vol. 11, No. 1, pp. 3–22.

Burgess, S. (2011). Measuring Financial Sector Output and Its Contribution to UK GDP [R]. *Bank of England Quarterly Bulletin*, Q3.

Cai, F. (2012). Historical Law and Gravity – Crossroads of China's Economic Growth [J]. *Academic Frontier under People's Forum*, Vol. 7, No. 2, pp. 6–15.

Chang, H-J., Andreoni, A. and Kuan, M.L. (2013). *International Industrial Policy Experiences and the Lessons for the UK, Centre for Business Research* [R]. University of Cambridge Working Paper No. 450.

Chen, D. (2014). Bubbles in China's Economic Cycle [J]. *China Development Observations*, Vol. 10, pp. 76–81.

Christensen, J. and Shaxson, N. (2013). *The Finance Curse: Exploring the Possible Impacts of Hosting an Oversized Financial Centre* [M]. Kent: Commonwealth Publishing, May.

Cœuré, B. (2014). *On the Optimal Size of the Financial Sector* [R], ECB Conference "The Optimal Size of the Financial Sector", Frankfurt am Main, 2 September.

Crotty, J. (2005). The Neoliberal Paradox: The Impact of Destructive Product Market Competition and 'Modern' Financial Markets on Nonfinancial Corporate Performance in the Neoliberal Era [A]. In *Financialization and the World Economy*, edited by G. Epstein. Northampton, MA: Edward Elgar.

Deng, X. (1993). *Selected Works of Deng Xiaoping* (Vol. III) [M]. Beijing: People's Publishing House, October.

Epstein, G. (2005). Introduction: Financialization and the World Economy [A]. In *Financialization and the World Economy* [M], edited by G. Epstein. Northampton, MA: Edward Elgar.

Goldin, C. and Katz, L. (2008). Transitions: Career and Family Life Cycles of the Educational Elite [J]. *American Economic Review*, Vol. 98, No. 2, pp. 363–369.

Greenwood, R. and Scharfstein, D. (2013). The Growth of Finance [J]. *Journal of Economic Perspectives*, Vol. 27, No. 2, pp. 3–28, Spring.

Henderson, N. (1987). Translated by H. Huajun. Britain's Fall and Its Causes and Consequences – Valedictory Despatch by Sir Nicholas Henderson, Senior Diplomat of Britain [J]. *Research on Western Europe*, Vol. 5, pp. 67–76.

Jensen, M. and Murphy, K. (1990). Performance Pay and Top-Management Incentives [J], The Journal of Political Economy, Vol. 98(2), 225–264.

Johnson, S. (2009). The Quiet Coup [N]. *The Atlantic*, May 1.

Kay, J. (2013). Why Business Loves Capital Markets, Even If It Doesn't Need Capital [N]. *Financial Times*, May 14.

Kedrosky, P. and Stangler, D. (2011). *Financialization and Its Entrepreneurial Consequences* [R]. Ewing Marion Kauffman Foundation Research Paper, March 1.

Kneer, C. (2013). *The Absorption of Talent Into Finance: Evidence From US Banking Deregulation* [R]. DNB Working Paper 391.

Krippner, G. (2005). The Financialization of the American Economy [J]. *Socio-Economic Review*, Vol. 3, pp. 173–208.

Krippner, G. (2012). *Capitalizing on Crisis: The Political Origins of the Rise of Finance* [M]. Cambridge, MA: Harvard University Press, May.

Lazonick, W. and O'Sullivan, M. (2000). Maximizing Shareholder Value: A New Ideology for Corporate Governance [J]. *Economy and Society*, Vol. 29, No. 1, pp. 13–35.

Levine, R. (2002). Bank-Based or Market-Based Financial Systems: Which Is Better? [J]. *Journal of Financial Intermediation*, Vol. 11, pp. 398–428.

Levine, R. (2005). Finance and Growth: Theory and Evidence. In *Handbook of Economic Growth* [A], edited by Philippe Aghion and Steven Durlauf. Amsterdam: Elsevier, pp. 865–934.

Li, Y. (2014). Finance Reforms in the Deep Water Zone [J], *China Finance*, Vol. 19, pp. 68–70.

Liu, S. (2013). *China's Economic Growth in Ten Years (2013–2022) – Seeking New Engine and Rebalance* [M]. Beijing: China Citic Press.

Lu, L. (2012). Banks Will Maintain High Profits, Whether We Like It or Not [N]. *21st Century Economic Report*, January 5.

Lucas, R. (1988). On the Mechanics of Economic Development [J], *Journal of Monetary Economics*, Vol. 22, No. 1, pp. 3–42.

Minsky, H. (2010). Translated by S. Baofeng and Z. Huihui. *Stabilizing an Unstable Economy: A Perspective From Financial Instability* [M]. Beijing: Tsinghua University Press, January.

Mukunda, G. (2014). The Price of Wall Street's Power [J]. *Harvard Business Review*, June, pp. 70–78.

Murphy, K., Shleifer, A. and Vishny, R. (1991). The Allocation of Talent: Implications for Growth. *The Quarterly Journal of Economics*, Vol. 106, pp. 503–530, May 2.

Oulton, N. (2000). *Must the Growth Rate Decline? Baumol's Unbalanced Growth Revisited* [R]. Bank of England Working Paper Series No. 107, January.

Palley, T. (2007). *Financialization: What It Is and Why It Matters* [R]. Economics Working Paper Archive wp525, Levy Economics Institute.

Philippon, T. (2008). *The Evolution of the US Financial Industry From 1860 to 2007: Theory and Evidence* [R]. NBER Working Paper No. 13405.

Philippon, T. (2010). Financiers Versus Engineers: Should the Financial Sector Be Taxed or Subsidized? [J]. *American Economic Journal: Macroeconomics*, Vol. 2, No. 3, pp. 158–182.

Philippon, T. and Reshef, A. (2012). Wages and Human Capital in the U.S. Finance Industry: 1909–2006 [J]. *Quarterly Journal of Economics*, November, pp. 1551–1609.

Sachs, J. and Warners, A. (2001). The Curse of Natural Resources [J]. *European Economic Review*, Vol. 45, pp. 827–838.

Schumpeter, J. (1911). *A Theory of Economic Development* [M]. Cambridge, MA: Harvard University Press.

Shi, Y. (2014). *Research University: Never Oriented by Employment* [N]. Third Annual Meeting of Western Returned Scholars Association, September 16.

Shiller, R. (2012). Translated by S. Yu. *Finance and the Good Society* [M]. Beijing: China Citic Press.

Stiglitz, J. (2011). *Freefall: America, Free Markets, and the Sinking of the World Economy* [M]. Beijing: China Machine Press, January.

Tobin, J. (1984). On the Efficiency of the Financial System [J]. *Lloyds Band Review*, Vol. 153, pp. 1–15.

Volcker, P. (2014). Volcker Lambasts Wall Street Lobbying [N]. *Financial Times*, December 19.

Wang, D. (2014). Address at Tsinghua PBOCSF Global Finance Forum [N]. *http://finance.sina.com.cn*, May 10.

Wang, K. and Huang, M. (2011). Billions of Private Lending May Threaten National Financial Security. *Economic Information Daily*, November 7.

Wang, Q., Zhang, J. and He, Z. (2009). *China's Economy Before 2020: It Is Not Whether Economic Growth Will Slow Down But How* [R]. Morgan Stanley-China's Economy, Morgan Stanley Research Department (Asian/Pacific), September 20.

Wiener, M. (2013). *English Culture and the Decline of the Industrial Spirit (1850–1980)* [M]. Beijing: Peking University Press.

Wu, J. (2008). Further Releasing the Entrepreneur's Innovation Vitality [J], *China Entrepreneur*, Vol. 23, pp. 156.

Xie, P. and Zou, C. (2013). *Thought on China's Financial Reform* [M]. Beijing: China Financial Publishing House, April.

Yu, Q. (2013). *China Foreign Exchange Reserve and Global Industrial Investment* [N]. Beijing: The Commercial Press.

Zhang, W. (2012). *Logic of Market* [M]. Beijing: People's Publishing House.

Zhao, C. and Zhu, H. (2012). Industry and Finance Integration: Trap or Flower [J]. *Capital Shanghai*, Vol. 12, pp. 24–26.

4 The formation of "extractive" financial systems

However, this system is only designed to address deficiencies in a certain period of time and should not last too long. Just as we take medicine to cure disease, but won't take any more when we recover; otherwise, we will be sick too if we take more medicine. . . . Therefore, the nine-rank system is not all bad, since it helped to solve certain problems, but ended up with even more severe ones, because it remained unchanged when conditions and situations were different.

– *Merits and Demerits of Chinese Dynasties* by Qian Mu (2001, p. 53)

China's "extractive" financial system is a result of many factors, including financial factors and factors outside the financial sector. Among financial factors, the postponed withdrawal of financial restraint centred on interest margin protection is most important (Hellmann, Murdock and Stiglitz, 1998). Irrational financial regulation, unbalanced financial structures and irrational accounting standards are also reasons that cannot be ignored. Important factors outside the financial sector were institutional and structural factors which led to the swelling of the financial system. Factors leading to too slow economic transformation and upgrading are important because "extraction" is a concept in a relative sense.

The financial restraint system

The most important reason underlying the "extractive" financial system or financial "overdevelopment" in China is that financial restraint does not cease at the correct time.

Financial repression or financial restraint

There is bitter controversy and misunderstanding about China's financial system. If we suppose there are only two kinds of states of finance: financial repression and financial liberalization, the only thing to conclude is that China is in the state of financial repression since it has not realized financial liberalization yet and its financial policies are accordingly financial repression policies. However, financial restraint is drastically different from financial repression. Given that, we think it is necessary to clarify relevant definitions to prevent policy mistakes due to mis-understanding. Currently, most foreign and domestic literature regards China's financial system as financial repression. For example, Bai and Qian (2009), Liu Ruiming (2011), Kong (2011), He and Wang (2011), Jia and Meng (2013), Niu (2013b), Lardy (2008), Feyzioglu (2009) and Johansson (2012), etcetera. As a matter of fact, during the transformation from a planned economy to a market economy, or at least since the previous round of financial reforms, China has chosen a different way to reform its financial system, which is summarized as financial restraint by the Nobel Laureate Stiglitz and others (Wang, 2001; Chen, 2002; Chen and Qian, 2011; Tian and Bai, 2012). Then why in most literature is China's financial system or financial development described as financial repression rather than financial restraint?

One explanation is that all this literature holds that financial repression and financial liberalization are the only two kinds of states of finance. Since China has taken many measures to regulate the financial sector and has not introduced financial liberalization, it is natural to regard China's financial policies or financial system as financial repression. However, between financial repression and finan-cial liberalization there is a third state: financial restraint. From the perspective of financial reform, non-financial liberalization does not equal financial repression.

Another possible explanation is that some literature generalizes the connota-tion of financial repression. Financial repression in this literature is used differently from its classic meaning (Shaw, 1973; McKinnon, 1973). For example, in some literature, manifestations of financial structure imbalance, such as laggard devel-opment of the capital market, are identical with financial repression. Therefore, it is necessary to clarify the relevant concepts so as to avoid misunderstanding.

According to Hellmann, Murdock and Stiglitz (1998), financial restraint and financial repression have obvious differences. As shown in Table 4.1, the two differ from each other in policy target, tools, preconditions and effect, etcetera. Financial restraint cannot be confused with financial repression. If we have to find some commonalities between them, then we should say neither of them is financial liberalization. Despite that, financial restraint enjoys a higher level of liberalization than financial repression.

Financial policies implemented in China should be classified as financial restraint whether gauged by their target, tools, conditions or their effect. First of all, China's financial policies aim at increasing financial supply rather than extracting rent from the private sector. Second, the major tools used to imple-ment such policies are typical financial restraint tools, for example, interest mar-gin protection to maintain positive real interest rate, access restriction and assets substitution restriction, rather than negative interest rate and overvaluation of the domestic currency. Third, as the previous round of financial reform proceeds, the financial system, including state-owned and state-holding financial institu-tions, becomes much more commercialized, with partial and indirect govern-ment intervention. Fourth, in terms of implementation conditions, China boasts lasting macroeconomic stability, a low and stable inflation rate and non-excessive taxes for the financial sector. Finally, China's financial system is not financially

Table 4.1 Financial restraint vs. financial repression

	Financial restraint policy	*Financial repression policy*
Target	By creating "rent opportunities" for the financial and production sectors, especially financial intermediaries (banks), the policy targets at reducing the banks' moral hazard, encouraging financial intermediaries to provide more goods and services that might be undersupplied in purely competitive markets, such as regulating loans and absorbing more deposits.	Extract rent from the private sector
Tool	Keeping the deposit interest rate below the competitive equilibrium level and creating "rent opportunities" by producing interest margin; imposing control over access and even directly restricting competition to maintain the availability of "rent"; restricting assets substitution to maintain "rent".	Controlling the interest rate to keep the nominal interest rate far below the inflation rate; suppressing the exchange rate, or overvaluing the domestic currency.
Government intervention	Selective intervention	All-around intervention
Implementation conditions	Stable macroeconomic environment, low and predictable inflation rate, no high tax levied from the financial sector (direct or indirect tax), more importantly, positive real interest rate (to curb the loss of deposits)	Low financial development level, weak institutional organization, poor capability of encouraging saving, and negative return on financial assets.
Effect	Promoting financial deepening and enhancing credit allocation efficiency	

Source: Aoki, Murdock and Okuno-Fujiwara, "A New Interpretation of the Role of Government in East Asian Economic Development: Market Enhancing View (Vol. I)", *Comparative Economic and Social Systems* (1996) 5: 6; Hellmann, Murdock andStiglitz, "Financial Restraint: Towards a New Paradigm", quoted from *The Role of Government in East Asian Economic Development—Comparative Institutional Analysis* by Aoki, Hyung and Okuno-Fujiwara, Economic Press China, April 1998: 183–235.

repressive, as far as the policy effect or the financial and economic performance. At the end of 2012, China's financial depth (proportion of credit provided by the banking sector in the GDP) reached 152.7 percent. In the decade between 2003 and 2012, China's annual average growth rate hit 10.45 percent. Such a stunning achievement is hardly imaginable in a country in which the financial restraint system dampens the resource allocation efficiency and impedes the development of the financial sector.

Some literature argues that China has financial repression because its deposit interest rate is negative. Two points should be made clear. First, China's deposit interest rate is negative only in certain periods of time. "If based on one or two decades of observation, the deposit interest rate is positive in general" (Zhou, 2012c). Second, an episodic negative deposit does not necessarily imply financial repression, since it also exists in advanced economies.

Besides the aforementioned analytic paradigm and psychological inertia, there are two reasons why China's financial restraint system is easily misunderstood to be financial repression. On the one hand, financial restraint and financial repression look similar; for example, they both stress interest rate control and extract benefits from the household sector; on the other hand, China has a unique economic system.

The essential difference between the two states lies in the distribution of rent, which, however, is ignored by the public because of China's special economic system. Unlike in a repressive financial system, rent is partially extracted from the household sector, and partially created by banks which are more motivated to encourage depositing and strengthen loans management. Rent created by financial restraint goes largely to the financial sector and less to the production sector. Nevertheless, state-owned banks dominate China's banking sector, while many scholars, especially those paying special attention to the ownership structure, usually regard the state-owned banks as government departments. In fact, after the previous round of financial reform, especially after many banks were re-organized and listed, state-owned banks have become highly marketized financial institutions. Therefore, it is improper to equate them as government departments. Therefore, China's financial restraint is misunderstood as financial repression.

Interest margin protection

Interest margin protection is the core policy of financial restraint and the most important financial policy factor underlying the "extraction" of China's financial system. To demonstrate interest margin protection as the key reason for excessively high profits of the financial sector, we must answer the following three questions:

1   Is there interest margin protection in China?
2   If there is, is the interest margin too high?
3   If the high interest margin is protected, does it constitute a major source of profits for the banking industry?

There should not be many disputes over the first question. After all, the interest margin is artificially made by the monetary authority which set the deposit and lending rate as well as the ceiling and floor. As of July 20, 2013, the interest rate floor of all types of loans other than home loans was cancelled. As of May 11,

2015, the deposit rate cap was enhanced to 1.5 times the benchmark interest rate. Besides, financial policymakers publicly admitted and justified a policy-generated interest margin. Therefore, it is not whether there is interest margin protection in China, but whether the interest margin of China's banking sector is too high.

The second question "If there is interest margin protection in China, is the interest margin too high?" is fiercely disputed. Some hold that China's banking sector does not have an interest margin higher than its international counterparts. For example, the Research Team of the Monetary Policy Department of the PBOC (2014) finds that the average annual net interest margin was 2.51 percent in China's banking sector during 2000 to 2011, lower than for most emerging economies. Pan Gongsheng (2012a) points out that the average interest margin of China's banking sector stood at 2.46 percent in 2010 and was not too high, compared with that of the world's top ten banks, which was 2.31 percent. However, the interest margin of China's banking sector was much lower than that of the four BRIC countries which are at a similar degree of development to China. In the seven years from 2003 to 2010, the average interest margin of the banking sector was 2.7 percent in China, 3.05 percent in India, 11 percent in Brazil and 6.4 percent in Russia. Yang (2012, 2014a) and Tang (2012) as well as some others also agree that the interest margin of China's banking system is not high. Some other scholars insist that China's banking sector has a high or relatively high interest margin (for example, Pan Yingli (2007), Ba (2011), Huang Qifan (2012), Yang and Wu (2012), Shi (2012) and Ma Weihua (2012)).

The emergence of the two opposite ideas is partially because literature uses different indicators and samples. In terms of indicators, some literature uses the difference between the deposit and lending interest rate as the interest margin, while in some others, the interest margin refers to the net interest yield (the proportion of net interest income in total interest-earning assets, also called the net interest rate differential). In terms of samples, some literature selects samples from countries or regions, while some others use individual banks as samples. Striking disparity appears when banks are involved in international business.

Is the interest margin high or not in China's banking sector? International comparison is the usual method to determine this. For more convenient comparison, this book defines the interest margin as the net interest income. Generally speaking, three indicators can reflect the interest margin. The first is the interest rate spread, or the difference between the lending rate and the deposit rate. For example, the interest rate is 3 percent, if the one-year deposit rate is 3 percent and the lending rate for six months to one year is 6 percent. The second is the net interest yield, also called net interest margin, referring to the proportion of net interest income in average interest-earning assets and the weighted average of the net interest margin of all kinds of interest-bearing assets. The third is the net interest spread, referring to the differential between the average interest-earning asset yield and average ratio between interest-bearing liabilities and cost. We chose the net interest yield as the interest margin when considering data availability.

We compare the interest margin of China's banking sector with that in major advanced economies and BRIC countries after 2003. As revealed by the comparison, China's net interest margin is higher than that of OECD countries except the US, but is lower than all other BRIC countries (Table 4.2). In general, data reflect that the net interest margin of China's banking sector is at a moderate level.

Is China's interest margin not high or at a moderate level, just as shown by data in Table 4.2? We may give a negative answer, because the data of China and other countries are incomparable to some degree due to differences in economic performance, financial policies and financial environment, etcetera. Simple comparison of interest margins without considering these differences will lead to misleading conclusions. If we take stock of all such factors, we may get another story.

First, China and other BRIC countries are not comparable in terms of performance in economic development. In recent years, BRIC countries other than China have "discoloured" and their economic development is less than satisfactory (Table 4.3). Given China's outstanding achievement in economic development and its financial system as an important factor, we have reasons to believe it is unreasonable to use financial systems of other BRIC countries as a reference, and their high net interest margin cannot be the basis for concluding that China's net interest margin is not high. If we do so, we are falling back on a substandard method.

Second, China's deposit reserve rate is consistently high, leading to an artificially low net interest margin. According to the usage of assets, business contributions to banks' interest income roughly fall into four categories: deposits in the

Table 4.2 International comparison of the banking sector's net interest yield (%)

	2003	2004	2005	2006	2007	2008	2009	2010	2011	2012
China	2.12	2.41	2.05	2.77	4.02	3.11	2.30	2.47	2.72	2.61
OECD countries										
	2003	2004	2005	2006	2007	2008	2009	2010	2011	2012
US	3.71	3.50	3.29	3.28	3.35	3.06	3.38	3.79	3.64	3.54
Germany	0.98	1.04	0.87	1.04	1.07	0.93	1.11	0.93	0.78	1.64
Japan	1.39	1.22	1.14	1.20	1.25	1.13	1.12	1.11	1.01	
France	1.07	0.89	0.65	0.63	0.47	0.79	0.91	0.88	0.89	
Britain	1.48	1.92	2.04	1.44	2.01	1.28	1.39	1.35	1.06	
Italy	2.49	3.07	3.02	2.04	2.04	1.73	1.42	1.40	1.30	2.05
South Korea	2.30	3.92	5.39	2.53	2.09	1.71	2.06	4.98	2.65	
BRIC countries										
Brazil	8.00	7.50	6.50	9.90	9.04	3.45	6.23	5.02	5.09	
India	3.72	3.52	2.96	3.34	3.46	2.72	3.08	3.29	2.95	
Russia	4.72	8.02	3.94	5.48	5.96	4.53	4.31	4.19	3.93	5.05
South Africa	11.67	4.94	2.84	4.08	4.15	2.71	3.08	3.07	2.76	

Source: World Bank.

Table 4.3 BRIC countries' economic development achievement in post-crisis era

GDP growth rate (%)	2009	2010	2011	2012	2013
China	9.21	10.45	9.30	7.80	7.70
Brazil	−0.33	7.53	2.73	0.87	2.30
India	5.04	11.23	7.75	3.99	4.70
Russia	−7.80	4.50	4.30	3.40	1.60
South Africa	−1.53	3.09	3.46	2.55	1.90

Inflation rate (%)	2009	2010	2011	2012	2013
China	−0.70	3.30	5.40	2.60	2.6%
Brazil	4.89	5.04	6.64	5.40	5.9%
India	10.88	11.99	8.86	9.31	11.1%
Russia	11.65	6.86	8.44	5.07	6.8%
South Africa	7.13	4.26	5.00	5.65	5.7%

Source: National Bureau of Statistics of the PRC, Wind database.

central bank (the deposit reserve); fixed-income investment; inter-bank business, and credit operation. A bank's net interest margin is the weighted average of the net interest yield of the four types of business. Among the four types of business or assets, the yield of the deposit reserve in the central banks is the lowest. Due to reasons like the economic development pattern, the need to maintain basic stability of the exchange rate and the expectation of RMB appreciation in the long run, China's deposit reserve rate is higher than that of most major economies. This reduces the banks' net interest margin and leads to artificially low data for the net interest margin.

Finally, the low non-performing loan (NPL) ratio also artificially reduces the net interest margin. To some degree, the interest margin is the risk premium, and higher risks imply higher interest margins; and a higher NPL ratio means a higher interest margin. The analysis of the operation mode of China's banking sector reveals a high proportion of mortgage loans and relatively low risks of banks' credit in general. International comparison of the NPL ratio also shows a fairly low NPL ratio in China (Table 4.4). Therefore, we should take into consideration the very low NPL ratio or the low credit risks in China and realize the fact of the high interest margin by seeing through the seemingly not-high level as shown by relevant data.

The third question is: If the high interest margin is protected, does it constitute a major source of profits for the banking industry? Disputes over the third question are bitter, since interest margin protection has been there for about two decades. However, why did the banking sector suffer from extremely lean profits and even losses at the end of the 1990s and the beginning of the 21st century? About this, Zhou (2012a) says:

> *From the outbreak of the Asian financial crisis to date, the benchmark interest rate spread of China roughly stands at 3 percent and only reached 3.6 percent*

Table 4.4 International comparison of banks' non-performing loan ratio

	2003	2004	2005	2006	2007	2008	2009	2010	2011	2012
China	20.40	13.20	8.60	7.10	6.20	2.40	1.60	1.10	1.00	0.95
OECD countries										
	2003	2004	2005	2006	2007	2008	2009	2010	2011	2012
US	1.10	0.80	0.70	0.80	1.40	3.00	5.40	5.17	4.35	3.86
Germany	5.20	4.90	4.10	3.40	2.70	2.90	3.30	3.20	3.00	
Japan	5.20	2.90	1.80	1.80	1.50	1.40	1.60	2.50	2.40	2.40
France	4.80	4.20	3.50	3.00		2.90	4.20	4.30	4.30	4.40
Britain	2.50	1.90	1.00	0.90	0.90	1.57	3.50	3.95	3.96	3.96
Italy	6.70	6.60	5.30	6.60	5.80	6.30	9.50	10.00	11.70	12.90
South Korea	2.60	1.90	1.20	0.80	0.70	1.10	1.20	1.90	1.40	1.60
Other BRIC countries										
	2003	2004	2005	2006	2007	2008	2009	2010	2011	2012
Brazil	4.10	2.90	3.50	3.50	3.00	3.10	4.20	3.10	3.50	
India	8.80	7.20	5.20	3.50	2.70	2.40	2.30	2.40	2.40	3.60
Russia	5.00	3.30	2.60	2.40	2.50	3.80	9.50	8.20	6.60	6.00
South Africa	2.40	1.80	1.80	1.10	1.40	3.90	5.90	5.80	4.70	4.00

Source: World Bank.

> *during the crisis. However, we all know that all banks suffered from loss when hit by and recovering from the crisis. . . . But the interest rate spread was high then and is narrowed down now. Therefore, high profits should not be totally attributed to the interest rate spread. Further research is needed.*

Interest margin protection is not the only reason for the high profits of the banking sector. Some attribute the high profits to better operation of the banking sector. Undoubtedly, great progress was made in the previous round of financial reform in which the corporate governance, operation and management and degree of marketization were all improved. That explains why, as noted by Zhou (2012a), the banking sector suffered from sweeping losses when hit by and recovering from the Asian financial crisis but makes handsome profits now with the same or higher interest margin. In advanced economies with a similar or high level of corporate governance, operation, management and marketization and with a profit rate far below that of China, the banking sector has profits: therefore improved operation may not be the major reason for the high profits of the banking sector.

Some others think the high profits are the result of the rapidly expanding credit scale (Liu Yuhui, 2012; Niu, 2013a; Yang, 2014a). It should be made clear that some economists like Pan Gongsheng (2012b) and Liu Yonggang (2012), regard the interest margin as a major source of the banking sector's income but they do not necessarily think that high bank profits come from a high interest margin. These scholars take the perspective of business structure, just like those who think an expanding credit scale is the source of bank profits, because credit scale expansion results in an increase of the interest margin income. According to Liu Yuhui (2012), in recent years the profit growth of the banking sector was derived from extraordinary expansion of the credit scale, rather than from interest margin regulation and restriction on access to the sector, both of which assist banks to make money. The two control measures have been used for a long time but they provided less and less protection in recent years. According to Yang (2014a), the relative stability of assets quality, constant technical progress and strict control over operation cost also contribute to profit increase of the banking sector as well as the increase of total assets of the banking sector. This idea does make sense. Since credit assets take the lion's share of the bank's interest-earning assets and income from the interest margin is the major source of the bank's profit, we can roughly equate the bank's income with the product of the balance of credit assets and the interest rate differential. If the interest rate differential remains the same and the profit keeps growing, then credit scale expansion is the direct cause for profit growth.

However, that is not the most cogent reason to deny that interest margin protection is a major source of high bank profits. On the one hand, bank upsizing is caused to some degree by interest margin protection. According to the financial restraint theory, this policy is designed to stimulate banks with incentives, because with this policy as a precondition, a predictably stable interest margin means more lending brings more profits. Therefore, the expansion of the credit scale is a result of interest market protection to some degree. The expansion impulse of commercial banks is a result of many factors including interest margin protection. The expansion impulse was strong in the early 1990s, for example the deposit-to-loan ratio was introduced in 1994. The strong expansion impulse or "unstoppable competition for profits" is also associated with the reform to commercialize banks in which commercial banks went public, and the incentive mechanism for their executives and employees was changed, and bank expansion is associated with the culture of comparison or competition inside the commercial banks.

On the other hand, to provide support for the idea that the credit scale expansion is a major reason for high bank profit, we also have to explain why the level of interest margin can be maintained during credit expansion. Theoretically, if demand remains constant, capital supply expansion will lead to a drop in capital price and then to a decrease of interest margin. However, after the effect of interest rate increase caused by inflation is deducted, China's interest margin did not narrow down. We attribute the concurrence of credit expansion and interest margin maintenance to interest margin protection and the access restriction closely related to it, and also to the fast expansion of credit demand. For example, economic development relies more on credit: and the self-circulation of "land finance – real estate – financial system" for financial expansion was formed. Such factors are discussed in more detail later in this chapter. Therefore, despite credit expansion as the direct cause of high profits of banks, we still regard interest margin protection as a major cause, at least it is a major financial reason.

Restrictions on access and asset substitution

Two other policies under a financial restraint system are as supportive to the interest margin protection policy: restrictions on access and asset substitution. The interest margin protection policy cannot be formulated without two restrictions. Fiercer competition inside the financial system, inside the banking sector or between banks and the capital market will erode the interest margin and make it hard to maintain a high interest margin. Restrictions on access and asset substitution help with the implementation of the interest margin protection policy by restricting competition or reducing the intensity of competition.

For over a decade, China has imposed strict restriction on access to the banking sector, due to lack of a smooth withdrawal mechanism and the need to maintain financial stability. The China Minsheng Bank was the only depository financial institution established in the period from 1996 to 2013. The number of financial institutions in China's banking sector keeps declining due to the reform of rural credit cooperatives. At the end of 2006, there were 19,797 financial institutions with legal status in the banking sector, including 19,348 rural credit cooperatives; and at the end of 2013, these two figures were down to 3,949 financial institutions with legal status and 1,803 rural credit cooperatives. According to the financial restraint theory, such strict access control helps prevent excessive competition inside the banking sector and maintains the banks' "rent" or "franchise value" endowed by the interest margin protection policy.

China has formulated no policies concerning asset substitution restriction. Instead, China developed the multi-layer capital market and enhanced the proportion of direct financing as the main features of its financial policy. Then, does that deny actual existence of asset substitution restriction in China?

The answer is no. As a matter of fact, excessive expansion of the banking sector squeezes development space for other financial sectors in the financial system. Considering the stage of economic development that China was in and its special economic and financial system, China's had a typical bank-dominated financial system before the financial restraint policy was adopted. Banks had the upper hand, compared with the financial market. Against such a backdrop, interest margin protection, as a strong stimulus to the banking sector, further reinforces the advantageous position of banks, and plays the same role as the asset substitution restriction. Laggard development of non-bank financial institutions restricts asset substitution. Therefore, as far as the effect of the previous round of financial reform is concerned, despite constant financial deepening, residents have few options for financial investment other than deposit and investment products provided by banks (Table 4.5). That means there are asset substitution restrictions in China's financial system.

It is because of actual access control and objective asset substitution restriction that the high interest margin in the banking sector as well as its post-2008

Table 4.5 Allocation of household financial assets (Unit: RMB1 trillion)

	2005		2006		2007		2008		2009		2010	
	Amount	Proportion	Amount	Proportion	Amount	Proportion	Amount	Proportion	Amount	Proportion	Amount	Proportion
Financial assets	20.91	100.00%	25.16	100.00%	33.55	100.00%	34.29	100.00%	41.09	100.00%	49.48	100.00%
Domestic currency	1.99	9.54%	2.25	8.93%	2.52	7.51%	2.86	8.35%	3.20	7.78%	3.77	7.62%
Deposit	15.06	72.01%	17.17	68.26%	18.18	54.20%	22.85	66.64%	26.87	65.39%	31.56	63.79%
Securities	1.44	6.89%	2.39	9.52%	5.83	17.38%	2.51	7.33%	5.00	12.17%	5.92	11.96%
Bond	0.65	3.13%	0.69	2.76%	0.67	2.00%	0.50	1.45%	0.26	0.64%	0.27	0.54%
Stocks	0.79	3.76%	1.70	6.76%	5.16	15.38%	2.02	5.88%	4.74	11.53%	5.65	11.41%
Fund	0.24	1.17%	0.56	2.23%	2.97	8.86%	1.70	4.96%	0.84	2.04%	0.73	1.48%
Securities margin	0.16	0.75%	0.31	1.24%	0.99	2.95%	0.48	1.39%	0.57	1.39%	0.44	0.90%
Reserve for insurance	1.83	8.76%	2.27	9.01%	2.71	8.08%	3.78	11.03%	4.62	11.25%	5.27	10.64%
Wealth management in financial Institutions											1.50	3.03%
Equities in trust fund schemes											0.31	0.62%

Source: China Financial Stability Report 2012.

high profit rate can be maintained. Thus the law of the average rate of profit fails (Marx, 2004).

Let us consider the function mechanism through which the financial restraint system contributes to the "extractive" financial system. First, by pressing down the deposit rate and maintaining the positive real interest rate, it sets high interest rate spread. By doing this, the per unit profit margin of bank loans is enhanced on the one hand; on the other hand, banks are encouraged to expand the credit scale and provide more loans to obtain "rent" or "franchise value". Second, the positive deposit rate is pressed down to a low level, and with asset substitution restriction, this prevents the loss of too much deposit, thus keeping the banks' interest margin at a high level. Finally, newcomers are blocked by access control from participating in completion and eroding "rent", so that the high profit rate of the banking sector is maintained, rather than returning to the social average rate of profit. Meanwhile, insufficient completion caused by access control and asset substitution restriction directly leads to overly high financing cost in the real economy and low financial efficiency which is discussed in detail later.

Merits and demerits of the financial restraint policy

The financial restraint policy centred in interest margin protection is adopted as a measure to implement financial reform. Interest margin protection is launched or maintained for the purpose of "online repair" of the banking sector. According to Zhou (2012b, p. 497):

> As per the then standard, the NPL ratio of the financial system in 1998 was 25 percent; but the figure actually soared to 40 percent if measured by the stricter international standard, and a practical NPL crisis has been materialized. Many banks saw their net value become negative and were technically insolvent.

To reform and rescue the "technically insolvent" banking sector in China, we have to maintain the banks' capability to keep serving the real economy and impose no more pressure on the state finance. To this end, interest margin protection is completely proved right, it repairs banks' balance sheets online, and has contributed to the success of the previous round of financial reform. The contribution of the interest margin protection policy to online repair is closely associated with other measures in the previous round of financial reform (such as improving banks' corporate governance, helping banks to go public, establishing China Banking Regulatory Commission [CBRC], responsible for supervising banks) and economic system reforms in other fields (like the reform on SOEs and the fiscal reform). Interest margin protection, having existed since the 1990s, did not help with online repair; instead, it dampened banks' performance and caused the accumulation of over RMB3 trillion of NPLs and finally the technical insolvency of the banking sector. About this, Zhou (2012b, p. 453) writes:

> In early 2000, China's big banks, which were about to be restructured and trying to repair their balance sheet and seek more capital, may be less enthusiastic

on playing a role in capital intermediation, and they were too worried about their asset quality. People have realized the importance of interest margin management, since appropriate interest margin can stimulate banks to providing loans while cleaning themselves.

Zhou (2012b, p. 189) also says:

> *We regard the period from 2003 to date as a stage of "online repair" of most commercial banks in China, during which banks try to eliminate their NPLs and urgently need additional capital. Therefore, it is necessary to maintain appropriate interest margin for commercial banks, to reinforce their resilience and help them become robust. On the other hand, the central bank should properly manage interest margin to arouse banks' enthusiasm on serving real economy, prevent excessive pro-cyclicality and strengthen banks' resilience on the same time. During the reform to transformation and when countering risks, the central bank perhaps should be taken into consideration the enthusiasm and resilience capability of commercial banks.*

It is safe to say that the interest margin protection policy is rational and did more good than harm in the early stage of the previous round of financial reform or before banks finished repairing their balance sheets. Nevertheless, it is not rational anymore and should be withdrawn after the repair is completed. According to Hellmann, Murdock and Stiglitz (1998, p. 187),

> *financial restraint is not a static policy instrument. . . . As financial depth increases, and in particular, as the capital base of the financial sector strengthens, these interventions may be progressively relaxed and the economy may transition to a more classic "free markets" paradigm.*

The problem is how can we can determine the best time to withdraw the interest margin protection policy and how to judge whether the balance sheet repair is complete?

Pan Yingli (2007) suggests the time for withdrawal should have been around 2007 because state-owned commercial banks, except for the ABC, recovered from insolvency and reached a good condition with the capital adequacy ratio arranging from 12 percent to 15 percent around 2007; besides, banks' earnings after restructuring were ten times that of four years before (about 2003). Agreeing with Pan Yingli (2007) generally, we think the window for financial restraint to withdraw should have begun, theoretically, at least from the end of 2008. Regarding the balance sheet repair of commercial banks, at the end of 2008, the NPL ratio dropped from 6.17 percent in 2007 to 2.42 percent, the provision coverage ratio increased from 39.2 percent from the end of 2007 to 116.4 percent and the capital adequacy ratio grew to 12 percent from 8.4 percent at the previous yearend. In terms of profitability, the ROE of listed banks was close to that of non-bank listed companies in 2007 and far above the latter in 2008. However, profit disproportion between finance and the real economy has been getting worse and interest margin protection has remained, despite frequent new all-time highs set since 2008. It is an evident mistake when we look back, but remains uncorrected. Why? Liu He (2012) points out in *Comparative Study on Two Major Global Crisis* that

> *These mistakes are obvious and ridiculous in hindsight, but for those involved in, it is extremely hard to implement correct ones. That is because decision makers lack experiences since they may encounter only one such sweeping crisis in their lifetime.*

There might be two reasons for the timely withdrawal of financial restraint to fail.

The first is policy inertia. Just as written by Hellmann, Murdock and Stiglitz (1998, p. 229), "In fact, it will most likely become the vested interest of the bureaucrats running the system to uphold it long beyond its economic justification". The second is the outbreak of a global financial crisis, which rarely occurs even in a century. On the one hand, the crisis increased uncertainty in financial development and thus the priority of financial stability in all policy goals. Against the backdrop of the global financial crisis, the maintenance of financial stability is among the most important policy goals of almost all major economies in the world. Prolonging interest margin protection for commercial banks helps to build up their capital strength and keep the whole financial system sound when it is hit by powerful external shocks.

On the other hand, interest margin protection as an incentive can promote the implementation of stimulus policies designed to maintain "stable growth". Hit by the global financial crisis, all major economies competed to adopt economic stimuli to recover from the crisis as soon as possible. Unfortunately, due to the strong pro-cyclicality of the financial sector, banks are naturally reluctant to lend when financial crisis occurs. To ensure the effectiveness of the economic stimulus, the state should provide adequate incentives to commercial banks, so that they can expand their balance sheet counter-cyclically and provide more credit to the real economy. Interest margin protection is obviously effective. Zhou (2012b) also regards it as an important experience for China to counter the financial crisis.

Financial regulation and supervision, financial innovation and shadow banking expansion

Besides the financial restraint policy, the linkage of "financial regulation and supervision – financial innovation – shadow banking expansion" is another important mechanism for the formation of the "extractive" financial system. This chain increases the high profits and high employees' income in the financial sector, and also leads to the high financing cost of the real economy.

Financial regulation and supervision: size control and industrial restriction

Size control is closely associated with the financial restraint system and is a "patch-making" regulation policy. Under the financial restraint system, interest margin is high and stable, and the banking sector has a natural impulse of credit expansion. Size control is an inevitable choice to meet the macro-control requirement of maintaining a "rational" credit growth rate and insisting on financial restraint at the same time. Besides, the financial restraint system, commercialization and financial institutions going public are an important cause of size control. Once commercialized, banks, driven by their own pursuit of excellent performance and corresponding incentives, compete to outshine others with higher profits and bigger size. "Everyone is dancing before the music stops".

Regulation measures for size control in China's banking industry fall into three categories: capital adequacy ratio regulation, loan-to-deposit ratio restriction and credit control. Capital adequacy ratio regulation is a universal and core principle of an effective banking supervision that must be implemented, and has nothing to do with the formation of the "extractive" financial system. On the contrary, other kinds of regulation policies with distinct Chinese characteristics are directly associated with the "extractive" financial system.

Recently, the loan-to-deposit ratio was called a minor system but a big problem (Gao, 2014). The loan-to-deposit ratio has been discussed regarding its pros and cons, abolishment and reform direction, for example, by Ba (2012), Huang (2013b), Chen and Sun (2013), Wu X (2013), Gao (2014), Zeng (2014) and Li and Xu (2014). Indeed, the loan-to-deposit ratio regulation played an important role in the formation of the "extractive" financial system.

The loan-to-deposit ratio regulation can be dated back to the *Notice of the People's Bank of China on the Administration of Asset Liability Ratio of Commercial Banks* released in early 1994, which capped the loan-to-deposit ratio of commercial banks at 75 percent. Later, it was enshrined in the *Law of the People's Republic of China on Commercial Banks* enacted in 1995 that the ratio of the loan balance to the balance of deposits should be less than 75 percent. At that time, the loan-to-deposit ratio was controlled because of the macro-economic environment. For example, it was applied as a tightening policy to check inflation, as discussed in the literature (Ba, 2012; Huang, 2013b; Chen and Sun, 2013; Zeng, 2014). The inflation rate was 14.7 percent in 1993 and 24.1 percent in 1994.

Microeconomic conditions also counted. For example, the loan-to-deposit ratio was restricted as a supplementary measure to poor management of asset liabilities and the liquidity of commercial banks to tighten restriction on non-prudential behaviours (Wu, 2013; Ba, 2012). It can enhance the flexibility of the credit scale control, break the confinement of directive administration of lending and improve independence of commercial banks (Wu, 2013; Zeng, 2014).

Introduced as early as 1994 and 1995, the loan-to-deposit ratio control was strictly enforced before 2004, and the ratio was still above 75 percent (Zeng, 2014). Four reasons might underlie the failure of implementation. First, the initial condition of the banking sector when the policy was released might be relevant. The loan-to-deposit ratio was high then, 90 percent both in 1994 and 1995, and could hardly be reduced to 75 percent. Second, changes in the macroeconomic environment might be a reason. During 1998 to 2002, China was at the bottom of the economic cycle and under great pressure from deflation. The third is the changes in the regulation system. The CBRC was established in

2003 to supervise the banking sector. The fourth is the introduction of the joint stock system to state-owned commercial banks at the end of 2003. Although China's financial system, with a poor foundation, was far from an "extractive" one in 2004, the loan-to-deposit ratio restriction, once enforced strictly, quickly enhanced the cost of financing.

The financing cost through loans was significantly enhanced (Figure 4.1). In the fourth quarter of 2004, the weighted average rate of one-year fixed-rate RMB loans increased to 6.75 percent and the loan rate was 1.21 times the benchmark rate.

The proportion of loans in the social financing of the economy declined. As shown in Figure 4.2, in 2004 when the loan-to-deposit ratio was strictly controlled, the loan proportion dropped significantly from 2003. Loan proportion decline means higher financing costs across the economy, since loans were less costly than other means of financing.

Many years later, the general loan-to-deposit ratio of the banking sector from 2010 to 2014 was kept at 65 percent (Figure 4.3). Does that mean the loan-to-deposit ratio control was not an effective restriction on the banking sector any more and thus would not affect banks' behaviours and the financing cost of the real economy? The answer is no.

Firstly, due to imbalance between the assets and liabilities of commercial banks, even with a generally low loan-to-deposit ratio of the banking sector, control of this ratio may in practice restrict some types of banks. In recent years, the average loan-to-deposit ratio of small and medium-sized banks other than the five largest state-owned banks and joint stock banks was roughly 55 percent, and the average

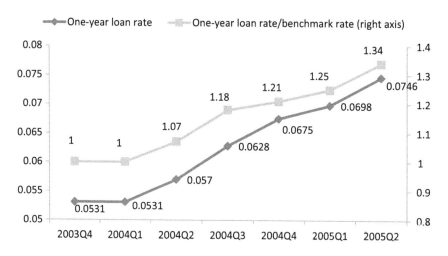

Figure 4.1 Weighted average interest rate of fixed-rate RMB loans

Note: "Q" means quarter, for example, 2003 Q4 means the fourth quarter in 2003.

Source: Report of the People's Bank of China on the Implementation of the Monetary Policy (2003Q4–2005Q2).

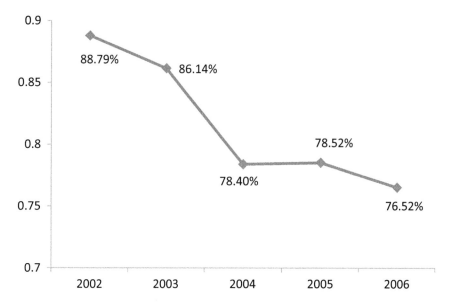

Figure 4.2 Proportion of RMB loans in adjusted social financing

Note: The adjusted social financing refers to social financing of the economy with undiscounted acceptance bills of banks. The deduction is because the undiscounted acceptance bills are neither banks' assets nor enterprises' debts to banks. Instead, they represent the commercial credit between businesses in nature. It is improper to include the undiscounted acceptance bills of banks into the social financing of the economy, since they have nothing to do with capital formation and stock.

Source: PBOC.

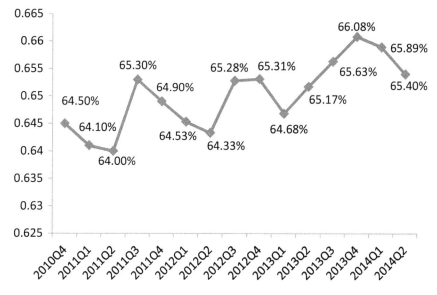

Figure 4.3 General loan-to-deposit ratios of commercial banks in recent years

Source: CBRC.

loan-to-deposit ratio of the five largest state-owned banks was about 65 percent, much below the regulation red line of 75 percent; nevertheless, the average loan-to-deposit ratio was about 70 percent or above for joint-stock banks. Some small and medium-sized banks had a loan-to-deposit ratio above 70 percent (Figure 4.4). Therefore the loan-to-deposit ratio has strong restriction on joint-stock banks.

Secondly, the loan-to-deposit ratio indicator value failed to reflect the restriction of this ratio on the banking sector. To circumvent such restriction, commercial banks substituted some loans through shadow banking, such as trust loan and interbank loan. If shadow banking were taken into consideration, the loan-to-deposit ratio of the entire banking system would be much higher than the current level.

Credit scale control is deemed a regulation measure with strong characteristics of the planned economy and was abolished in 1998. However, it has been restored by the central bank which was forced to issue money due to a lasting imbalance of payments. At present, the central bank uses the consensus loan formula to determine the loan increment of commercial banks (Wu, 2013). Notably, credit scale control is rational to some degree for small- and medium-sized financial institutions. Among over 3,000 depository financial institutions, most are rural, small and medium-sized financial institutions that have not established a complete corporate governance framework yet. The credit scale control based on the amount of credit in the previous period plays a role of prudential regulation, helping to curb the loan impulsion of small and medium-sized financial institutions when interest margin protection is effective and demands for loans are strong, and thus reducing financial risks.

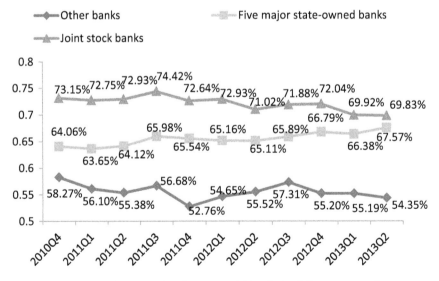

Figure 4.4 Loan-to-deposit ratio of commercial banks in different categories

Source: CBRC.

According to Zhang Chenghui (2012), regulation authorities even impose monthly control over the credit scale. Given the considerable influence of the base number (credit granted in the previous year by the bank), the credit scale control is more influential for banks with a relatively low loan-to-deposit ratio. "Some small- and medium-sized banks, whose loan-to-deposit ratio is only 40 percent, can hardly expand credit to small and micro-sized businesses due to limited size".

Financial regulation and supervision may also restrict loans to specific industries. For example, for the purpose of supporting regulation of the real estate industry, loans to property enterprises might be restricted; in order to encourage energy saving and environmental protection, enterprises in high-polluting and high energy-consuming industries might get less loans; and to address overcapacity, the government may restrict loans to enterprise in industries with severe overcapacity. Undoubtedly, such restrictions are designed to maintain sustainable economic development and are rational to some degree. However, the problem is that if the development of industries subject to loan restrictions is commercially sustainable over a long period, then in a market-based system, demand automatically spawns supply; therefore, loan restrictions for such industries only lead to increasing reliance on shadow banking for financing and thus to a higher financing cost.

Financial innovation and the shadow banking sector

Despite supply restriction caused by control measures on access, size and loans to businesses in specific loans as well as other regulation policies, demand generates the supply in China's financial system which is highly commercialized. To meet such strong financing demand, a gigantic shadow banking sector is derived, through which people keep pursuing high profits. To be specific, access control spawns shadow banking with informal financial institutions or informal finance as major suppliers, and size control and loan restrictions targeting specific industries catalyze the formation of the shadow banking sector with financial institutions as the major supplier.

Financial innovation, a major cause of the recent global financial crisis (the Financial Crisis Inquiry Commission 2011), was once bitterly attacked. However, in China it is generally positive and is encouraged and supported. According to differing mainstream ideas, the US features excessive financial innovation, and China features inadequate innovation (Hua, 2008; Zhang Xiaopu, 2012). Indeed, China lags far behind the US in terms of diversity and complexity of financial products. From this perspective, financial innovation is inadequate in China and anything but excessive.

Does excessive financial innovation exist in any aspect in China? The answer is yes.

To explain, we have to define excessive or inadequate financial innovation. Obviously, the major criteria is not the amount of financial innovation but "whether the financial innovation helps to enhance the efficiency of finance in serving the real economy and reduce financial market volatility" (Li, 2013) and whether it is beyond the risk management capability of financial institutions and the capability of financial regulators (Zhang, 2014b). In other words, it is the quality that really matters rather than quantity.

Financial innovation may be good or bad. Good innovation, within the reach of risk management of financial institutions and the financial regulation and supervision, helps to optimize the functions of such institutions and better serve the real economy. On the contrary, bad innovation impedes improvement of financial functions and threatens financial stability. According to the financial dichotomy, financial innovation might be excessive and inadequate at the same time. Inadequate quantity and capability of financial innovation does not necessarily deny the existence of excessive financial innovation.

Second, we would like to analyze how excessive or bad financial innovation comes into being. Excessive financial innovation in the US is attributed to two causes. First, financial regulators are incapable of regulating and supervising financial innovation. Second, due to improper restriction mechanisms of financial incentives, financial institutions are incapable of managing risks brought by financial innovation. These factors also exist in China. In terms of financial regulation and supervision, both China and the US are disadvantaged by improper or low-efficiency regulation and supervision, but they differ from each other, as financial regulation was lacking in the US before the financial crisis but is excessive in China. China's financial regulation and supervision is averse to risk, and excessive regulation and supervision result in, among others, costly financial innovation (Yi, 2008), which is beyond the regulation and supervision capability of competent authorities and the risk management capability of financial enterprises themselves and does not enhance the efficiency of serving the real economy. As China's financial reform proceeds, especially the commercialization of the financial system, the restriction mechanism for financial incentives is not fully effective as improper or excessive financial incentives are widely used in China. Therefore, theoretically, excessive financial innovation finds soil in China and has already germinated. Li (2013) points out that "people are concerned that institutional-arbitrage-based innovation of China's financial institutions, too fast and too intensive, is beyond the actual capability of regulation and supervision as well as risk control and encourages the improper profit-making pattern of financial institutions". That testifies to the existence of obvious and excessive financial innovation in China.

A typical manifestation of excessive financial innovation is the drastic expansion of shadow banking. Not all shadow banking falls to the category of excessive financial innovation. For this, Zhang (2014a) points out that "shadow banking and financial innovation are two sides of a coin. In other words, if financial regulators completely 'eliminate' shadow banking, they suffocate financial innovation". Shadow banking should be defined from the perspective of actual functions, attributes and risk features and by considering whether there are legal or regulatory loopholes or arbitrage factors (Lei, 2014). Calculation results show rapidly swelling shadow banking.

Financial innovation and shadow banking expansion make the financial system even more "extractive". First of all, the profits of the banking sector increase even more. On the one hand, swelling shadow banking brought further expansion of the banking system. The banking system is the core of shadow banking in China, such as trust loan, assets management of brokers and entrusted loans; therefore, "shadow banking" swelling is by nature the expansion of the banking system. On the other hand, swelling "shadow banking" produces the "crowd-out effect" in the capital market and non-bank financial institutions and makes it harder to maintain the high interest margin of the banking sector. For example, against the backdrop of "rigid redemption", high-yield wealth management products and trust products systematically enhance the risk-free return rate, curbing the development of both the stock market and the insurance industry.

Second, financial ecology is damaged and the financing cost of the real economy is increased. Considerable capital other than bank credit is wrapped up and made more expensive by trust funds, securities firms, leasing companies, venture capital and private equity as well as other institutions beyond, which increases the financing cost of enterprises and builds up "higher risks than bank credit in the financial system" (Huang, 2013a). In this case where everyone is a rentier, the financial system takes away the benefits of the real economy and obtains more profits.

Financial structure imbalance and other reasons

Financial structure imbalance

China is confronted with severe financial structure imbalance which features overdevelopment of the banking system, underdevelopment of the capital market and non-bank financial institutions and low proportion of direct financing. According to literature comparing financial systems (Levine, 2002; Allen and Gale, 2002), bank-dominated financial systems and market-dominated financial systems are not superior to each other in promoting economic growth; however, severe imbalance in the financial structure contributes to the formation of the "extractive" financial system. Whether based on banks' assets or their liabilities, we find a clear link between financial structure imbalance and the "extractive" financial system.

An undeveloped capital market means there are inadequate assets to supply finance to business which, slowing down financial disintermediation, makes it harder for big enterprises to finance from the capital market instead of the banking system. As a result, the banking system maintains a high interest margin due to inadequate competition with the capital market on the one hand; on the other hand, given size control and loan-to-deposit ratio restriction imposed on the banking system, SMEs are confronted with difficult and expensive financing.

An undeveloped capital market means depositors have few alternative investment options. Depositors, especially those with low balance of deposits, have no choice but resort to low-rate deposits, which allows banks to keep financing at a low cost and maintain a high interest margin.

The financial structure imbalance is not only manifested in an undeveloped capital market but also in undeveloped non-bank financial institutions. As with the undeveloped capital market, undeveloped non-bank financial institutions result in the extraction of the financial system because they are insufficiently competitive to the banking system. The financial structure imbalance has many causes. First, the financial restraint system endows the banking system with advantages in competition and thus reinforces the imbalance in the financial structure. Second, the swelling shadow banking system provides low-risk and high-yield products to dampen the development of the capital market and of non-bank financial institutions. Finally, the institutional design for the capital market and non-bank financial institutions has deficiencies.

Unreasonable accounting standards

The irrational accounting standard is an important reason for extraction of the financial system. The high profits of the banking sector are an "accounting phenomenon". On the one hand, the current accounting standards, especially those for NPLs, are deficient. Loan classification is "retrospective" rather than "forward looking". In accounting, NPS are incurred losses and not potential ones, and cannot predict hidden risks (Zhang, 2014a). On the other hand, the implementation of accounting standards is in many cases subject to the judgement of financial institutions and might be lax due to improper incentive constraints. Before financial risks are widely materialized, losses from NPLs and assets impairment are often underestimated, leading to artificially high profits and higher employees' income in the financial sector.

Non-financial reasons

In a closely knit economic and social system, all fields affect each other. Financial problems are just "mirror images" of issues in other aspects of society and economy in the sphere of finance in many cases. The formation of the "extractive" financial system also owes much to factors outside finance, which affect the relative status of finance and the real economy by promoting financial expansion and checking the transformation and upgrading of the real economy. In particular, financial expansion is fuelled by the self-circulation of "land finance – real estate – financial system", heavy reliance on credit, financial overloading, and lack of anti-finance forces. Deficiencies in traditional industrial policies and education and research systems constrain transformation and upgrading of the real economy.

The loop of "land finance – real estate – financial system"

The loop of "land finance – real estate – financial system" is a key factor outside the financial sphere. Chen Daofu's elaboration of this self-circulation is brilliant (Chen, 2014, p. 78):

> *Huge demand for housing, once repressed, was released when subsidized apartments were not provided any more, and was met since people the real purchasing*

power and obtain external funds thanks to instalment payment to banks and higher real effective exchange rate of RMB; therefore, it brought forth prosperity of the real estate market; land finance prevails, as revenue increase through land transfer through bidding, auction and listing is line with local government's idea of urban development and encouraged the latter to introduce various local platforms as financing tools; and NPLs disposal and listing through capital restructuring encourage and enable banks to expand, leading to relaxed financial regulation and financial transformation and finally fast development of the shadow banking system during the transitional period. All these factors constitute a powerful self-circulation system.

Borrowing from local governments and real-estate-related loans provide foundations for credit expansion in the financial system. The credit line is further enhanced due to increased property and land price and guarantee for loans. Credit expansion related to land and real estate enhanced the purchasing power on the land and real estate market and further pushed up land and property prices.

Notably, similar self-circulation also occurred in late 1980s when the "extractive" financial system and economic bubbles were formed (Cong, 1998). For the "extractive" financial system, the importance of such circulation lies in their role in promoting the expansion of the financial sector.

Heavy reliance on credit

China certainly relies too much on credit for economic growth (Yang, 2014b). The proportion of credit from the financial sector in the GDP rocketed from 120.8 percent in 2008 to 162.96 percent in 2013, indicating significantly increasing reliance on credit for economic growth in China since the outbreak of the global financial crisis (Figure 4.5). This increase can by no means be interpreted as a continuous financial deepening; we can regard the decline of this proportion between 2003 and 2008 to be opposing financial deepening.

Two reasons underlie the heavy reliance on credit. First, stimulus is excessive and irrational after the outbreak of the global financial crisis. It is too intensive in terms of size and returns from the credit project. In 2009, new local and foreign currency loans hit RMB10.5 trillion, 2.06 times that in 2008. Most loans were not liquidity loans: instead, they were used to support newly started projects; therefore, credit blowout precedes gigantic follow-up financing in future years. In 2010 and 2011, due to the high growth rate of the nominal GDP, reliance on credit remained stable. Continuous economic slowdown and decline of inflation meant the proportion of credit in the GPD surged again. Stimulus irrationality means over reliance on monetary policies and the financial system and insufficiently powerful fiscal policies. This is discussed in detail in Chapter 5.

Second, economic growth keeps slowing down and the real economy sees benefits declining. Earnings decline in the real economy dampens debt repayment capability of enterprises in the real sector and increases their dependence on debt.

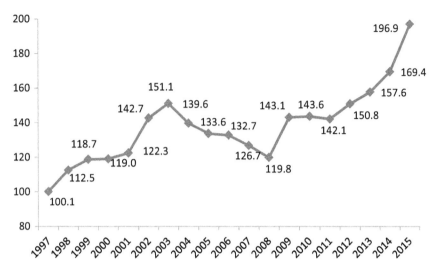

Figure 4.5 China domestic credit provided by financial sector (% of GDP)
Source: World Bank.

In addition, in the short term, this benefit drop implies higher income in the financial sector. It is because of increasing dependence on credit for economic growth and survival and development of individual enterprises that the asset or credit of the financial system swells drastically. Due to the time lag of risks and enterprises' behaviours like refinancing (borrowing more money to repay old debts), mean more returns and thus promotes the formation of the "extractive" financial system.

It is worth examining why the "extractive" financial system was not formed in the period from 1997 to 2003 when economic growth relied on credit much more heavily. The reason is the financial system at that time was weak with poor profitability, and the combination of swelling credit with interest margin protection functioned as "online repair".

An overloaded financial system

The financial system has undertaken many non-obligatory duties or tasks. "Rigid redemption" is an example. At present it is common to see "rigid redemption" at markets of banks' wealth management products, trust products and corporate credit bonds. "Rigid redemption" is associated with poor risk knowledge of investors and the intention of financial institutions to maintain their reputation as well as many other factors. However, the more important reason is the concern that the absence of "rigid redemption" might impair social stability due to an inadequate social safety net. "Rigid redemption" contributes the formation of the "extractive" financial system in two aspects. First of all, it spawns fast expansion of wealth management products and objectively functions as an asset substitution restriction. In this way, it produces the "crowd out" effect on the development of multi-layer capital market and non-bank financial institutions. Secondly, although it avoids financial risk in the short term, "rigid redemption" prolongs the time lag of risks and reinforces future risks, making the "extractive" financial system potentially more harmful.

Another typical example is loan restrictions targeting specific industries, like loans to enterprises in the real estate industry. Such restrictions are imposed against the backdrop of a property price hike fuelled by improper regulation. The real estate sector should be regulated more effectively by adjusting policies concerning the land market and taxation of properties, rather than loan restrictions imposed on this sector.

A long time before the loan restrictions were imposed, the real estate sector obtained high profits, and property companies were commercially sustainable. However, restrictions on real-estate-related loans pressured property enterprises to finance through shadow banking at a higher cost. Another example is loan restriction targeting high-energy-consuming and high-polluting industries. For these industries, the environmental protection cost should be borne by individual enterprises through environmental policy adjustment and reinforced regulation and supervision. The performance appraisal of local government with GDP as the only criteria should be reformed.

Why is the financial sector obliged to undertake too many tasks? On the one hand, it might be because finance as the core of the modern economy is a pervasive concept so that people believe finance can solve all problems or can help to do so. On the other hand, it might be because of the incomplete market-based economic system, the improper relationship between the government and the market and failure to transform the functions of the government.

The lack of anti-finance forces

Having faith in finance as the core of modern economy, China has neither an anti-finance tradition nor anti-finance forces or interest groups. That is testified by the fact that the argument about windfall profits of banks vanished in the first half of 2012 and that competent authorities have seldom imposed harsh penalties on financial institutions. However, as the financial sector expands, a group representing the interests of the financial sector, mainly consisting of financial institutions, has taken shape. Upholding the concept that finance is the core of the modern economy, it emphasizes the risks of financial reform and the risks of opening up through public opinion and other channels and exerts influence on decision-making authorities, leading to more benefits for the financial sector and the failure to withdraw the financial restraint system on time and the loss of benefits to the real economy.

Anti-finance forces are necessary. They may not be able to prevent the formation of the "extractive" financial system and the outbreak of the financial crisis;

but at least they call attention to problems in the financial sector and thus play a positive role in eliminating institutional factors in the "extractive" financial system. After the global financial crisis, the US adopted the *Dodd-Frank Wall Street Reform and Consumer Protection Act*, a financial reform act deemed as more thorough than those in Europe and the most comprehensive and strictest since the Great Depression. An important reason for that is the confrontation between "Main Street" and "Wall Street". This act plays an important role in balancing finance and the real economy of the US.

Some drawbacks in traditional industrial policies

In the relationship between finance and the real economy, the finance sector is "extractive" because it is too powerful in the relative sense, while the real economy sees benefits decline. Indeed, benefit decline in the real economy is a result of many factors, including inevitable external factors and irreversible structural changes. For example, an economic bubble burst (Chen, 2014) leads to weak external demands, labour costs keep increasing after the Louis Turning Point, and more importantly, the real economy is not transformed and upgraded fast enough in the new situation. Besides the "siphonic effect" and "erosion" effect of such "extractive" sectors as finance and real estate on aggravating external conditions for innovation, transformation and upgrading of the real economy, behind the decline are also unignorable deficiencies in industrial policies and education and research systems.

A Chinese saying goes that while water can support a boat, it can also overturn it, therefore it is important that industrial policies cautiously upgrade the industrial structure and advance economic growth (Lin, 2012). We may see the presence of these policies in the economic history of such successful catch-up economies as the US, Germany, Japan and South Korea, and we must recognize the contribution of such policies to the "economic miracle" of China since its reform and opening up campaign was launched. However, as China enters a different stage of development, industrial policies are much less effective and may cause unignorable problems. Zhao and Zhu (2013) provide detailed discussion of this point.

Industrial policies are now much less effective for two reasons. First, factor-driven industrialization expedites the transition into a new economic development stage driven by innovation. Core competitiveness of products, enterprises, industries and economy will rely on quality, technique and brand, instead of price and scale. As a result, traditional industrial policies, which reduce the factor cost and maintain the competitive edge by taking advantage of preferential policies of land, tax, finance and labour, produce results much less than they used to. On the one hand, hiking factor cost squeezes the space for implementing such increasingly costly policies; on the other hand, such policies can neither efficiently bring forth a new competitive edge centring on quality, techniques and brand, nor enhance the contribution rate of innovation to economic growth.

Second, China now enters a stage of technical frontiers and leaves a stage of imitation. An important precondition for the success of traditional industrial policies is the late-comer advantage. In other words, experiences and lessons of advanced economies are an important basis for China to formulate industrial policies. However, according to domestic and foreign experience, in the stage of technical frontier, the government does not receive enough information for effective formulation and implementation of industrial policies any more. A bitter lesson from Japan's failure in its competition with the US in the late 1980s is that the direction for technical or industrial development was determined by the government rather than the market, and the state failed to replace industrial policies with innovation policies fast enough. According to *A Strategy for American Innovation* (2011), "historical experience shows that governments that try to select winners and promote economic growth through frequent intervention often waste resources and curb innovation ultimately. The reason for that is partially the limited predictability of governments".

Industrial policies imposed considerable negative effects on economic upgrading and transformation in recent years. First of all, traditional industrial policies have become an important source of overcapacity. Local governments have become a major executor of industrial policies. In a special political-economic ecology featuring fiscal decentralization and competition between local governments, economic growth rate is a priority compared with the growth quality. Therefore, to reach short-term economic growth goals, local governments make full use of preferential land, taxation, financial and labour policies and other traditional industrial policies and even alienate industrial policies, for example, market segmentation caused by local protection. As a result, the blind pursuit of rapid growth leads to severe overcapacity in many places, imposing a heavy burden on transformation and upgrading of the real economy.

Another negative effect of traditional industrial policies is that they restrain enterprise enthusiasm for innovation and impede the improvement of the overall innovation capability of the economy. Used as a risk-free arbitration tool by some enterprises, traditional industrial policy has encouraged the formation of many rent-seeking enterprises and dampened the whole society's motivation to innovate. For example, due to policies like "investment for land" or "investment for resources", the rise in land value and the resource development have become the major source of project income or the major purpose of investment by some enterprises. Some industrial policies alienate innovation by enterprises, innovation is guided by policies rather than being based on the market; and innovation for innovation's sake is commonly seen. The innovation environment is artificially made unfair by industrial policies. For example, innovation is not confined to a specific industry or only refers to technical innovation, but traditional industrial policies support innovation in high-tech industries and emerging industries with strategic importance much more than traditional industries, and with emphasis on technical innovation rather than other types of innovation.

Traditional industrial policies have other severe deficiencies. Take the industrial land policy, for example. The country provides low-priced industrial land by making land for other purposes more expensive. According to data from the Ministry of Land and Resources, despite a rise in the absolute price, the relative price of industrial land maintained a general decline compared with land for business and housing. From 2008 to the second quarter of 2014, the price ratio of land for commerce and service to industrial land increased from 6.83 to 8.97, and that of residential land to industrial land hiked from 5.73 to 7.22. The striking contrast significantly increases enterprises' rental cost and thus their total cost and innovation cost.

The education system and the scientific research system

According to the production function, laggard transformation and upgrading of the real economy is attributed to insufficient improvement in total factor productivity or technical progress, and to inadequate capability of technical innovation. From the perspective of enterprise competitiveness, the laggardness of the real economy equals laggard transformation and laggard upgrading of enterprises. The laggard upgrading of enterprises means a lack of significant quality improvement of products or services and failure to elevate to industrial chains and value chains with more added value.

Regarding innovation spending aggregation, China's annual R&D expenditure ranked second in the world, but the country's scientific and technical innovation capability is still inadequate. Why? An obvious answer is low innovation efficiency. Then why is the efficiency so low? Deficiencies in education and research systems are an important reason.

Deficiencies in the educational system lie in the biased outlook of college education. Just as Shi Yigong (2014) writes a major deficiency in the outlook of college education in China is the employment orientation, which leads to severe defects in the outlook of life and value of college students and overemphasis on material benefits. As a result, "graduates swarm to sectors where they can earn easy money". Of course, it is easy to understand, because the "rational economic man" is a basic condition for our analysis of economic problems, which, in general, is also applicable to job selection by individuals. However, according to the employment-oriented outlook of education, pursuit of personal benefit maximization is easily downgraded into pursuit of maximum short-term economic benefits for individuals. Against the backdrop of financial overdevelopment, a college education fails to counter the "siphonic effect" of the financial sector by erecting a correct outlook of life and value for college students; instead, it reinforces such an effect and drives excessive talents and capital as innovation factors into the financial sector.

Scientific and technical systems also have defects. For example, coordinated design is lacking in the macromanagement system for science and technology, leading to compartmentalization of different departments. Scholars in basic research are eager for quick success and instant benefits, and scientific researchers only focus on publishing papers to enhance their career profile due to the SCI (US Science Citation Index) and EI (US Engineering Index) orientation of colleges and scientific research institutions, rather than valuing the industrial and commercial value of these papers. The rigid evaluation mechanism for scientific research overemphasizes quantity rather than quality, and leads to useless and low-quality research results. Industries, colleges and universities and research institutions are not closely associated; and platforms are lacking to jointly address common technical difficulties for industrial development.

References

Allen, F. and Gale, D. (2002). Translated by J. Wang, C. Zhu, X. Ding, and Y. Hu. *Comparing Financial Systems* [M]. Beijing: China Remin University Press, June.
Aoki, M., Murdock, K. and Okuno-Fujiwara, M. (1996). A New Interpretation of the Role of Government in East Asian Economic Development: Market Enhancing View (Vol. I). *Comparative Economic & Social Systems*, Vol. 5, pp. 1–10.
Ba, S. (2011). Ba Shusong: A Rethink on Banks's Operation Model: Lasting Monopolistic Profits From "High Interest Margin" [N]. *Economic Information Daily*, March 30.
Ba, S. (2012). Conditional Mature for Lower Loan-to-Deposit Ratio as a Regulation Indicator [N]. *xw.qq.com*, December 27.
Bai, C. and Qian, Z. (2009). Who Crowds out Residents' Income – An Analysis of China's National Income Distribution [J]. *Social Sciences in China*, Vol. 5, pp. 99–115.
Chen, C. (2002). An Analysis of Financial Restraints in Progressive Reform [J]. *Economic Science*, Vol. 2, pp. 5–14.
Chen, D. (2014). Bubbles in China's Economic Cycle [J]. *China Development Observations*, Vol. 10, pp. 76–81.
Chen, D. and Sun, X. (2013). Analysis of the Rationality of the Current Loan-to-Deposit Ratio Regulation and Reform Recommendations [J]. *Financial Perspectives Journal*, Vol. 2, pp. 53–58.
Chen, Y. and Qian, L. (2011). SOEs and Economic Growth Under the Financial Restraint System [J]. *Shanghai Finance*, Vol. 8, pp. 12–17.
Cong, Y. (1998). Analysis of the Vicious Circle Mechanism Between Land Price "Bubbles" and Financial Expansion and Inspiration to China [J]. *Japanese Research*, Vol. 4, pp. 6–10.
The Financial Crisis Inquiry Commission (2011). *The Financial Crisis Inquiry Report* [R], January.
Feyzioglu, T. (2009). *Does Good Financial Performance Mean Good Financial Intermediation in China?* [R]. IMF Working Paper, WP/09/170, August.
Gao, S. (2014). Small System, Big Problem [J]. *Tsinghua Financial Review*, Vol. 6, pp. 27–30.
He, D. and Wang, H. (2011). Dual-Track Interest Rate Model and Implementation of China's Monetary Policy [J]. *Journal of Financial Research*, Vol. 12, pp. 1–17.
Hellmann, T., Murdock, K. and Stiglitz, S. (1998). Financial Restraint: Towards a New Paradigm. In *The Role of Government in East Asian Economic Development – Comparative Institutional Analysis* [A], edited by A. Masahiko, K. Hyung and O. Masahiro. Beijing: Economic Press China, April, pp. 183–235.
Hua, S. (2008). Financial Innovation in China: Insufficient Rather Than Excessive – An Interview with Economist Hua Sheng [N]. *China Securities Journal*, September 28.
Huang, J. (2013a). A Call for Low-Cost Financing Environment to Develop Real Economy [N]. *People's Daily*, February 4.

Huang, J. (2013b). Improvement of Loan-to-Deposit Ratio Cap Policy [J]. *China Finance*, Vol. 3, pp. 26–28.

Huang, Q. (2012). Easy High Profits for Banks Thanks to Special Privileges [N]. *The Beijing News*, March 6.

Jia, K. and Meng, Y. (2013). Vitalizing Financial Asset Stock Through Interest Rate Liberalization [J]. *China Report*, Vol. 8, pp. 70–72.

Johansson, A. (2012). *Financial Repression and China's Economic Imbalances* [R]. CERC Working Paper, No. 22, April.

Kong, J. (2011). International Background and Demonstration of "Middle-Income Trap" and China's Countermeasures [J]. *Reform*, Vol. 10, pp. 5–13.

Lardy, N. (2008). Financial Repression in China [N]. *Peterson Institute for International Economics Policy Brief No. PB08–8*, September.

Lei, W. (2014). Reform of Shadow Banking Regularization and Regulation [N]. *Shanghai Securities News*, February 28.

Levine, R. (2002). Bank-Based or Market-Based Financial Systems: Which Is Better? [J]. *Journal of Financial Intermediation*, Vol. 11, No. 4, pp. 398–428.

Li, J. (2013). Financial Reform: From Conception to Action [N]. *www.Caixin.com*, September 27.

Li, W. and Xu, J. (2014). Direction and Path of Loan-to-Deposit Ratio Reform [J]. *China Rural Finance*, Vol. 15, pp. 21–23.

Lin, J. (2012). *New Structural Economics* [M]. Beijing: Peking University Press.

Liu, H. (2012). *Comparative Study on Two Major Global Crisis, Comparative Studies* [M], Issue 62. Beijing: China Citic Press.

Liu, R. (2011). Financial Repression, Ownership Discrimination and Growth Burden – A Re-Investigation of SOE Efficiency Loss [J]. *China Economic Quarterly*, Vol. 1, pp. 603–618.

Liu, Yonggang. (2012). Blue-Whale-Phenomena in China's Banking Sector – Windfall Profits and Reform [J]. *China Economic Weekly*, Vol. 13, pp. 26–36.

Liu, Yuhui. (2012). Extraordinary Credit Scale: Root for Banks' High Profits [N]. *China Securities Journal*, April 11.

Ma, W. (2012). High Interest Margin Unsustainable for Banks [J]. *China News Week*, Vol. 10, pp. 46–47.

McKinnon, R. (1973). *Money and Capital in Economic Development* [M]. Washington, DC: Brookings Institute.

Marx, K. (2004). *Das Kapital* (Vol. III) [M]. Beijing: People's Publishing House, 2.

National Economic Council, Council of Economic Advisers, and Office of Science and Technology Policy (2011). A Strategy for American Innovation: Securing Our Economic Growth and Prosperity (R), Feb. Retrieved from: https://obamawhitehouse. archives.gov/sites/default/files/uploads/InnovationStrategy.pdf.

Niu, X. (2013a). Weak Risk Control in Internet Finance [N]. *www.finance. sina.com. cn*, June 2.

Niu, X. (2013b). Several Thoughts on Credit Asset Securitization [N]. *www.ce.cn*, July 26.

Pan, G. (2012a). Pan Gongsheng: Interest Margin Is Not High in China's Banking Sector [N]. *Beijing Youth Daily*, March 8.

Pan, G. (2012b). Retrospect and Prospect of the Reform of China's Banking Sector [N]. *21st Economic Report*, June 1.

Pan, Y. (2007). High Margin Between Deposit and Loan Rates Has Fulfilled Its Mission [N]. *China Securities Journal*, July 30.

Qian, M. (2012). *Merits and Demerits of Chinese Dynasties* [M]. Shanghai: SDX Joint Publishing Company.

Research Team of the Monetary Policy Department of the PBOC (2014). International Comparison in Deposit Rate, NPL Ratio and Net Interest Margin [N]. *www. caixin.com*, September 17.

Shaw, E. (1973). *Financial Deepening in Economic Development* [M]. New York: Oxford University Press.

Shi, J. (2012). Shi Jianping: Interest Margin in China's Banking Sector: High But Cannot Be Eliminated for Now [N]. www.stcn.com, March 15.

Tang, S. (2012). Two Sides of Banks' Profits [N]. *People's Daily*, December 21.

Tian, S. and Bai, Q. (2012). Financial Restraint, Financial Inclination and Economic Growth – An Empirical Research Based on China's Financial Resources Allocation [J]. *Shanghai Finance*, Vol. 12, pp. 3–7.

Wang, G. (2001). China's Interest Rate Regulation and Liberalization [J]. *Economic Research Journal*, Vol. 6, pp. 13–20.

Wu, X. (2013). Asset and Liability Management of Commercial Banks in Market-Based Financial Reform [J]. *Journal of Financial Research*, Vol. 12, pp. 1–15.

Yang, K. (2012). Yang Kaisheng, Comparatively Low Profit Margin of China's Banking Sector: A Comprehensive Interpretation Is Need [N]. *China Economic Net*, March 5.

Yang, K. (2014a). Misunderstandings to Be Clarified About China's Banking Sector [N]. *www.caixin.com*, June 2.

Yang, K. (2014b). Yang Kaisheng Talks about Excess Credit: Heavy Reliance on Credit for Economic Growth and Corporate Development [N]. *http://money.163. com*, September 11.

Yang, X. and Wu, X. (2012). Interest Rate Spread Above 3%: Higher than International Average [N]. *www.caijing.com.cn*, March 12.

Yi, G. (2008). Path and Logic for Opening up of China's Financial Sector. In *China's Opening up for Three Decades: Growth, Structure and Institutional Evolvement* [A], edited by Jiang Xiaojuan. Beijing: People's Publishing House.

Yigong, S. (2014). Research University: Never Oriented by Employment [Z]. *The Third Annual Meeting of Western Returned Scholars Association Chinese Overseas Scholars Association*, September 16.

Zeng, G. (2014). Loan-to-Deposit Ratio: Past, Present and Future [J]. *Modern Banks*, Vol. 8, pp. 68–69.

Zhang, C. (2012). Removing Loan Restriction of Commercial Banks as Soon as Possible [N]. *China Economic Times*, June 1.

Zhang, X. (2012). Insisting on Coordination of Financial Innovation and Financial Regulation – A Review on RMB Derivatives (3rd edition) [N]. *Financial Times*, June 29.

Zhang, X. (2014a). International Shadow Banking Regulation and Inspiration for China [J]. *Tsinghua Financial Review*, Vol. 6., pp. 23–26.

Zhang, X. (2014b). Several Thoughts on Further Improving Financial Regulation [N]. *China Business News*, September 18.

Zhao, C. and Zhu, H. (2013). Upgrading China's Economy by Building an Innovation Polity System [N]. *Science and Technology Daily*, October 28.

Zhou, X. (2012a). Zhou Xiaochuan: China's Banking Sector Have Handsome Profits But Far From Windfall Profits [N]. *xinhuanet*, March 12.

Zhou, X. (2012b). *Zhou Xiaochuan, International Financial Crisis: Observation, Analysis and Countermeasures* [M]. Beijing: China Financial Publishing House, October.

Zhou, X. (2012c). Zhou Xiaochuan: We Cannot Say the Negative Interest Rate Lasts in the Long Run, But Just at a Certain Stage [N]. *xinhuanet*, March 12.

5 Insufficient competition, implicit guarantee and financial inefficiency

When Yin dominates, Yang declines, and vice versa.
— *The Yellow Emperor's Classic of Medicine*

According to the financial coopetition outlook, the principal problem is financial "overdevelopment" or the extraction of finance from the real economy, and low financial efficiency and financial risks are only a secondary aspect. Giving appropriate attention to financial "extraction" and the establishment of transformation of the financial system as the goal of financial reform does not mean we can ignore the problem of low financial efficiency and financial risk. On the contrary, financial reform should be designed to effectively eliminate the "extraction" of the financial system and at the same time enhance financial efficiency and maintain basic financial stability.

Drawing on Mao Zedong's *The Question of Independence and Initiative within the United Front* (Mao, 1991) as a frame of reference, we can describe the relationship between eliminating the "extraction" of the financial system and enhancing financial efficiency and maintaining basic financial stability as follows: "The resource allocation efficiency of the whole economic system should be enhanced by realizing compatibility between finance and the real economy". In other words, addressing financial "underdevelopment" should include the elimination of financial "overdevelopment". That is the fundamental principle of financial reform. According to this principle, the capability of finance to serve the real economy is enhanced by addressing financial "underdevelopment", rather than supporting compatibility at the price of financial efficiency and stability. That helps compatibility and provides a precondition for compatibility: otherwise, finance and the real economy may impair each other, and the financial reform will undoubtedly be sacrificed. During the reform, efforts to enhance financial efficiency and to maintain financial stability take the form of addressing financial "overdevelopment".

Maintaining compatibility between finance and the real economy in a particular historical period is the condition for realizing long-run benefits of the financial sector. All requirements for higher financial efficiency and better financial stability should help improve the resource allocation efficiency of the whole economy. By so doing, we finally coordinate compatibility improvement with financial efficiency enhancement and financial stability maintenance in the financial reform and combine financial "overdevelopment" elimination with a solution to financial "underdevelopment".

Low financial efficiency is an important reason for the formation of the "extractive" financial system. To rebalance finance and the real economy, we must maintain basic financial stability and keep improving financial efficiency. Without higher financial efficiency and financial stability, rebalance between finance and the real economy, even if realized, is unsustainable. As the interaction between finance and the real economy is improved, the negative externality of the financial sector is significantly reduced. Otherwise systematic financial risks pile up, financial efficiency or stability become the principal aspect of the contradiction, and the focus or goal of the financial reform will be changed accordingly. This chapter deals with low financial efficiency.

Disputes over financial efficiency

Since the previous round of financial reform began, Chinese financial institutions have seen their strength rocket whether gauged by size indicators like assets and profits or by stability indicators, such as asset adequacy ratio and NPL ratio. However, there is disagreement about whether or not the efficiency of finance to serve the real economy is enhanced too.

Some argue there has been a considerable increase in financial efficiency in recent years, because many relevant indicators have been greatly improved. For example, the cost-to-income ratio of commercial banks saw a continuous and significant drop in recent years (Figure 5.1).

Others deny the significant improvement in the efficiency of finance in serving the real economy. On the one hand, many efficiency indicators are enhanced because of the expansion of the financial sector, for example, the obvious decline of cost-to-income ratio of listed banks. On the other hand, the efficiency of the financial sector in serving the real economy is different, and the efficiency of finance is the fundamental standard to measure financial efficiency. The improvement of efficiency indicators like the cost-to-income ratio is attributed more to higher efficiency of the financial sector than the efficiency of finance in serving the real economy. If measured by financing cost of the real economy and accessibility of finance, the efficiency of finance in serving the real economy is not significantly enhanced.

We agree with the second idea. Moreover, given the degraded service capability of the financial sector, the severe resource mismatch and high financing cost of the real economy, we hold that China's financial efficiency is low, rather than "not high" or "not low".

This judgement might be challenged in two ways. First, the financial efficiency or the efficiency of financial institutions is not low. This doubt is explained in previous sections. Second, China's financial system shows efficiency in mobilizing savings, even in resource allocation, for example, fund raising for infrastructure.

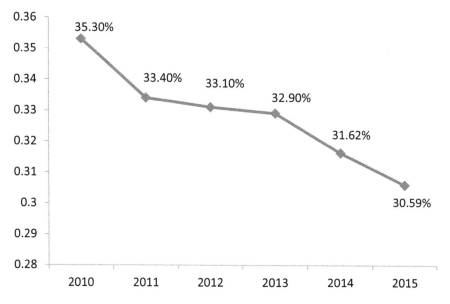

Figure 5.1 Cost-to-income ratio of China commercial banks
Source: CBRC.

Although the efficiency of finance in serving the real economy is considered, the efficiency of the financial system in resource allocation is more important and decisive than the efficiency in mobilizing savings, since high savings mobilization efficiency does not necessarily mean high efficiency of finance in serving the real economy. Indeed, the current financial system provides adequate support to infrastructure construction projects, which is a significant advantage, compared with other developing and developed countries. However, we have to recognize that some projects are low-efficiency and even severely wasteful of resources. That is revealed by the debt management measures taken by local governments.

Typical characteristics of low efficiency

The declining service capability of finance

In recent years, the capability of finance to serve the real economy degenerated rather than improved (Wang, 2014). A typical manifestation is that the proportion of unsecured and guaranteed loans provided by listed banks has been declining since 2008. At the end of 2013, unsecured loans accounted for 25.66 percent, 1.24 percentage points lower than that at the end of 2008; the combination of unsecured loans and guaranteed loans took 46.02 percent, down by 4.05 percentage points at the end of 2008 (Figure 5.2). That means the banking system's

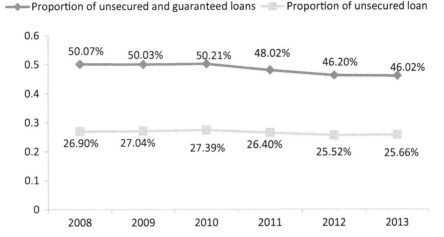

Figure 5.2 Proportion of non-loans and secured loans of A-shared listed banks
Source: Wind database.

capability of risk identification and control did not improve along with the asset and profit upsizing.

Severe resource misallocation

The effect of financial resource allocation reflects a severe mismatch. Many market-based sectors and SMEs with great growth potential lack financial support (Ba and Shen, 2013), and financial resources are poorly accessible. Ma (2013) points out "China's financial sector, especially the banking sector, provides service to only 20 percent of its clients". Even compared with major emerging economies, support from the financial sector to small and micro businesses is insufficient in China. According to an investigation by the World Bank, only 13.9 percent of small and micro businesses receive loans from banks in China, a percentage significantly lower than that of such emerging economies as Turkey, Brazil, Mexico and Indonesia (Figure 5.3).

A large amount of financial resources are allocated to the public sector and SOEs. From the perspective of local government debt, between 2009 and 2010, the loan balance through financial vehicles increased by about RMB5 trillion, nearly one-third of new RMB loans provided in the two years. From 2011 to the first half of 2013, local governments borrowed another RMB5 trillion, accounting for about 13 percent of aggregate social financing. According to data from the Ministry of Finance, SOEs' liabilities totalled RMB67.1 trillion at the end of 2013. According to statistical standards of the Ministry of Finance, SOEs include local governments' financial platform companies. Supposing 50 percent of them

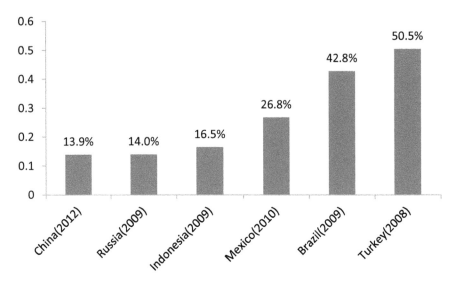

Figure 5.3 Proportion of loan-receiving small and micro businesses in major emerging economies

Source: World Bank Enterprise Surveys (2008–2012).

were from bank loans, the loan balance of SOEs took about 64.5 percent of loans of non-financial enterprises in the same period, and about 44 percent of loan balances of all businesses in the same period. However, "In China's GDP, SOEs contribute less than 35 percent" (Li, 2014).

High financing cost for the real economy

At present, the high financing cost of the real economy has constituted a severe restraint on China's economic development and is of general concern to society including decision makers. To address the problem of the high financing cost of the real economy, the government has considered many measures. It was proposed at the Central Economic Work Conference convened in early 2013 that the financing cost of the real economy should be considerably reduced. In August 2014, the General Office of the State Council released *Guiding Opinions on Reducing High Financing Cost of Enterprises through Multiple Measures*. Some economists still doubt whether or not the financing cost of the real economy should be deemed high, considering, for example, that the average loan rate is not high.

Indeed, China's average loan rate is relatively low whether according to the so-called "golden rule" or international comparison based on the loan rate (Research Team of the Monetary Policy Department of PBOC, 2014). The "golden rule" may be defined as the equilibrium interest rate of an economy necessarily being higher than the nominal growth rate of its GDP. In the current financial system or financial structure, we regard a low average loan rate to be only a reflection of the low financing cost of medium- and large-sized enterprises, and low banks' on-balance-sheet financing cost. What concerns governments and much of society is the high financing cost of SMEs and small and micro businesses, as well as many enterprises being unable to get access to banks' on-balance-sheet financing.

SMEs and small and micro businesses are mainly financed through bank loans, entrusted loans, informal finance (including small loan companies), trust financing and rent financing. The ideal way to determine the financing cost of these enterprises is to calculate their comprehensive financing cost according to cost and proportion of financing from different channels, which is not feasible due to data unavailability. However, we derive evidence for the high financing cost of these enterprises from literature and the incomplete data and conclude that their financing cost is much higher than the standard required by the "golden rule". One report found the annualized interest rate of the financing cost of small and micro businesses to be 12.75 percent. Huang (2013a) points out "the entrusted loan rate is around 10 percent, and the composite interest rate of trust financing and lease financing is between 10 percent and 14 percent".

According to the *Survey Report on China Small and Micro Businesses* jointly formulated by Survey and Research Center for China Household Finance of

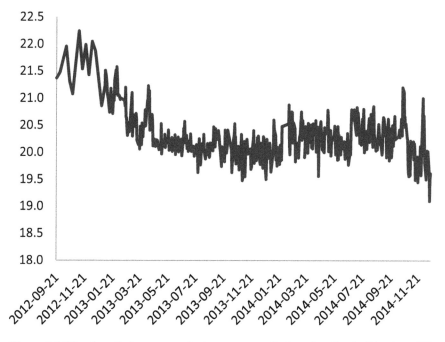

Figure 5.4 Wenzhou Index: composite interest rate of private lending in Wenzhou (%)
Source: Wind database.

Table 5.1 Calculation of the lending rate of small loan companies based on shareholder's expected return (The leverage ratio is 100% and tax evasion is not considered)[1]

Interest rate level (Business income/equity)	Business tax and surcharge/ equity	Operation and overhead expenditure/ equity	Asset impairment loss/equity	Total profit/equity	Income tax/ equity	Return on equity (ROE)	Shareholder return
A	B = A * 5.56%	C	D	E = A − B − C − D	F = E * 0.25	G = E * (1 − F)	H = G * (1 − 20%)
15.00%	0.83%	3.00%	3.00%	8.17%	2.04%	6.12%	4.90%
18.00%	1.00%	3.00%	3.00%	11.00%	2.75%	8.25%	6.60%
21.00%	1.17%	3.00%	3.00%	13.83%	3.46%	10.37%	8.30%
24.00%	1.33%	3.00%	3.00%	16.67%	4.17%	12.50%	10.00%
27.00%	1.50%	3.00%	3.00%	19.50%	4.87%	14.62%	11.70%
30.00%	1.67%	3.00%	3.00%	22.33%	5.58%	16.75%	13.40%

Note: Suppose the NPL ratio is not associated with the interest rate level.

Source: Calculation by authors. [1]For small loan companies, the cost is incurred from taxes, operation and overhead expenditures and asset impairment. Taxes mainly include business tax and surcharge and the income tax, the rate of which is about 5.56% and 15% respectively. Operation and overhead expenditures consist of salaries and office cost. According to statistics of small loan companies in a province of China, the ratio of operation and overhead expenditures to paid-in capital is about 1.8%. The operation and overhead expenditures are more like fixed cost, which, in general, tend to be lower in larger small loan companies. The average paid-in capital of small loan companies in this province stood at RMB160 million, 1.7 times the average value of the country. Therefore, the national ratio of operation and overhead expenditures to paid-in capital is about 3%. In Table 5.1, loss from asset impairment = NPL ratio * (1-NPL recovery rate). Suppose the expected NPL ratio is 5% and the NPL recovery rate is 40%, the asset impairment loss/loan balance or "asset impairment loss/equity" is 3%.

Southwestern University of Finance and Economics (SUFE) and China PNR Limited, interest-bearing loans from the informal financial sector are as high as 20.9 percent (Survey and Research Center for China Household Finance of Southwestern University of Finance and Economics (SUFE) and China PNR Limited, 2015). The Wenzhou Index also shows that the financing cost from the informal financial sector is above 19 percent (Figure 5.4).

The rate for small loan companies is high too. At present, the ROE target set by shareholders for management of such companies is around 15 percent. To achieve this goal, the average lending rate should be above 27 percent without leverage, considering the business tax and surcharge, business and overhead expenditure, asset impairment and income tax as well as other cost. The average lending rate should be no less than 20 percent; even the ROE target is reduced to 10 percent (Table 5.1).

Key financial reasons: insufficient competition

The ownership structure: not the ringleader

A kind of "Washington Consensus" is reached to attribute the low financial efficiency mainly to the insufficient commercialization of financial institutions, which is caused by the ownership structure, or the dominance of state-owned and state-holding financial institutions. According to the intuitive and simple logic of this idea, the ownership structure of the financial system affects the allocation of financial resources; thus, financial resources are undoubtedly allocated to state-owned sectors since the whole financial system is dominated by state-owned financial institutions. A large amount of financial resources are indeed allocated to state-owned enterprises, local governments and their affiliates. Therefore, this idea seems to have a strong basis in reality.

It is biased, however. It is not true to say that the commercialization of financial institutions is not high. Through the previous round of financial reform, financial institutions were highly commercialized through restructuring and listing. At the end of 2013, the proportion of 16 A-shares listed banks in all commercial banks in terms of loan balance and total assets reached 83.7 percent and 79.70 percent respectively. Unlisted commercial banks have also finished the shareholding reform. All these commercial banks, whether state holding or dominated by private capital, are clearly profit-oriented or financial-performance-oriented, and are much criticized for this orientation.

The major reason underlying the current resource allocation is not the dominance of state-owned financial institutions. Comparison between state-holding banks and non-state-holding banks of a similar size reveals commonalities in resource allocation. Both of them are inclined to allocate resources to SOEs and the financing vehicles of local governments. Therefore, a low degree of commercialization or the ownership structure, though perhaps a major reason, is not the most important one for low financial efficiency.

Insufficient competition and financial inefficiency

Competition outweighs the ownership structure as a reason for low financial efficiency. In the financial system, competition exists in the banking system, between the banking system and the capital market and between the banking system and the non-banking system.

Competition in the banking system mainly refers to direct rivalling in deposit and loan business. With fixed deposit supply, such composition will lead to a higher cost of absorbing deposits, which will bring forth changes in the loan rate and customer structure. Loan rate drop caused by competition helps to address the problem of "expensive financing"; for the other, "customers sink" due to competition, with a higher proportion of SME customers, which helps solve the "financing difficulty". Meanwhile, under prudential regulation, "customers sinking" will motivate banks to enhance their capability for financial innovation and risk control.

The capital market and the banking system compete with each other at the liabilities side (fund raising) and the assets side (capital utilization). At the liabilities side, the development of the capital market brings more alternative investment channels other than deposits, such as stocks and bonds, which, therefore, diverge deposits and increase the banks' cost of deposit absorbing. At the assets side, it provides alternative financing channels other than bank loans for enterprises in need of financing, leading to de-intermediation and diverging major corporate customers or quality customers. Confronted with competition from the capital market, banks have to pay more for fund raising and face lower quality loan demand. Under prudential regulation, non-bank financial companies compete with the banking sector (for example, in competition for high-grade bonds), producing a similar effect with the competition inside the banking system, since it will cause spontaneous "customer sinking" of banks.

Non-bank companies also compete with banks at the liability and asset sides. At the liabilities side, the development of non-bank financial companies makes investment channels to deposits available for investors, such as monetary market fund, trust products, insurance products for wealth management, diverging deposits and increasing deposit-absorbing cost. At the assets side, non-bank financing companies compete with banks in two aspects. First, on the credit market, they enable entities to finance through alternative channels to bank loans, such as debt investment schemes and policy loans of insurance companies and claims investment schemes. Second, non-bank financial companies compete with banks at the capital market. For example, insurance companies and fund companies compete fiercely with banks in investing high-grade bonds. Under prudential regulation, such competition leads to spontaneous "customer sinking" and produces similar effects with that of completion between banks and between the capital market and the banking system.

However, competition in all the three aforementioned aspects is actually insufficient. Banks make considerable earnings by only depending on major customers or relying too much on collaterals and guarantee, rather than being sufficiently motivated to capitalize and develop new credit techniques, resulting in "difficult financing"; or they have overly strong bargaining power on the credit market, leading to "expensive financing". The "two not-belows" policy means the loan growth rate for small and micro businesses is not below the average growth rate of all types of loans, and the loan increment is not below that in the same period of the previous year. Despite the strong impetus from the "two not-belows" policy and other incentives, difficulties and high cost of financing for SMEs and small and micro businesses are barely addressed.

Insufficient competition reflects problems in the financial structure to some degree; for example, insufficient competition between the banking system and the capital market and the overly high proportion of the banking system are two sides of a coin. However, unlike literature discussing China's financial reform from the perspective of the financial structure (Ba and Shen, 2013), this paper, by focusing on the competition mechanism, instead of superior resource allocation efficiency or some advantages of the capital market, holds that the most important reason for development of the capital market is not resource allocation efficiency but the competition effect on the capital market.

Three manifestations of insufficient competition in the financial system

1. Insufficient competition in the banking system

There is controversy about whether the competition in the banking system is sufficient or not. Some hold that competition in China's banking system is not insufficient, but in reality is fierce. China has more banks than other major economies. At the end of 2013, the number of banks in China was second only to that of the US, and was much higher than that of Germany and Japan (Table 5.2).

Secondly, as indicated by international comparison, the concentration degree of China's banking sector is not high. In 2011, the concentration degree was higher than that of the US but significantly lower than that of Japan, Germany, Britain and France as well as many other major economies (Table 5.3).

Thirdly, the "deposit war" between banks is common; besides, banks scramble fiercely for major customers.

However, we still think the competition in China's banking system is insufficient.

First, there are many banks, if they are regarded as corporate institutions. But the number of corporate institutions may not be an appropriate standard. It is an aggregate indicator rather than a per capita one, and the number of corporate institutions in China in 2006 is about 2.3 times that of the US, but that does not indicate fiercer competition between Chinese banks than in the US.

Second, from the perspective of the coverage of branches, the competition between banks in China is much less fierce than in other major economies. In 2012, there were 7.72 bank branches per 100,000 people, while the figure in the US, Japan, Germany and France was as high as 35.26, 33.92, 13.90 and 38.83 respectively. Since China's financial depth has reached the level of the major

Table 5.2 Number of banks in major economies

	US	China[1]	Japan	Germany
2006	8,681	19,797	N/A	N/A
2007	8,533	8,877	N/A	N/A
2008	8,305	5,634	N/A	N/A
2009	8,012	3,857	N/A	2,248
2010	7,658	3,769	N/A	2,228
2011	7,357	3,800	N/A	2,199
2012	7,083	3,747	N/A	2,149
2013	6,812	3,949	480	2,130

Note: (1) The amount of China's banks has dropped a lot since 2006, mainly because of the decline of rural credit cooperatives. The number of rural credit cooperatives in China is 19,348, 8,348, 4,965, 3,056, 2,646, 2,265, 1,927 and 1,803 each year between 2006 and 2013.

(2) The US data refer to the number of banks insured by the FDIC, and those not insured by the FDIC account for only a small part.

(3) Data of China also include non-bank financial companies which account for a proportion too insignificant to affect the international comparison.

Source: FDIC, Annual reports of the CBRC 2006–2013, Financial Service Agency of Japan and Deutsche Bundesbank.

Table 5.3 Concentration of the banking sector in major economies: asset proportion of the top three commercial banks (Unit: %)

	China	US	Japan	Germany	Britain	France
2008	48.62	35.48	44.74	72.22	62.60	60.46
2009	47.17	34.92	44.19	75.90	56.77	62.43
2010	44.71	34.55	44.16	77.46	56.66	63.81
2011	42.68	35.39	44.60	78.66	58.54	63.21
2012	40.71	35.25	N/A	64.68	N/A	N/A
2013	39.06	N/A	N/A	N/A	N/A	N/A

Note: Given the big difference between the Word Bank data about the asset proportion of China's top three commercial banks (58.32%, 55.89%, 51.23%, 51.96% and 68.49% for each year between 2008 and 2012) and the real proportion, we recalculate the concentration degree of China's banking sector according to data from the CBRC and Wind.

Source: World Bank, CBRC and Wind database.

economies in Table 5.4, the number of branches per 100,000 is an internation-ally comparable indicator in general (Table 5.4).

However, due to the great difference in the coverage between rural and urban financial institutions, the comparability of this indicator is affected by the dispar-ity in the urbanization rate between China and other major economies. Even if the effect of the urbanization rate is deducted, the coverage of China's bank branches is relatively low.

Third, the "deposit war" between banks is more a result caused by restrictions on the loan-to-deposit ratio than a manifestation of fierce competition in the

Table 5.4 Number of bank branches per 100,000 people in major economies

	2004	2005	2006	2007	2008	2009	2010	2011	2012
China	N/A	N/A	N/A	N/A	N/A	N/A	N/A	N/A	7.72
US	32.52	33.13	33.76	34.59	35.01	35.80	35.36	35.17	35.26
Japan	34.59	34.38	34.15	33.97	33.95	33.94	33.98	33.90	33.92
Germany	21.28	20.19	16.68	16.30	16.30	15.84	15.68	15.52	13.90
France	21.52	21.97	45.86	44.85	44.51	41.85	41.49	41.25	38.83
Britain	29.07	28.39	26.52	26.50	26.16	25.56	24.87	24.23	N/A

Source: World Bank.

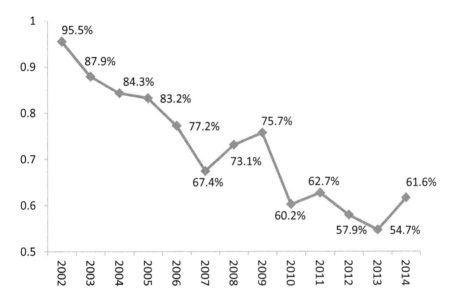

Figure 5.5 Proportion of bank loans in social financing

Source: PBOC.

banking system. Scrambling for major customers does not imply intense competition in the banking sector. In recent years, the interest margin and interest rate remained high, which is difficult in an industry with fierce competition.

2. Insufficient competition between the capital market and the banking system

From the perspective of the financing structure, despite a significant drop in the proportion of bank loans in recent years (Figure 5.5), the capital market has not yet become a powerful rival to banks. The decline of the bank loan proportion is not because of the increase proportion of funds from the capital market, but

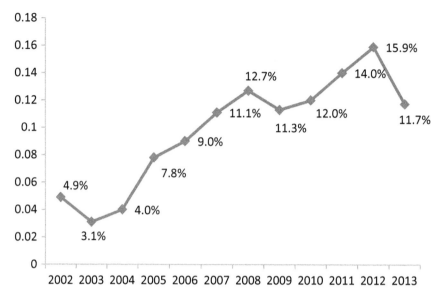

Figure 5.6 Proportion of multi-layer capital market financing in social financing

Note: Multi-layer capital market financing includes domestic equity financing of enterprises and non-financial enterprises.

Source: PBOC.

because of the higher proportion of off-balance-sheet financing or funds from shadow banking which is closely associated with banks.

As matter of fact, the proportion of multi-layer capital market financing has remained at a low level. In 2013, the proportion was only 11.71 percent, lower than that in 2008.

3. Insufficient competition between non-bank financial companies and banks

In terms of competition at the liabilities side, although the proportion of deposits in the financial assets of the household sector declined in recent years, the decline is largely offset by wealth management products provided by banks. Non-bank financial institutions affect the deposit market in a very limited way. In the credit market, policy loans, debt investment schemes of insurance companies and collective funds trust, although growing fast, have not impacted on the banks' credit market. On the capital market, non-bank financial companies are not power rivals either. In terms of the creditor structure, as of the end of November 2014, banks have held about two-thirds of all debts, while non-bank financial companies have held about one-fifth, only 5.1 percentage points higher than a decade ago (Table 5.5).

Table 5.5 Bondholder structure

	2005	2006	2007	2008	2009	2010	2011	2012	2013	2014.11
Banks	73.23%	74.13%	69.89%	66.22%	72.17%	71.94%	69.93%	68.58%	66.67%	65.12%
Non-bank financial institutions	15.40%	17.15%	12.67%	18.68%	14.67%	16.82%	18.83%	20.26%	20.19%	20.50%
Among them: trust companies, etc.	4.49%	6.53%	0.57%	0.77%	0.48%	0.43%	0.39%	0.34%	0.29%	0.25%
Securities companies	0.07%	0.16%	0.35%	0.86%	0.65%	0.75%	0.87%	0.67%	0.61%	0.67%
Insurance institutions	6.62%	7.37%	7.58%	9.23%	8.99%	9.73%	9.65%	9.30%	8.97%	8.08%
Fund	4.22%	3.09%	4.17%	7.83%	4.54%	5.92%	7.92%	9.95%	10.33%	11.49%

Note: Non-financial institutions do not comply with standards of the CBRC, but refer to non-depositary financial institutions. The category of trust companies and others includes trust companies, financial companies, auto financing companies and financial leasing companies.

Source: chinabond.com.cn. Accessed on Feb 10, 2015.

In addition, to prove insufficient competition rather than the ownership structure to be the key reason for low financial efficiency, we have to determine whether or not insufficient competition is caused by the problem of ownership structure. The answer is in the negative. Insufficient competition on the capital and credit markets is hardly associated with the ownership structure, and insufficient competition in the banking sector is mainly because of the high threshold for market access set to maintain financial stability, which is barely linked with the ownership structure.

Key non-financial reasons: pervasive implicit guarantee

Implicit guarantee and financial inefficiency

Pervasive implicit guarantee is a cause of low financial efficiency as well as the financial factors. In this book, implicit guarantee is defined as a guarantee provided by the government to entities in need of financing. These entities may include industrial SOEs, financing vehicles of local governments, or urban infrastructure investment companies, and real estate enterprises.

High-efficiency functioning of the financial system requires the involvement of qualified players with demand, and a financial environment in which they can compete fairly. A government implicit guarantee allows unqualified players to enter the market, such as local governments' financing vehicles which may have severe budget constraints and not be sensitive to the interest rate. A government implicit guarantee systematically reduces the real risks for SOEs, and the risk-return structure of financing SOEs is severely distorted. Under these circumstances, even with qualified entities with demand, there is no environment where SOEs and non-SOEs may compete fairly for financial resources. Although SOEs face higher risks than non-SOEs when doing their business in the banking system or the bond market, state-holding banks or private banks will allocate financial resources to SOEs under the rule of commercialization. With pervasive implicit guarantees, the bigger role of the market in the financial system implies a more severe mismatch of financial resources.

Laggard SOE reform

Why is implicit guarantee so common? The reason varies a lot for different types of entities in need of financing. An implicit guarantee is common for industrial SOEs because of the laggard or delayed reform of such enterprises. Despite great achievements made in previous rounds of SOE reforms and significant improvement in size and profits of SOEs, the government administration has not been completely separated from the management of enterprises and state assets, and a considerable part of SOEs are still "half government tools and half market players" (Chen, 2014). Even during the global financial crisis, the emergence of financing platform companies and the swelling debts of local governments reinforced the central government's intervention in the management of enterprises and state assets and made SOEs play a bigger role as "half government tools and half market players".

Therefore, the government has close or distant relationships with enterprises under different ownership systems, and SOEs enjoy advantages (Chen, 2012). In other words, due to delayed SOE reform, the government keeps providing implicit guarantees to such enterprises. We can say that the implicit guarantee is a valuable consideration provided by the government to SOEs, so that the latter plays a role as "half government tools and half market players". There is another possibility. Due to problems left over from the past in SOEs and unsolved by public finance, enterprises can only obtain financial resources with a government implicit guarantee. This implicit guarantee is equal to a consideration payment to solve "problems left over from the past" (Zhao, 2014).

Excessive policy burdens

The implicit guarantee is so pervasive because financing vehicles and urban infra-structure investment companies of local governments bear too many policy burdens. Policy burdens lead to soft budget constraints. Yet policy burdens cannot completely explain the soft budget constraints of financing platforms of local governments and government implicit guarantee. In addition to policy burdens, time inconsistency of investment is also an important reason (Dewatripoint and Maskin, 1995; Qian, 1994). Local governments or their financing platforms may be motivated to invest more in inefficient investment projects that are not completed, because the marginal revenue of additional investment may be higher than the marginal cost of abandoning the projects, and they will try to avoid leaving projects unfinished. For financial institutions, the soft budget constraints of the financing platforms and urban infrastructure investment companies equal the government's implicit guarantee. Li Yifu and other scholars systematically discuss the policy guarantee (Lin, Cai and Li, 1997, 1999; Lin and Li, 2004; Lin, Liu and Zhang, 2004).

According to their research, policy burdens are the root of soft budget constraints on SOEs and fall into two categories. One category is the strategic policy burden. Under the influence of the traditional catch-up strategy, investment in industries without comparative advantages generates the emergence of enterprises without viability and thus cause burdens. Another category is social policy burdens. SOEs are burdened with redundant personnel and benefits for employees or social security. Although the aforementioned studies focus on industrial SOEs and the classification of policy burdens are not applicable to financing vehicles or urban infrastructure investment companies of local government, their analysis framework clearly explains these burdens.

Why do financing vehicles and urban infrastructure investment companies bear too many policy burdens? Why did such burdens not exist or were not obvious before the outbreak of the global financial crisis? First, the proactive fiscal policies failed to provide sufficient fiscal support. Since the outbreak of the global financial crisis, fiscal policies have not been supportive enough, despite the high deficit ratio or proportion of deficits in the GDP (Figure 5.7).

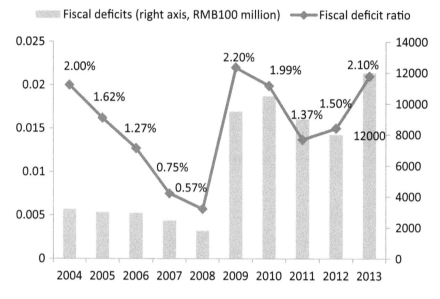

Figure 5.7 Fiscal deficits and the deficit ratio

Source: Ministry of Finance.

According to the "fiscal pulse" indicator, active boost from fiscal policies with cyclical effects deducted, is much less than reflected by the deficit ratio (Ma, 2014). Second, the leverage ratio of the central government remains almost unchanged. Since the outbreak of the global financial crisis, the central government has barely elevated its leverage. In 2008, debts of the central government accounted for 37.05 percent of the GDP, and the leverage ratio of the central government slightly increased to 37.52 percent at the end of 2013 (Figure 5.8). According to a vertical comparison, the central government significantly increased its leverage in the previous round of economic downturn. Its leverage ratio was enhanced from 21.20 percent in 1997 to 42.31 percent in 2003, an increase of 21.11 percentage points.

As shown by horizontal international comparison, since the outbreak of the global financial crisis, central governments of major economies have experienced the rocketing leverage ratio (Figure 5.9). For example, the leverage ratio of the US Federal Government was elevated from 64.02 percent in 2008 to 93.81 percent in 2012; and the figure for Germany, which is known for its strict restriction on governmental debts, was increased from 43.15 percent to 56.91 percent over the same period.

Due to insufficient support from fiscal policies in general and the lack of effectiveness of proactive fiscal policies, fiscal problems have to be financialized; and without significant enhancement of leverage by central government, local governments have to borrow more money from banks and other financial institutions.

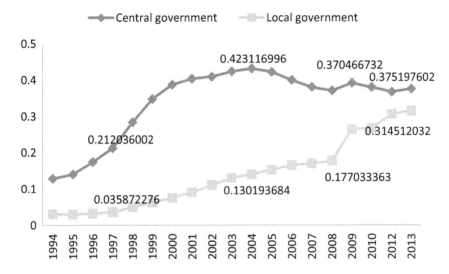

Figure 5.8 Leverage ratio of the central and local governments

Note: (1) The leverage ratio of local governments in 2013 only covers the first half of 2013.

(2) Central government debt includes treasuries, policy financial bonds, bonds issued by Central Huijin, NPL debts, debts of the National Railway Administration and China Railway and sovereign debts, with special treasuries deducted which are issued for spinning off NPLs. Data of local government debts comes from the National Audit Office or is calculated based on statistics from the National Audit Office. Notably, the calibre for central and local governments' debts used in this book is different from No. 32 of 2013: Audit Results of National Governmental Debts released by the National Audit Office (www.audit.gov.cn/n1992130/n1992150/n1992379/3432165.html). The first difference is that policy bank debts and bonds issued by the Central Huijin as well as many other items are included in the calculation of the central government's debt in this book. Second, we do not distinguish debts for which the government is obliged to pay, debt for which the government is responsible for providing guarantee and debts that the government may have the duty to rescue. In addition, debts of different types are not converted as per specific coefficients when we calculate the leverage ratio.

Source: National Audit Office, Wind, State Administration of Foreign Exchange, annual reports of the Ministry of Railway or China Railway and annual reports of the Industrial and Commercial Bank of China (ICBC), Construction Bank of China (CBC), ABC and Bank of China (BOC).

That is the essential reason why local government financing platforms bear excessive policy burdens. Due to these policy burdens, some business of the financing platforms is not commercially sustainable, and the implicit guarantee of government is a compulsory precondition for these companies to borrow money.

The performance evaluation mechanism of local governments is not viable. Under the mechanism with the GDP as the sole criteria, local governments generalize responsibility for expenditure, and exercise many unnecessary powers of administration in the name of "developmental governments", which significantly increases the expenditure demand. Disposable fiscal resources of local governments are restricted due to defects in the tax distribution system and the transfer payment system (for example, special transfer payment). To narrow the gap

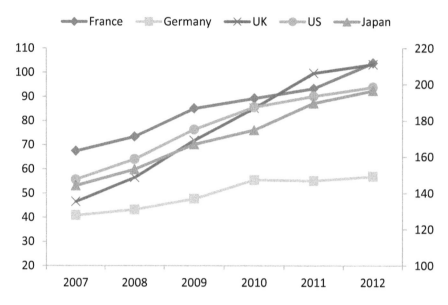

Figure 5.9 Leverage ratio of central governments in major economies
Source: BIS.

between the huge expenditure demand and limited disposable fiscal resources, local governments usually impose more policy burdens on the financing platforms or SOEs under their control. Then the implicit guarantee comes from the government as a consideration.

"Too-big-to-fail" real estate companies

Two kinds of players in the financial market are not sensitive to change in the interest rate and both of them are closely associated with implicit guarantees. One player is the entity under the soft budget constraint, mainly referring to financing vehicles of local governments. The soft budget constraint is also seen in some industrial SOEs, but generally speaking, such constraints have been significantly reduced after the previous round of SOE reforms establishing their listing. The association of these entities with implicit guarantee is discussed in previous sections. The other category of player is the real estate company.

Generally, real estate companies are not sensitive to the interest rate for two reasons. First, they are in a high-profit industry. Second, due to restrictions imposed by regulation policies, capital accessibility is more important than capital cost for real estate companies. Explained from the perspective of demand, they do not take supply into consideration. Why is the financial sector, regardless of risks, willing to invest in real estate companies although they are not sensitive to the interest rate, especially when the adjustment and control of the real estate sector became normal? According to the credit rationing theory, financial institutions may exclude entities insensitive to the interest rate through credit rationing to avoid adverse selection, but it is not true in reality.

An exploratory explanation is that the real estate industry obtains a sort of implicit guarantee because it is too big to fail. From the perspective of economic composition, the real estate industry has become a one-hundred-percent pillar industry. In 2013, its added value accounted for 5.9 percent of the GDP, and this proportion would be higher if related sectors are considered. In terms of composition of the fixed asset investment, real estate investment in 2013 accounted for nearly 20 percent. Regarding financing risks, the financial system is severely exposed to real estate risks. At the end of 2013, the land mortgage loan balance reached RMB7.76 trillion; at the end of the first half of 2013, among debts that the government is liable for, the government pledged to repay 37.23 percent of the revenue from land transfer; the proportion of commercial real estate loan balance in banks' loan balance reached 20.32 percent, and loans with land and housing as collaterals accounted for an ever-higher percentage in the total loan balance of banks.

In these circumstances, the real estate industry has become vital for macroeconomic stability and financial stability and is "too big to fail". Given its extreme importance, the financial sector has reasons to expect that the government will provide an implicit guarantee for the real estate market in order to avoid violent fluctuations and underpin the industry. This expectation is testified to by recent policy adjustment. The implicit guarantee is similar to Greenspan's put. The Board of the Federal Reserve, when chaired by Greenspan, capitalized on monetary policies to prevent the continuous plummet of the market and to maintain market confidence and financial stability. The Chinese implicit guarantee equates to providing a "Greenspan put" to investors.

Other reasons for financial inefficiency

Besides insufficient competition in the financing system and a pervasive implicit guarantee, there are other reasons for low financial efficiency that we must recognize.

Monetary policies

Since 2007, China has undergone a "roller-coaster" of monetary regulation and control. China sharply tightened its monetary policy between 2007 and August 2008, and suddenly switched to monetary easing and even to an excessively relaxed monetary policy in the period from September 2008 to the end of 2009; yet from the beginning of 2010 to October 2011, the monetary policy was tightened again.

Monetary policy greatly affected the financial resource allocation. First, a too relaxed monetary policy led to a credit surge; as a result, a large amount of financial resources may have been allocated to low-efficiency projects. Second, frequently reversing the monetary policy produced an obvious squeeze-out effect on loans for small and micro businesses. When the monetary policy was tightened, banks usually reduced loans to small and micro businesses to counter the credit crunch, since their major clients usually have more bargaining power than small-sized and medium-sized customers. In the case of monetary easing, facing credit expansion, banks usually granted large loans to quality big enterprises or enterprises with an implicit guarantee from the government, since it is hard to accumulate enough projects of small and micro businesses. Some loans provided to quality big enterprises may go to medium, small, and micro-sized businesses in such forms as entrusted loans. Enterprises with a government implicit guarantee, represented by financing platforms of local governments, may directly consume loans, leading to low efficiency in financial resources allocation.

A weak financial infrastructure

To some degree, since the financial infrastructure is so weak, the effect of low financial efficiency is just like the Chinese proverb says: even a clever housewife cannot cook a meal without rice. For example, information asymmetry and low default cost caused by an incomplete credit reporting system increase the risk premium of loans for medium, small and micro-sized enterprises or reduce the banks' willingness to provide loans, and finally lead to difficult and expensive financing for such enterprises. Another result is that the proportion of secured loans does not decline. Loopholes in the financial legal system are one of the essential factors curbing the healthy development of China's stock market, which then causes insufficient competition in the financial system.

Rigid redemption

According to the Financial Stability Analysis Group of the PBOC (2014, p. 129),

> *rigid redemption refers to the situation when wealth management products may default or fail to deliver targeted interest payment, the commercial banks, trust companies and insurance companies as the issuers or conduits must guarantee to pay off the principal and interests to the investors by means of seeking the third party's take-over, paying by own funds or providing compensation to investors, etc., so as to maintain their own reputation.*

The influence of "rigid redemption" is mainly manifest in the fact that it impedes the functioning of the price mechanism in the financial market and severely damages the risk pricing capability of the financial market. "Rigid redemption" of banks' wealth management products systematically enhances the risk-free yield and the financing cost. In such a case, the interest rate does not reflect the real capital demand. "Rigid redemption" of trust products and bonds dampens the risk pricing capability of the trust market and the bond market. "Rigid redemption" provides a breeding ground for the habit of paying no attention to risks and the excessive pursuit of returns. It drastically increases the risk appetite and the piling up of financial risks.

Economic bubbles

Despite the overwhelming advance of information technology in the banking sector after the previous round of financial reform, credit assessment techniques used by banks are still at a relatively low level. Banks rely on collaterals, properties and land mortgage and lack capabilities to grant unsecured loans and effectively control risks. Therefore, banks are dubbed to be the pawnshop. The economic bubble is an important backdrop for this phenomenon.

With economic bubbles, property and land are preferred by banks as high quality collaterals. Their rising price indicates the rocketing value appreciation of collaterals. Considering the discount rate when evaluating collaterals, collaterals can excessively overlay all risks of bank loans. Therefore, banks only have to pay attention to collaterals as the secondary source of payment rather than as the primary source of payment. Under such a circumstance where collaterals become the safest way of risk control, banks are not interested at all in developing new risk control techniques. As a result, they gradually lose their risk control capability due to excessive reliance on collaterals like land and property.

References

Ba, S. and Shen, C. (2013). Improving Financial Sector's Efficiency in Serving Real Economy Needs Perfecting Financial Structure [N]. *Guangming Daily*, July 19.

Chen, Q. (2012). From SOE Reform to State-owned Asset Reform [J]. *Capital Shanghai*, Vol. 6, pp. 20–23.

Chen, Q. (2014). State-Owned Asset Reform Roadmap [N]. *Caijing Magazine*, February 24.

Dewatripont, M. and Maskin, E. (1995). Credit and Efficiency in Centralized and Decentralized Economies [J]. *Review of Economic Studies*, Vol. 62, No. 4, pp. 541–556.

Financial Stability Analysis Group of the PBOC (2014). *China Financial Stability Report 2014* [M]. Beijing: China Financial Press.

Huang, J. (2013a). A Call for Low-Cost Financing Environment to Develop Real Economy [N]. *People's Daily*, February 4.

Li, Y. (2014). On Several Frontier Issues Concerning the Current Economic Situation [N]. *Beijing Daily*, October 27.

Lin, J., Cai, F., and Li, Z. (1997). *Sufficient Information and SOE Reform* [M]. Shanghai: Shanghai Sanlian Book Store, Shanghai People's Publishing House.

Lin, J., Cai, F. and Li, Z. (1999). *China's Miracle: Development Strategy and Economic Reform* (additional edition) [M]. Shanghai: Shanghai Sanlian Book Store, Shanghai People's Publishing House.

Lin, J. and Li, Z. (2004). Policy Burden, Moral Hazard and Soft Budget Constraints [J]. *Economic Research Journal*, Vol. 2, pp. 17–27.

Lin, J., Liu, M. and Zhang, Q. (2004). Policy Burdens and Enterprises' Soft Budget Constraints: An Empirical Study on China [J]. *Management World*, Vol. 8, pp. 81–127.

Ma, J. (2013). Financial Sector Needs a Spoiler [N]. *People's Daily*, June 21.

Ma, J. (2014). Several Opinions on Taxation, SOE Profits and Local Government Debts [N]. *21st Economic Report*, August 25.

Mao, Z. (1991). The Question of Independence and Initiative Within the Unified Front [A]. In *Selected Works of Mao Zedong* (2nd edition) [M]. Beijing: People's Publishing House, pp. 537–540.

Qian, Y. (1994). A Theory of Shortage in Socialist Economies Based on the Soft Budget – Constraint [J]. *American Economic Review*, Vol. 84, No. 1, pp. 145–156.

Research Team of the Monetary Policy Department of the PBOC (2014). International Comparison in Deposit Rate, NPL Ratio and Net Interest Margin [N]. *www.caixin.com*, September 17.

Survey and Research Center for China Household Finance of Southwestern University of Finance and Economics (SUFE) and China PNR Limited (2015). *Survey Report on China Small and Micro Businesses* [R], March 10.

Wang, D. (2014). Address at Tsinghua PBOCSF Global Finance Forum [N]. *http://finance.sina.com.cn*, May 10.

Zhao, C. (2014). SOE Reform Should Focus on the Principal Contradiction [N]. *Caijing Magazine*, December 8.

6   Financial risks

Bring your umbrella just in case of rain, take enough food although you are full.
– A Chinese proverb

The accumulation of financial risks

Financial reform is definitely concerned with financial risk. Chen (2014) regards addressing financial risks as one of the two major tasks of financial reform. Financial risks can be classified as internal risks and external risks. External risks are associated with the exchange rate and short-term cross-border capital flows, such as financial risk caused by short-term cross-border capital flow reverse and a drastic drop in the exchange rate. External risks are associated with financial opening and the exchange rate regime. Yi (2008) holds that China's financial system has five lines of defence: current account surplus, a great amount of foreign direct investment, a giant foreign exchange reserve, capital account control and the increasing international competitiveness of the Chinese economy. Given the strong resistance of China's financial system to external financial risks, external risks can be controlled if the principle of orderly regulation and prudent liberalization of the capital account is followed. The internal financial risks remain to be discussed. Drawing on the classification criteria of financial crises, we classify internal financial risks as solvency risks or liquidity risks.

Solvency risks: the biggest at present

The NPL ratio of banks keeps recovering and increases rapidly. The NPL ratio of commercial banks returned to 1.25 percent by the end of 2014. Although rather lower than that of international counterparts, this ratio reflects a tendency towards continuous and accelerated recovery. In 2014, the NPL ratio rallied by 0.25 percentage points, while this ratio has rebounded only by 0.05 percentage points in 2013 (Figure 6.1).

Secondly, driven by heavier debt burdens and the declining earnings of the real economy, the solvency risk will be higher in the future.

More debt burdens are imposed on the real economy. For one thing, the leverage ratio of the non-financial sector surged. Although the leverage ratio is much

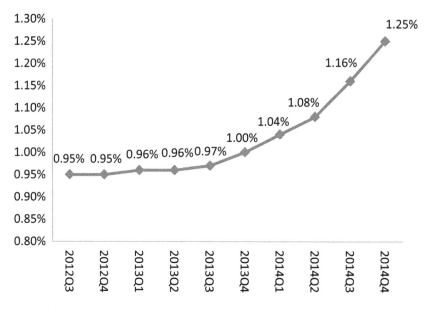

Figure 6.1 NPL ratio of China commercial banks

Source: CBRC.

lower than that of advanced economies like the US, Japan and Britain, in the short term that does not imply that China has in comparison weaker solvency, considering the high financing costs in China. According to our calculation, since the outbreak of the global financial crisis, China has undergone a process of credit boom and a fast increase of the leverage ratio. The leverage ratio of China's non-financial sector and corporate sector reached 208 percent and 124 percent respectively at the end of 2013, 66 and 40 percentage points higher than at the end of 2008, and 17 and 11 percentage points higher than at the end of 2012, indicating an increase significantly deviating from the historical trend. According to international experience, a credit boom or upward deviation of the leverage ratio from the historical trend implies huge latent debt risks and even the risk of a financial crisis (Dell'Ariccia et al., 2012; Borio and Lowe, 2002; Mendoza and Terrones, 2008; Schularick and Taylor, 2009; Mitra et al., 2011). Yet financing costs remains high. The weighted loan rate for the non-financial sector and other sectors reached 7.2 percent in the fourth quarter of 2013, the average interest rate of bonds reached 7.15 percent in 2013, the average yield of collective funds trust as loans was 9.15 percent, and the average rate of small loan companies and private lending was above 18 percent. The financing cost of average interest rate of bonds is even higher if all other financing fees are added. On the other hand, due to overcapacity and economic downturn, the earnings and solvency of the real economy are in decline. The income tax from industrial enterprises increased by only 2.61 percent and 0.99 percent respectively in 2012 and 2013.

The following three factors also trigger or increase solvency risks. The first factor to trigger or increase solvency risks is the downside risk in the real estate market. Due to rocketing housing prices and the excessive reliance of banks on collaterals, China's financial system faces a large risk of exposure. At the end of 2013, real estate development loans and loans with properties mortgaged by major banks accounted for 38 percent of all loans. Meanwhile, China began to face oversupply (SUFE Survey and Research Center for China Household Finance, 2014) or structural surplus (Ni, Zou and Gao, 2014) at the real estate market, and the demand for real estate may culminate somewhere around 2015 (Liu, 2013). Therefore, the real estate market is confronted with downside risks, even the risk of a bubble burst, which will severely damage the banks' asset quality.

The second factor to trigger or increase solvency risks is mutual and joint guarantee risks which have developed in the delta areas of the Yangtze River and the Pearl River and triggered severe risks in Wenzhou and other places. These risks, once materialized, may contribute to debt evasion by enterprises, damage the financial ecology, put enterprises into a liquidity crisis due to the banks' reluctance to provide loans, loan withdrawal or refusal to renew loans and dampen their solvency; also, high-quality guarantors might be affected and the solvency of "quality enterprises" might be weakened.

The third factor to trigger or increase solvency risks is maturity mismatch in the real economy. In the past three years, mid-term and long-term financing accounted for only 19.6 percent of the total investment in fixed assets. That means the investment in fixed assets was funded by short-term capital and enterprises were confronted with severe maturity mismatch. If the enterprises' operation keeps worsening or the financial system is tightened, enterprises will be exposed to solvency risks due to liquidity difficulties.

Liquidity risks that cannot be ignored

Due to a severe maturity mismatch in the shadow banking system, the interbank market was confronted with a sweeping "money shortage" in June 2013, although the liquidity ratio of commercial banks reached 43.68 percent and the excess reserve ratio of commercial banks reached 2.63 percent. Despite the regulation on shadow banking, severe maturity mismatch and latent liquidity risk in this sector have not yet been radically addressed.

Deteriorating structural risks

First, structural risks are more latent and contagious. Due to separate regulation and the lack of an effective regulation coordinating mechanism, interbank business is active, the chain of trading is prolonged and risks are more invisible and transmissible; as a result, enterprises' financing cost is increased, and systematic risks are also enhanced.

Second, most financial risks are in the banking system. In 2013, assets of the banking sector in China accounted for 83.92 percent of total assets of the whole financial system. Although the proportion of loans in social financing declined year on year (54.7 percent in 2013), banks accounted for 80.58 percent in social financing across society. This calculation includes various kinds of bonds held by banks and off-balance-sheet business like trust loans, entrusted loans and unaccepted bills.

Reasons for piling up financial risks

The legacies of counter-crisis policies

Irrational counter-crisis policies are a major reason for piling up financial risks. Since the outbreak of the financial crisis, the biggest irrationality in China's counter-risk policies is the mismatch between fiscal and monetary policies, and inactive fiscal policies. China's fiscal policies are inactive or not proactive enough (Ma, 2014), and the central government has not substantially enhanced leverage. To counter the crisis, fiscal and monetary policies should be coordinated with each other. The weakness of each of them leads to excessive reliance on the other, leading to an imbalance of macroeconomic policies and even to macroeconomic risks. Inactive fiscal policies directly cause financialization of fiscal problems and lead to severe consequences in two aspects.

The first severe consequence is the serious error in monetary policies. The monetary policies were too relaxed, considering the growth rate of M2 reached 28.4 percent in 2009, much higher than the average in years shortly before and after 2009 (Figure 6.2). In terms of the proportion of credit in the GDP, the year 2009 witnessed a "credit boom". The proportion of credit in the private sector increased by 23.5 percentage points over the previous year in 2009, meeting the two standards or indicators of a credit boom proposed by Dell'Ariccia et al. (2012). The first standard is when the annual proportion of private credit in the GDP increases by over ten percentage points and the divergence tendency is over 1.5 standard deviations. The second standard is when the annual proportion of private credit in the GDP increases by over 20 percentage points (Figure 6.3). A credit boom means a large amount of financial resources were allocated to low-efficiency or inefficient projects, and implies high financial risks.

The second severe consequence is the increasing debt of local governments. As discussed in Chapter 5, the central government did not enhance the leverage, leaving local governments no choice but to do so. Local governments cannot present deficits, leading to financialization of their debts. Regulations on local governments' debt since 2011 focus on blocking this debt and only consider the financial supply side, leading to a piling up of risks for local governments' debts. The most prominent manifestation is debt upsizing and increasing high-cost debts and an increasing proportion of opaque debts.

Defects in the incentive and the disincentive mechanisms of financial institutions

The global financial crisis reveals severe defects in the incentive and disincentive mechanism of financial institutions and the pervasive moral hazard of attributing

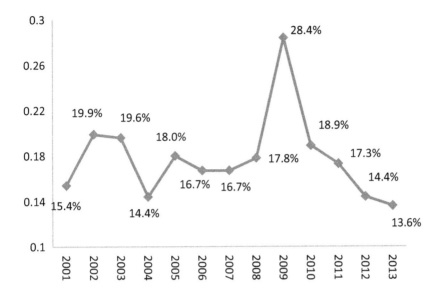

Figure 6.2 M2 growth rate

Source: PBOC.

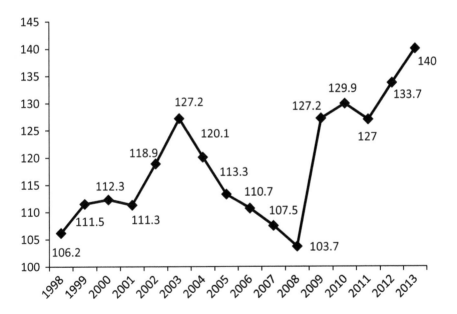

Figure 6.3 Proportion of private credit in the GDP

Note: In some literature the standard for a credit boom is based on comparable data around the world. World Bank data are used here, which are different from data calculated by the authors.

Source: World Bank.

earnings to individuals and of risk socialization. The benefits are taken by individuals, but the risk is borne by society. China's financing institutions are confronted with the same problem. After the shareholding reform and public offering, listed banks compete with each other in terms of performance and size. Under the performance competition pressure and even the window guidance in special periods, banks relaxed the loan-granting requirements or risk control criteria; as a result, risks piled up. One example is the repeated pledge by warehouse receipts in steel trade in the delta area of the Yangtze River. Another example is the mutual and joint guarantee risks. In the case of mutual guarantee, banks should make sure parties to the mutual guarantee are familiar with each other; in the case of joint guarantee, they should make sure the guarantor does not undertake excessive burdens. However, mutual and joint guarantee risks materialized in some places reveal that parties to the mutual guarantees barely know each other, and guarantors undertake too many burdens. All these imply severe defects in banks' risk control.

Other reasons

Deficiencies in financial regulation are an important reason for piling up financial risks. For example, while implementing counter-crisis policies, financial regulators have relaxed the regulation. Another example is that financial risks are enhanced along with the expansion of local governments' debts, since financial regulation did not coordinate with other policies and too strict regulation significantly pushed up the opaque and high-cost debts of local governments.

The "extractive" financial system is also a reason for building up risks. Finance relies on the real economy. The "siphonic effect", "erosion effect", interest group and corporate financial mechanism form an "extractive" financial system which damages the foundation of the real economy, resulting in worse underlying asset quality and more financial risks.

A financial crisis will hit China: yes or no?

A sweeping financial crisis affects the whole country in a systematic way and features extensive tightening or the loss of almost all functions of the financial system. According to static and dynamic calculation based on the asset adequacy ratio, China will not be hit by financial crises if it makes no major mistake in macro policies, and if its financial system has enough reserve to counter risk.

China's capability to withstand risks: static calculation

China's financial system has a strong resistance to solvency risks. The banking system generally has triple risk buffer zones. The first is the loan loss reserve. In the third quarter of 2014, about RMB1.90 trillion was provisioned for loan impairment by commercial banks; the provision coverage ratio was 247.15 percent and the loan provision rate was 2.88 percent. That means under the shock of financial risks, profits are affected only when the NPL ratio is higher by 1.72 percentage points than that at the end of the third quarter of 2014, if the requirement of the provision coverage ratio is down to 100 percent. The second is the capital buffer. In the third quarter of 2014, the net value of core tier-one capital was RMB8,639.5 billion, tier-one capital was RMB8,639.5 billion and capital was RMB10,668.3 billion. The adequacy ratio of core tier-one capital was 10.47 percent, tier-one capital was 10.47 percent and capital was 12.93 percent. If the average core tier-one capital adequacy ratio of commercial banks is 5.7 percent, the core tier-one capital can provide RMB3,94 trillion as the risk buffer, well able to absorb an impact of 5.95 percent of NPLs. The third buffer is the operating profit. Since profits for the current period are reflected in the net capital of the period, operation profits are not taken into consideration in static analysis. Given the aforementioned risk buffers, based on the point data of the third quarter of 2014, it is bearable for China's banking system if the NPL ratio is 9.83 percent.

China's financial system can well resist liquidity risks. Regulation indicators for banks' liquidity are still in a rational range. At the end of June 2014, the liquidity ratio of commercial banks was 47.52 percent, the loan-to-deposit ratio was 65.4 percent and the excessive reserve ratio was 2.5 percent. Additionally, the central banks can provide sufficient liquidity support. Commercial banks hold a vast amount of treasury and policy bank debt. At the end of August 2014, commercial banks held treasury and policy bank debts worth RMB13.43 trillion, including RMB5.68 trillion for the former. Commercial banks can obtain sufficient liquidity by pledging enough high-grade bonds only if the central bank performs its duty as the lender of the last resort. The deposit reserve is high; it reached RMB21.66 trillion at the end of June 2014. The central bank can inject enough liquidity by reducing the deposit reserve.

China's capability to withstand risks: dynamic calculation

Unlike the static calculation, the dynamic calculation takes stock of future performance and the profitability of financial institutions. We set three basic scenarios in the calculation.

Scenario 1: The NPL ratio released intensively in 2015.
Scenario 2: The NPL ratio released uniformly in the three years between 2015 and 2017.
Scenario 3: The NPL ratio released uniformly in the six years between 2015 and 2020.

We propose these hypotheses.

Hypothesis 1: The net interest margin of listed banks remains at the level of 2013, 2.57 percent.
Hypothesis 2: The proportion of net interest income and non-interest income of listed banks remains at the level of 2013, respectively 76.9 percent and 23.1 percent.
Hypothesis 3: Weighted risk assets grow synchronously with the average interest-earning assets and loan balance, and their annual growth rate remains at 13 percent, the same level as in 2013.

Hypothesis 4: The proportion of business tax and surcharge in the operating income and the cost-to-income ratio of listed banks remain at 6.35 percent and 30.88 percent respectively, which is the same as in 2013.

Hypothesis 5: The net core tier-one capital is only affected by the profitability (net profit). The following factors are not taken into consideration: add-on equity offering, allotment, swap of convertible bonds into equity, conversion of preferred stock and other equity financing, changes of capital surplus caused by fair value difference, changes in reputation, other intangible assets (excluding the land use right), net deferred tax assets, and the gap in loan impairment reserve.

Hypothesis 6: The annual dividend yield between 2014 and 2020 remains at 31.83 percent, the same level as in 2013.

Hypothesis 7: Before the loss provisioning coverage ratio is reduced to 100 percent, commercial banks adjust this ratio for the purpose of avoiding loss in the long run.

Hypothesis 8: Regardless of NPL write off, the NPL loss rate is 100 percent.

Hypothesis 9: The NPL ratio is released in the period set by each scenario at an average rate.

Hypothesis 1 should be further explained. Although a great deal of literature holds that interest rate liberalization will impose great pressure on the interest margin of commercial banks, we assume the net interest margin of listed banks between 2014 and 2020 remains the same as in 2013 for three reasons. First, suppose each value of the net interest margin is subjective. Second, even if unchanged, the net interest margin is an optimistic assumption; it can be offset by the hypotheses of unchanged proportion of non-interest income and cost-to-income ratio. Finally, the initial conditions for interest rate liberalization should be considered to evaluate its effects on the net interest margin. We are fully convinced that the net interest margin of commercial banks will not drop significantly in six to seven years.

According to the definition of the new interest margin, its calculation formula can be broken down as follows:

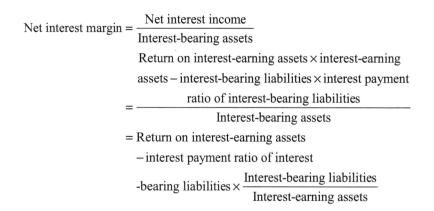

$$\text{Net interest margin} = \frac{\text{Net interest income}}{\text{Interest-bearing assets}}$$

$$= \frac{\begin{array}{c}\text{Return on interest-earning assets} \times \text{interest-earning}\\ \text{assets} - \text{interest-bearing liabilities} \times \text{interest payment}\\ \text{ratio of interest-bearing liabilities}\end{array}}{\text{Interest-bearing assets}}$$

$$= \text{Return on interest-earning assets}$$

$$- \text{interest payment ratio of interest}$$

$$\text{-bearing liabilities} \times \frac{\text{Interest-bearing liabilities}}{\text{Interest-earning assets}}$$

Evidently, the net interest margin is determined by the return on interest-earning assets, the interest payment rate of interest-bearing liabilities and the ratio of interest-earning assets to interest-bearing liabilities, among which the return on interest-earning assets is very important. Meanwhile, changes in the interest rate of interest-bearing liabilities will not be completely transmitted to the new interest margin.

The asset structure of commercial banks affects the return on interest-earning assets. The preconditions for interest rate liberalization of the asset structure of commercial banks in advanced economies are unlike the preconditions for China in two ways: the preconditions for China area high deposit reserve ratio or a high proportion of deposits in the central bank but low loans for SOEs. In years to come, interest rate liberalization will bring forth two great changes in the asset structure of commercial banks in China, which will help to elevate the return on interest-earning assets to offset the increase in the interest rate of interest-bearing liabilities.

First, the proportion of deposits in the central bank will be reduced. At the end of 2013 among the total interest-earning assets of listed banks, deposits in the central banks accounted for about 20 percent, with the yield roughly standing at 1.6 percent, almost three percentage points more than the return on interest-earning assets. Considering changes in the international balance of payment environment and channels of base currency insurance, the deposit reserve ratio or the proportion of deposits in the central bank will follow a significantly downward trend; as a result, the return on interest-earning assets will be enhanced.

Second, SME loans or credit bonds will occupy a bigger part respectively in loans and bond investment. Since interest rate liberalization is usually accompanied by "financial de-intermediation", the credit bond market will embrace fast development. To offset the loss of major corporate customers, commercial banks may increase the proportion of loans to SMEs, so as to increase the return on loan interest-earning assets or the proportion of corporate credit bonds they hold to increase the return on interest-earning assets for bond investment.

According to calculation based on the nine hypotheses, if financial risks are intensively materialized in 2015, the bearable NPL ratio would be 10.45 percent, and the calculation based on the loan balance at the end of 2013, this ratio can reach 13.34 percent. If financial risks were uniformly materialized in the three years between 2015 and 2017, the bearable NPL ratio would be above 13 percent, and based on the loan balance at the end of 2013, the ratio would be over 21.5 percent. If financial risks become uniformly materialized from 2015 to 2020, the ratio would be more than 12.5 percent, and higher than 30 percent based on the loan balance at the end of 2013.

References

Borio, C. and Lowe, P. (2002). *Asset Prices, Financial and Monetary Stability: Exploring the Nexus* [R]. BIS Working Paper No. 114.

Chen, D. (2014). Financial Reforms Should Effectively Address Financial Risks [N]. *Shanghai Securities News*, January 16.

Dell'Ariccia, G., Igan, D., Laeven, L. and Tong, H. (2012). *Policies for Macrofinancial Stability: Dealing With Credit Booms and Busts* [R]. IMF Staff Discussion Notes 12/06, International Monetary Fund.

Liu, S. (2013). *China's Economic Growth in Ten Years (2013–2022) – Seeking New Engine and Rebalance* [M]. Beijing: China Citic Press.

Ma, J. (2014). Several Opinions on Taxation, SOE Profits and Local Government Debts [N]. *21st Economic Report*, August 25.

Mendoza, E. and Terrones, M. (2008). *An Anatomy of Credit Booms: Evidence from Macro Aggregates and Micro Data* [R]. NBER Working Paper No. 14049.

Mitra, S., Beneš, J., Iorgova, S., Lund-Jensen, K., Schmieder, C. and Severo, T. (2011). Toward Operationalizing Macroprudential Policies: When to Act? [R]. Chapter 3 in *Global Financial Stability Report*, September. Washington, DC: International Monetary Fund.

Ni, P., Zou, L. and Gao, G. (2014). *(Mid-Term) Report on Housing Development in China 2014* [M]. Beijing: Social Sciences Academic Press (China).

Schularick, M. and Taylor, A. (2009). Credit Booms Gone Bust: Monetary Policy, Leverage Cycles and Financial Crises, 1870–2008[R]. CEPR Discussion Paper No. 7570, Centre for Economic Policy Research, London.

Survey and Research Center for China Household Finance of Southwestern University of Finance and Economics (2014). *Vacancy Rate of Urban Residences and Development Trend of the House Market* [R], June.

Yi, G. (2008). *Path and Logic for Opening up of China's Financial Sector*. In *China's Opening up for Three Decades: Growth, Structure and Institutional Evolvement* [A], edited by Jiang Xiaojuan. Beijing: People's Publishing House.

7 Withdrawal of the financial restraint system

Reform of the financial system

People naturally heal when Yin and Yang are in harmony.
– Treatise on Febrile Diseases Caused by Cold
by Zhang Zhongjing in the Han Dynasty

The current financial system is "extractive" featuring the co-existence of "overdevelopment" and "underdevelopment" and a severe imbalance in economic relationships. Therefore, the aim of financial reform should be to transform the "extractive" financial system to become "inclusive". This may be achieved by improving resource allocation efficiency across the entire economic system and promoting sustained and healthy economic development by rebalancing the relationship between finance and the real economy while maintaining financial stability. This chapter and the next chapter discuss the financial reform strategy from a holistic perspective, rather than analyzing reform measures in isolation as in the first six chapters.

The extractive-to-inclusive transformation requires reforms inside the financial system and supportive reforms in other sectors. This chapter is concerned with reforms inside the financial system. The recommended reform aims to withdraw the financial restraint system by liberalizing the interest rate and improving the competition mechanism of the financial market. Efforts should be made to implement financial regulation and monetary control and strengthen the financial infrastructure. Interest rate liberalization, relaxed market access and fostering multi-layer capital markets as well as other reform measures may be necessary. These measures cannot be carried out separately and a minor error may cause severe negative effects; or they need a long period of time to be effective. Therefore, in the short term, we should attempt to rebalance finance and the real economy by optimizing financial regulation and identifying and addressing financial risks promptly.

Interest rate liberalization

The significance of liberalization

Interest margin protection is the core pillar of the financial restraint system and a major cause of the formation of China's "extractive" financial system. Therefore, liberalizing the interest rate and reducing interest margin protection is a top priority of financial reform. The main reason for interest rate liberalization lies not in its function of directly enhancing the resource allocation efficiency of the finance, but its contribution to rebalancing the relationship between finance and the real economy in terms of profit distribution, rebalancing the relationship between the financial sector and other sectors and reducing the financial cost of all businesses. Interest rate liberalization is only a helpful method rather than a decisive one because it does not necessarily result in a rebalance of finance and the real economy. Competition inside the financial system should be enhanced and the competition mechanism should be improved. Interest rate liberalization neither necessarily reduces the financing cost nor enhances resource allocation efficiency. To reduce financing cost and enhance the allocation efficiency, unqualified financing entities should be eliminated to reshape the real economy. Reforms other than SOE reform and fiscal system reform are needed to achieve this. We can see the complexity of the financial system and should realize that there is no tool or method that can solve all problems in one move; instead, we need coordinated reform measures.

Interest rate liberalization slowdown: yes or no?

Some progress has been made in interest rate liberalization since the Third Plenary Meeting of the 18th CPC Committee was convened. According to the central government spokesman Governor Zhou Xiaochuan (2014), the deposit rate was totally liberalized before the first quarter of 2016. As of May 11, 2015, the deposit rate ceiling was 1.5 times the benchmark rate. However, there is a quite influential idea that the liberalization should be slowed down because it is an important reason for the constantly high cost of financing.

Does interest rate liberalization really push up financing cost in the current period? Theoretically, an elevated deposit rate ceiling will directly raise the financing cost of banks. The banking system, under competition pressure, will transfer the added financing cost completely or partially to entities in need of financing and increase the financing cost in the short term. This can be avoided if in the short term the supply capacity and the competition intensity and service efficiency of financial service suppliers are improved, the asset allocation structure is significantly changed, and financing demand is reduced. According to international experience, interest rate liberalization is initially accompanied by rising financing cost. Changes in domestic financing cost in recent years reveal a coincidence of financing cost increase and interest rate liberalization. Consequently, financing cost rise appears to be a result of interest rate liberalization.

Detailed analysis reveals that the rise in financing cost has other causes. For example, improper monetary adjustment and control ("money shortage in June 2013") elevated the risk-free yield, and delinking benefits of the real economy and rising leverage ratio as well as partial deterioration of the financial ecological environment pushed the risk premium.

Should interest rate liberalization be slowed down since it may actually increase the financing cost? The answer is no. Firstly, slower interest rate liberalization will exacerbate the imbalance between finance and the real economy. The major deficiency of the present financial system is financial "overdevelopment" and the excessively high profits and high employees' income in the financial sector. The lower pace of liberalization will not address the problem of high financing costs. The lower pace of liberalization will reinforce the imbalance in profit distribution, and exacerbate the mismatch in the primary distribution of social resources. We can say that slowing interest rate liberalization to circumvent the principle aspect of the contradiction will only waste the opportunity of financial reforms.

The second reason that interest rate liberalization should not be slowed down is that given the actual conditions in China, the financing cost is increased due to faulty interest rate liberalization and not by the liberalization itself. At present, the banks' wealth management products drive the liberalization. At the end of May 2014, the balance of banks' wealth management products reached RMB13.97 trillion, accounting for 28.7 percent of all residents' saving deposits in the same period and 12.3 percent of the total deposits across the country. This liberalization approach is positive in some aspects. The banks' wealth management products are provided to help liberalize the interest rate provided that the deposit rate ceiling is not removed. Wealth management products from banks promote liberalization in a gradual way and can reduce excessive market fluctuations during the liberalization. On the one hand, the deposit rate ceiling might suddenly change, for example jumping from 10 percent to 20 percent; and banks' wealth management products can promote the smooth liberalization of the interest rate. On the other hand, usually, wealth management product investors are high-net-worth clients of banks, while saving customers in small and medium-sized financial institutions are low-net-worth clients. Wealth management products help to mitigate the impact of interest rate liberalization on small and medium-sized financial institutions, especially rural financial institutions.

We must not neglect the negative effects of this approach, since it pushes up the financing cost. First, it systematically increases the risk-free yield in the financial market. Due to "rigid payment" policies, wealth management products, which should have been risky, are almost risk-free. Higher risk-free yield implies a higher financing cost. Second, the approach curbs the development of a multi-layer capital market and of non-bank financial institutions. Wealth management products, with high yield and low or no risk, produce a "squeeze out" effect on the development of securities investment funds and insurance companies and thus reduce competition in the financial system. Thirdly, low-risk wealth management products are a major source of funds for shadow banking. As the sale of low-risk wealth management products increases, it leads to an expansion of shadow banking.

The proper way to liberalize the interest rate should be to gradually raise the interest rate ceiling, rather than provide more and more wealth management products. If wealth management products have to be a major tool for liberalization, they should be time-regulated (by applying a similar regulation framework to that used for securities investment funds) and the practice of "rigid redemption" should be eliminated, to avoid higher risk-free yield.

The third reason that interest rate liberalization should not be slowed down is that interest rate increase caused by liberalization can be countered by short-term measures. A key reason for interest rate increase is that commercialized financial institutions pursue profits. Therefore, short-term measures can be taken to ensure a basically stable income for financial institutions, so that they will not transfer the cost to entities in need of financing, and the financing cost increase will be curbed. This shares the cost of interest rate liberalization.

Given the monetary environment confronting China's financing system, there are three options. The first option is to increase the interest payment ratio of the deposit reserve to increase the yield of deposit assets of commercial banks in the central bank. At present, there is room for an increase in the deposit reserve interest payment ratio. The deposit interest payment ratio of commercial banks is higher than the interest payment ratio of the deposit reserve. Take listed banks for example. The average deposit interest payment ratio of 16 A-shares listed banks was 2.08 percent in 2012 and 2.00 percent in 2013, both much higher than the interest payment ratio of the deposit reserve (1.62 percent). When the average deposit reserve ratio is as high as around 20 percent, and the interest payment ratio of the deposit reserve is lower than the deposit rate, this effectively levies a tax on banks. Yet financial accounts reveal high accounting profits for the central bank (Qian and Yu, 2014). The central bank is a non-profit institution and serves as the monetary authority: it should not earn profits by levying tax on financial institutions. The second option is to reduce the deposit reserve ratio in order to lower the proportion of deposit assets reserved in the central bank, so as to enhance the composite return on banks' assets. The third option is to reduce financing costs through an interest rate cut. The last two options are significant and influential moves in implementing monetary policy; therefore, many other factors should be taken into consideration.

Laggard reforms in many areas are an important reason for the interest rate increase effect of liberalization, such as lifting control on market access and developing a multi-layer capital market. Competition in the financial system discourages banks from transferring added financing cost caused by interest-rate liberalization. If reforms for lifting market access control and developing a multi-layer capital market can be coordinated with each other, fiercer competition in the financial system will significantly discourage banks from transferring financing costs.

To conclude, interest rate liberalization should not be slowed down just because it may increase the financing costs of all businesses. Instead, we should keep promoting interest rate liberalization through an improved approach, and adopt counter-measures and carry out supportive reforms in the short term.

Interest rate liberalization: much more than just lifting restrictions

Interest rate liberalization is not just to lift restrictions. First, the interest rate is determined by the market under the guidance of the central bank's monetary policy (Ji and Niu, 2014). Therefore, interest rate liberalization means that the central banks should adopt a market-based method of interest rate adjustment.

To this end, efforts should be made to strengthen the treasury market structure and improve the treasury yield curve and the central bank's policy interest rate adjustment system. Moreover, the more fundamental reform is to eliminate unqualified financing entities in the financial market: this requires coordination of SOEs reform with fiscal system reform.

Second, interest rate liberalization does not mean 100 percent removal of control over the interest rate. Financial reforms need to balance the relationship among reforms to ensure development and stability (Chen, 2014a). On the one hand, the main aim of interest rate liberalization is to address the severe imbalance of profit distribution between finance and the real economy and reshape the relationship between the two. Interest rate liberalization will not be the top priority of financial reforms once finance and the real economy are in balance. On the other hand, interest rate liberalization will negatively affect financial stability. According to international experiences, it will in most cases intensify competition in the banking system and propose a major challenge to some financial institutions. Once interest rate liberalization becomes a significant threat to financial stability, it should be slowed down.

Third, interest rate liberalization should be coordinated with reshaping financing entities which are not qualified. There are local government financing platforms with severe soft budget constraints and also "zombie companies" relying on borrowing new debts to repay old ones. Financing entities insensitive to the interest rate absorb a great amount of financial resources like a capital black hole. In this case, interest rate liberalization will not enhance financing efficiency and reduce the financing cost. Instead, it will lead to lower financing efficiency and higher financing cost. Therefore, the interest rate cannot be liberalized without other supportive reforms.

Improving the competition mechanism of the financial market

Improving the competition mechanism in the financial market is another key task for financial reform. It is an important component of the financial restraint system withdrawal and a vital guarantee for it. Improving the competition mechanism, despite its contribution to enhancing the efficiency of finance in serving the real economy, is not the main reason for our emphasis on competition at the financial market. The important reason, as for interest rate liberalization, is that fiercer competition at the financial market helps to rebalance the reward structure for finance and the real economy. Therefore, the aim of improving the competition mechanism in the financial market is to establish a unified and open financial market where all players compete with each to create a sound environment for distributing the profits of the financial sector.

Lifting market access control

The primary purpose for reducing control over market access is to improve competition in the banking system. The key to bank competition improvement is to reduce the market access control, or eliminate access restrictions in the financial restraint system, in order to form an open competition environment. Access control should be lifted for banks and other financial institutions and all types of financial products including administrative examination, and approval procedures should be reduced for financial products. At present, there is still much room for more intense competition in the banking system.

We recommend starting with improvement of the withdrawal mechanism. An open competition environment should feature both relaxed restrictions over market access and smooth withdrawal. The withdrawal mechanism for banks is not yet smooth, which prevents access control from being lifted. To improve the withdrawal mechanism, the country has to improve the bankruptcy law and formulate and enact a bankruptcy law for financial institutions to provide a legal basis and procedures for the withdrawal of financial institutions. The deposit insurance system is intended to help the judicial authorities play a more effective role in dealing with the bankruptcy of financial institutions. Deposit insurance institutions can directly enhance the capability of disposing of problematic financing institutions. However, the deposit insurance system may also trigger risks like intensive "deposit moving" or trigger moral hazards in small and medium-sized banks or in high-risk banks and their depositors and lead to the "Texas Premium". On the other hand, there are still a good number of high-risk rural credit cooperatives which reform of the deposit insurance system in China should remove from the financial market. The state should facilitate smooth withdrawal of problematic financial institutions by providing legal support and by adopting policies which facilitate mergers and acquisitions as well as restructuring the banking system.

We suggest three methods of lifting market access control to mitigate market access restrictions for the banking system. First, the threshold should be lowered for various types of capital to enter the market and allow private capital to be used to establish private banks. For example, the CBRC approved a pilot program for five private banks and WeBank opened before the end of 2014. Indeed, relaxed access control may create risks, especially when interest rate liberalization takes place at the same time; therefore, an active and sound method is necessary. At present, access control is being lifted in way that is "too steady and insufficiently active", considering the urgent need to redress the imbalance between finance and the real economy in terms of profit distribution and enhance the efficiency of finance in serving the real economy. Of course, there are valid reasons for this caution. Regulators may undertake too many responsibilities to be able to maintain financial and social stability because the withdrawal mechanism is incomplete (Xia and Chen, 2011). Improving the withdrawal mechanism of financial institutions should solve these problems.

The second recommendation is that market access control should be looser for foreign banks. Since its entry in the World Trade Organization (WTO), China has been working to open its banking sector to the outside world. Before entry to the WTO, a great deal of literature dealt with risks that might be caused by banks' opening up: for example, homegrown banks might be marginalized (Yi and Guo, 2002). However, such risks have become minor after the previous round of financial reform when home grown banks saw a drastic improvement in their strength and competitiveness. As long as they take the dominant position, it is acceptable to allow a much higher proportion of foreign capital into the financial sector. Opening the banking sector reinforces competition and helps to average out its profit margin and balance profit distribution between finance and the real economy. On the other hand, the opening of the banking sector can help to introduce effective increments, enhance the financial innovation capability and better serve the real economy. Rather than only considering the financial sector, financial reform should take a holistic view by considering the whole economic system.

The third recommendation is that more bank branches should be allowed to open. The competition intensity in the banking system does not solely depend on the number of bank corporations, but also on how many branches they have. Market access requirements for Chinese bank branches should be further lowered to improve the coverage of Chinese banks. Strict regulation on market access for more branches is intended to avoid efficiency loss caused by excessive competition, but insufficient competition is a major problem.

Developing a multi-layer capital market

The major reason for developing a multi-layer capital market is not its advantage in allocating financial resources. Literature comparing financial systems has not reached any conclusion yet on whether the banking system or the capital market is more effective in resource allocation. We attribute the importance of the multi-layer capital market to its role in reinforcing competition with the banking system. Fiercer competition helps not only average out the profit margin of the financial sector and rebalance finance and the real economy, but also enhances financial accessibility and the efficiency of finance in serving the real economy.

The multi-layer capital market can be categorized into the bond market and the stock market. The bond market and the stock market can keep pace with each other, but differ in the law and conditions of development; as a result, their development level may differ from each other at different stages. Ranking the priority of different layers is important for effectively developing the multi-layer capital market, as is deciding whether the bond market or the stock market should be developed first. The two kinds of markets face different problems. For example, there are phenomena in the bond market like regulation competition and rigid redemption which do not exist in the stock market.

Some economists emphasize the importance of the stock market. Allen and Gale (2002) argue that the stock market is more effective in supporting innovation. However, we think that the bond market should have higher priority when developing the multi-layer capital market. First, the multi-layer capital market is developed mainly for the purpose of reinforcing competition between the capital market and the banking system. The bond market, rather than being at a disadvantage, can do better than the stock market, as reflected by the comparison of annual financing totals. The second reason for prioritizing development of the bond market is the bond market is more feasible to develop. According to literature about the law and the finance, economies with an advanced stock market in most cases adopt the common law system rather than the civil law system. Under the civil law in China, it is more feasible to develop the bond market than the stock market. Finally, even if the stock market is more effective in supporting innovation, "importing" a stock market can only be a short-term method to boost innovation, considering the high internationalization of the stock market. A typical example is China's internet industry which is supported by the overseas capital market rather than the "home-grown" stock market. For example, internet giants like Baidu, Alibaba and Tencent all went public at NASDAQ, the New York Stock Exchange, the Hong Kong Stock Exchange and other overseas capital markets.

An unavoidable problem in development of the bond market is the regulation system. The bond market is currently subject to regulation by multiple authorizes, hence the highly controversial regulation competition. The National Development and Reform Commission (NDRC) regulate corporate bonds. The National Association of Financial Market Institutional Investors under the guidance of the central bank regulates inter-bank bonds, and exchange-traded bonds are regulated by the CSRC.

Some hold the regulation competition in the bond market is negative since it sabotages market unity and impedes the development of the bond market; besides, by pushing regulation authorities to lower the issuance threshold so as to become more competitive, it leads to a worse quality of issuers who pile up risks at the bond market, especially with "rigid redemption". Some scholars advise elimination of the "regulation competition" and entitlement of one single authority to provide unified regulation.

Other scholars find the positive effect of regulation competition to be undeniable. Regulation competition actually enhances the examination and approval efficiency of the regulation authority and boosts the growth of the bond market. Although the issuance threshold is lowered with the intention of surviving competition, the actual result of such behaviour is a more rational threshold, since the current threshold is already high. The lower average quality of bond issuers indicates more risks at the bond market; however, it will not become a major problem to impede sustainable development of the bond market, as long as "rigid redemption" is eliminated to mitigate risks at the market. We find a positive effect of regulation competition on market development when comparing the development of the stock market and the bond market. Scholars suggest maintaining regulation competition in the current period.

We think regulation competition has pros and cons. It enhances the efficiency of the regulation authorities, helps to lower the issuance threshold to a more reasonable level, and facilitates the development of the bond market by at least promoting its growth to compete with the banking system. On the negative side it leads to a discrepancy in the markets, such as the settlement and clearing markets, and reduces the market efficiency. If the current regulation competition continues, threshold lowering will lead to a further accumulation of risks in the bond market. Therefore, a mixed regulatory system should be designed to encourage orderly competition in a unified and open market. One option is to prepare consistent regulation rules and infrastructure for settlement and clearing but maintain the pattern of regulation by multiple authorities which are entitled to formulate specific regulation rules. On the one hand, consistent basic regulation rules and interconnection of clearing and settlement infrastructure help to form a unified and open bond market; on the other hand, with consistent basic regulation rules, multiple regulation authorities help to form orderly competition.

Another impediment to bond market development is "rigid redemption". A bond market is not a normal one and cannot develop in a sustainable way if no default ever occurs in this market. Due the "rigid redemption" regime, the bond market cannot develop its capability of risk pricing and its efficiency in resource allocation is affected. More importantly, "rigid redemption" has produced a "squeeze out" effect on private enterprises in the bond market. In recent years, the proportion of private enterprises in unsecured bond issue dropped, and the interest rate of bonds issued by private enterprises was much higher than other bonds with the same rating. According to Liu Xiaoping (2014),

> *Between January to August 2014, a total of 1,482 non-financial enterprises in China publicly issued unsecured bonds worth RMB3.15 trillion. The number of issuers and the amount of issuance increased by 234 and RMB560 billion respectively over the same period in the previous year. Among others, 267 private enterprises issued bonds with the total value of RMB178.153 billion, respectively 84 and RMB50.467 billion less on a year-on-year basis.*

The average interest rate of issuance by AA-rating private enterprises was 81 base points higher than that of SOEs at the same rating, and the disparity was 109 base points for those rated as AA-, with private enterprises higher.

Rigid redemption is an important reason underlying such phenomena. SOEs (including the urban infrastructure investment companies) backed by the government's implicit guarantee are more capable of sustaining "rigid redemption" and thus are more favoured by both risk-adverse regulators and investors seeking returns after risk adjustment. In 2014, "rigid redemption" was broken asymmetrically; in other words, "rigid redemption" imposed on private enterprises was mitigated to some degree, while that for SOEs remained unaltered. Such phenomena are reinforced when "rigid redemption" is broken. Therefore, to improve sustainability of the bond market, "rigid redemption" must be eradicated as soon as possible since the pressure on financial stability will grow in the future and the majority of participants in the bond market are institutional investors. To eliminate "rigid redemption", the first step should be to change the philosophy and conduct of regulation authorities. They cannot fake a no-risk "illusion" and prevent risk release by taking various measures (for example, local governments impose unnecessary pressure on market participants) with the excuse of maintaining financial stability.

Despite being a lower priority than the bond market, the stock market is also critical and can compete with the banking systems more directly. The stock market is not effective in supporting innovation. A typical manifestation is that many world-famous innovative enterprises in China, like Alibaba, Tencent and Baidu, failed to meet domestic requirements for stock issuance and went public at overseas stock markets. To some degree, the domestic stock market features "adverse selection" for innovative enterprises. In recent years, the stock market almost lost the function of raising funds and cannot compete with banks. Between 2011 and 2013, a total of RMB986.5 billion was raised through the stock market, only 2.33 percent of the social financing across the society over the same period. There was a slight improvement in 2014, the stock market provided RMB435 billion, 2.64 percent of the social financing in the same period.

Why did the stock market lose its ability to raise funds? One underlying reason is the poor performance of the secondary market. However, China's stock market began to surge from the second half of 2014. For example, the Shanghai Composite Index rocketed by over 50 percent in the second half of 2014. China's stock market is tasked too much and regulators are responsible for maintaining its stability. The initial public offering (IPO) market was criticized and was occasionally frozen for the sake of stability and also considering the "three highs" (high offering price, high price-earning ratio and high over-financing ratio).

Occasional IPO freezing has severe deficiencies. The stock market's failure in financing severely imposes negative effects on reinforcing competition at the financial market and improving the stock market's service for the real economy. It neither helps to optimize the profit distribution between finance and the real economy nor to enhance the efficiency of finance in serving the real economy. It disturbs the pace of issuance and will undoubtedly lead to a new round of "three highs" when the IPO is resumed.

Therefore, the top priority in developing the stock market is to maintain a reasonable rhythm for the IPO, rather than sabotage the basic function of the stock market. Other reforms and policy measures can be developed and implemented on this basis, such as reinforcing information disclosure, better protecting investors, combating insider trading and maintaining the market order.

We would do well to examine the reason underlying poor performance of the stock market. Some scholars attribute it to economic slowdown, since the stock market is the barometer of economy. We venture to have a different idea. After all, the stock market cannot reflect all developments in a macro-economy, and the two are inconsistent with each other in many cases. Other scholars blame the too high risk-free yield for the poor performance of China's stock market. Under the "rigid redemption" scheme, banks' wealth management products produce risk-free yield. We agree with them and regard the management of shadow banking and the elimination of "rigid redemption" as necessary for the sustained and healthy development of the stock market.

Registration system reform is another influence on stock market development and is widely discussed. Many measures have been proposed to reform the registration system. Amongst them all, we emphasize supportive reforms. The first is to improve the withdrawal system. The registration system can be regarded as the threshold to enter the stock market. A mechanism should be established to lift market access control for financial institutions so they can withdraw smoothly and the implementation of the registration system needs an improved withdrawal system for listed companies. The second is the investor protection system. The priority for investor protection, besides reinforced education, is to impose more severe punishment on infringements by investors, for example effective punishments for insider trading. To this end, securities regulators should intensify their regulation and the legal system for finance should be improved on the basis of the actual conditions in China and a class action system should be established.

Developing non-bank financial institutions

Non-bank financial institutions should be developed mainly to intensify the competition between banks and non-bank financial institutions. By adjusting asset allocation, banks can compete in the multi-layer capital market in two ways.

First, they can shift their focus on large enterprise to SEMs when granting loans. Under such a circumstance, the capital market has constituted real competition to the banking system, and the financial accessibility (or the proportion of loans accessible for SMEs and micro businesses) will be significant improved. In addition, higher financial accessibility does not result from non-market-based mechanisms like "two no-less-thans", but to "customer sinking" which occurs naturally under the market mechanism. With effective regulation and reasonable incentive mechanisms, "customer sinking" will be accompanied by a great amount of financial innovation, significant capability enhancement of SMEs and micro businesses (including credit techniques) and much higher efficiency of finance in serving the real economy.

Will such change make the financial system even more "extractive", given the higher interest margin of loans to SMEs and micro businesses than to large enterprises? The answer is no. Considering the high risk of SMEs and micro-businesses and high service costs, a higher interest margin does not mean higher profits. The absolute profits of the financial sector grow but the real economy will make more profits too. Therefore, the relative profits of the financial sector may decline. Underlying the higher profits of the real economy is the switch from high-cost informal financing to low-cost bank loans as financing sources of more and more SMEs and micro-businesses, as banks' customers sink or financial accessibility is improved. An increasingly growing proportion of bank loans in all financing of SMEs and micro businesses indicates declining financing cost in the real economy. Meanwhile, better accessibility to loans can help such SMEs and micro-businesses develop.

Second, banks turn to purchase bonds from large enterprises instead of granting loans to them. In this case, the multi-layer capital market does not compete substantially with banks, and banks, which still target mainly at major clients, can neither enhance their capability of serving SMEs nor lower their relative profits. To prevent such a scenario from being materialized, non-bank financial institutions are vital in competing with banks in the capital market. Out of all such institutions, insurance companies, trust companies and fund management companies are our focus in this book.

Generally speaking, China's insurance industry lags far behind. In 2013, the assets of the insurance industry in China only totalled RMB8.29 trillion, compared to RMB151.4 trillion of the banking sector over the same period. In 2010, insurance assets only accounted for 10.64 percent of all financial assets held by the household sector; in 2013, the depth and intensity of insurance in China was respectively 2.93 percent and RMB1,265.67, not only much lower than that of Western developed economies but also far below that of many major emerging economies (see Table 7.1). Insurance laggardness is caused by many factors. Besides the influence of culture, laggard premium fee liberalization and shock from shadow banking are important reasons. Therefore, efforts should be made to promote the development of the insurance industry.

The trust industry has made huge progress. The total trust assets reached RMB12.95 trillion at the end of the third quarter of 2014, 5.45 times that at the end of the first quarter of 2010. This fast development promotes competition inside the financial system, but not as much as is reflected by data about trust assets and trust loans, since the majority of trust assets are single fund trusts mainly from banks and function as a channel of "shadow banking".

The rapid development of the trust industry is accompanied with two interconnected problems. The first is the "rigid redemption" policy. On the one hand, rigid redemption makes risks in the trust industry converge, which impedes development of the whole industry in the long run: on the other hand, it also pushes up the risk-free yield and thus dampens the development of whole financial industry. Therefore, "rigid redemption" must be eliminated as soon as possible. Notably, breaking "rigid redemption" means trust companies will not be held accountable as long as they fulfill their duties. To reinforce the market discipline and prevent ignorance of the "duty performance of sellers" and overemphasis of "buyer's accountability", trust companies must be subject to "rigid redemption" in the case of default due to failure to perform their duties.

The second interconnected problem related to the rapid development of the trust industry is the fast growing "leverage ratio". The leverage ratio in the trust

Table 7.1 Comparison in insurance industry development between China and other countries

										(Unit: %)
	China	*US*	*Japan*	*Germany*	*France*	*Britain*	*South Korea*	*Brazil*	*India*	*South African*
Insurance depth	2.74	7.00	10.37	5.22	7.98	11.23	14.26	2.81	3.32	12.91

Source: World Bank.

industry soared in recent years, whether calculated on the basis of entrust assets or Collective funds trust assets. At the end of the third quarter of 2014, the trust assets and assembled funds trust assets were 44.92 and 13.08 times the net assets of the trust industry, while the figure was only 21.85 and 2.75 in the first quarter of 2010 (Figure 7.1). If "rigid redemption" remains, the rocketing leverage ratio will drastically increase risks in the trust industry. Therefore, while reinforcing regulations to make sure trust companies fulfill their duties, the state should break "rigid redemption" as soon as possible. The state should improve the resistance of the trust industry to risks, for example by improving and fully capitalizing on the security funds of the trust industry.

In recent years, fuelled by the emerging internet monetary market funds, the fund industry grew considerably and saw its efficiency improve. That means active increment, once introduced, has produced immediate effects on the development of the trust industry. Efforts should focus on relaxing access to the fund industry to let in energetic increment. Besides promoting the development of the internet monetary market funds, further opening up to foreign capital is another important policy option. In addition, healthy and sound development of the stock market is significant for the development of the trust industry.

Reform of commercial financial institutions

The aim of further reforming financial institutions is to establish an environment of orderly competition. The reform of commercial financial institutions is not

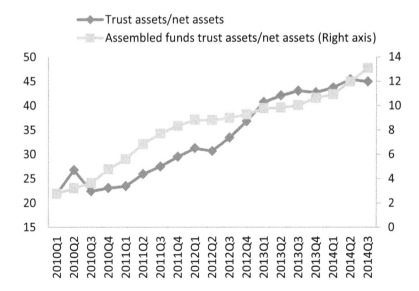

Figure 7.1 Leverage ratio of the trust industry

Source: China Trustee Association.

only at the institutional level, but also involves the state-owned financial assets management system. Regarding the reform at the institutional level, a widely proposed recommendation is to lower the proportion of the state-held assets, which is necessary in the new round of financial reforms, especially for the four largest state-owned commercial banks.

On the one hand, the largest shareholder holds too many shares (Table 7.2). According to corporate governance theory, the existence of a "dominant share-holder" leads to the low efficiency of corporate governance. On the other hand, since the four major commercial banks have a massive amount of assets and may expand credit if their earning power declines in the future, a huge capital increase stress will be imposed on the public finance if the four major commercial banks account for an excessively high proportion.

However, in respect to reducing state-owned shares of stock, two issues should be taken into consideration. First, the reduction cannot be made in haste and just for reduction's sake. Listed simultaneously at the A-shares and H-shares market, the four major commercial banks have adequate liquidity; besides, considering the overall low price-to-book ratio at the market, the Central Huijin Investment Ltd company has purchased more stocks of banks. The key issue for state-owned shares of stocks reduction is not the state-owned shareholders' willingness but whether other investors are willing to increase their holdings. The second issue is the introduction of strategic investors. The new round of financial reforms differs from the previous one in a remarkable way. Domestic and foreign qualified insti-tutions, rather than only foreign institutions, should be introduced as strategic investors on equal terms.

The incentive mechanism is also a target of the commercial financial institu-tions as well as the ownership structure. A rethink of the secondary mortgage crisis in the US reveals that their rational incentive mechanism is an important factor triggering the outbreak of the financial crisis (The Financial Crisis Inquiry Commission, 2011). After implementing shareholding reform, especially going public, China's financial institutions suffer under a problematic incentive mecha-nism. At present, the irrationality of incentive mechanisms is reflected by fast swelling bank assets and shadow banking, the rampant spreading of inter-bank business, the steel trade crisis and the mutual guarantee crisis.

Table 7.2 Proportion of state-owned shares of stocks of four major commercial banks in 2013

	ICBC	ABC	BOC	CBC
Largest shareholder	35.33%	40.28%	67.22%	57.03%
State-owned shares of stocks	70.42%	79.49%	67.22%	57.03%

Note: BOC refers to the Bank of China, and CBC refers to the Construction Bank of China. The proportion of state-owned shares of stocks means the level of equity held by the Ministry of Finance and institutions invested on behalf of the state. It does not include holdings by National Council for Social Security Fund and SOEs.

Source: Annual reports for 2013 of relevant banks.

There are two types of irrational incentive mechanism in the financial system. The first is the irrational performance appraisal mechanism for financial institutions, featuring excessive performance competition between institutions. The second is the irrational incentive mechanism for employees in financial institutions, which, based on performance in the current period, leads to short-term behaviours. The core principle for redressing faulty mechanisms is to properly handle the contradiction between time laggardness and current-period earning. The first priority is to reinforce forward-looking risk management, the second is to strengthen the counter-cyclical regulation, and the third is to limit or even reduce earnings.

Small and medium-sized banks must be reformed. These banks can be classified into commercial and non-commercial banks. In the first category are listed and unlisted banks (including joint stock banks, urban commercial banks, rural commercial banks and rural credit cooperative banks), and the unlisted banks refers mainly to rural credit cooperatives. Reforms of unlisted small and medium-sized commercial banks are implemented mainly by letting them go public. To this end, the threshold for small and medium-sized financial institutions to enter the capital market should be lowered.

Rural credit cooperatives will be restructured into rural commercial banks and go public. Due to the disadvantageous position of "agriculture, farmers and the countryside", many refuse to restructure all rural credit cooperatives into rural commercial banks out of the concern that complete commercialization in the rural financial reform may obliterate consideration of agricultural and rural issues. Theoretically, rural finance should be diverse, with a cooperative system, a joint stock system and joint stock partnership co-existing. There are successful rural cooperative financial institutions in foreign countries. Then why do we insist on the establishment of rural commercial banks? The reasons are as follows.

First, over 100 of them are high-risk cooperatives, and most rural credit cooperatives are more disadvantaged than rural commercial banks in terms of asset quality, risk resistance and government governance efficiency. Only with healthy rural financial institutions can sustainable rural finance be supplied. To this end, rural commercial banks should be established to improve asset quality, risk resistance and corporate governance efficiency. This should be done rapidly because financial reforms like interest rate liberalization and access control removal are proceeding; the deposit insurance system is established; economic development has entered a "new normal", and many financial risks might materialize soon.

Second, even though competition is fiercer in the banking sector and agriculture is being industrialized and modernized, rural commercial banks are unlikely to distance themselves from the concerns of agriculture, farmers and rural areas as long as their legal status is maintained.

The third reason we insist on the establishment of rural commercial banks is that current rural credit cooperatives are not about "cooperation" and cannot function like their foreign counterparts even without reform. Rural cooperative finance can be solved by regularized and supervised credit cooperation in farmers' professional cooperatives. Credit cooperation should be supported by a comprehensive, strict and effective regulation system, and the regulation can be provided and implemented by authorities other than the existing financial regulation departments.

Although we insist that establishing rural commercial banks is the recommended policy, we also emphasize the importance of supportive policies. Due to the lack of such policies, current commercialization of rural credit cooperatives, with severe deficiencies, may dampen the capability to serve agriculture, farmers and the countryside. For example, preferential deposit reserve ratio and tax policies for rural credit cooperatives will be cancelled once they are restructured into rural commercial banks. For rural financial institutions in middle and western regions, the policy environment will be much worse, since the customer structure does not change after rural credit cooperatives are restructured into rural commercial banks. Therefore, supportive policies should be adopted in the process of commercialization reform of rural credit cooperatives. The standard of preferential policies should be changed from being based on institutions to supporting behaviours which maintain the basic stability of the policy environment for rural financial institutions.

The state-owned financial assets management mechanism is also a priority for reform. There is no unified pattern for the state-owed financial assets management framework. In central state-owned financial institutions, the management framework falls into three types according to whether the institution is invested in by the government-owned Central Huijin Investment Ltd, the Ministry of Finance or by both. Likewise, local state-owned financial institutions adopt three types of management framework, depending on whether they are invested by the SASAC, the Ministry of Finance or financial service offices. Central state-owned financial institutions and local state-owned financial institutions can adopt different management frameworks due to the large disparity in size and ownership structure.

There are two options for a framework for managing central state-owned financial assets. The first is to let the state-owned Central Huijin Investment Ltd fulfill the function of investor and the second is to establish one or two investment and operation companies with state-owned financial assets to perform the function as investors. The management framework of local state-owned financial assets depends on the size of local state-owned financial assets and the orientation of the financial sector, as well as other factors.

Reform of Policy-oriented Financial Institutions

The past decade saw a rampant expansion of policy-oriented financial institutions. By the end of 2013, assets of policy-oriented banks and the China Development Bank (CDB) totalled RMB12.53 trillion, 5.90 times that in 2003; in contrast, in 2013 total assets of financial institutions and large commercial banks were only 5.47 and 4.09 times that in 2003. The expansion of policy-oriented financial institutions outpaced large commercial banks and was faster than the average rate of the banking sector.

Why was this? The first reason is the irrational performance appraisal mechanism. According to the Performance Appraisal Method for Financial Enterprises issued by the Ministry of Finance, standard indicators are applicable to policy banks and to state-owned commercial banks and joint-stock commercial banks. Special features of bank policy are considered when some indicators are designed for them, such as capital adequacy ratio; core asset adequacy ratio leverage ratio; return on asset and return on equity; size indicators, such as cost-to-income ratio; the ratio of state-owned capital retention and increase and profit growth rate or other indicators closely associated with the business scale. An irrational performance appraisal mechanism drives policy-oriented financial institutions to blindly expand their scale of business.

Second, legal protection for policy-oriented financial institutions is lacking. There is no special law for policy-oriented financial institutions, leading to the absence of a legal basis for the existence of such institutions and making them feel less safe. To solve this problem with a "rational" solution, policy-oriented financial institutions survive by developing and expanding to become "too big to be cancelled" and become *de facto* legal.

Due to expansion of such institutions, their business increasingly overlaps that of commercial financial institutions, which has affected orderly competition in the financial market. To promote effective competition, these institutions should be effectively curbed from blind expansion, so as to maintain orderly competition at the market. First, special laws and regulations concerning policy-oriented financial institutions should be formulated and implemented rapidly; meanwhile, a different performance appraisal system based on special features of such institutions should be established and improved to inhibit the impulse for internal expansion.

Second, policy-oriented financial institutions should be restrained in the areas of the national strategy, shareholders and regulation. Restriction at the national strategy level means that policy-oriented financial institutions should aim at serving the national strategy; shareholder-related restriction means these institutions should pursue commercial sustainability and try to impose no more burdens on the public finance; and regulation restriction should be implemented to reduce risks. Restrictions in these three aspects maybe inconsistent and should be coordinated.

Finally, policy-oriented and commercial financial institutions should be encouraged to compete with each other. There are two options for this. The first option is to horizontally distinguish policy business and commercial business and make clear the scope of policy financial institutions. The difficulty is how to establish the standard of division and there is considerable ambiguity even with clear standards. Optional standards related to policy-oriented business are as follows. Government-approval standard: concerning financial services that the government designates that policy-oriented financial institutions are to provide is completely policy-oriented business. Commercial banks participation standard: concerning financial business in which commercial banks do not or seldom participate is policy-oriented business. Loan tenure standard: concerning business involving mid-term and long-term loans is policy-oriented business. Other standards: concerning special projects reflecting state behaviours and national strategies are policy-oriented business. A noticeable problem when distinguishing policy-oriented and commercial business is that the border between the two kinds of business is dynamic. Some business is policy-oriented, but may become commercial as it becomes more commercially sustainable with market development and increasing commercial banks participation, and vice versa.

The second option is to address the relationship between policy-oriented and commercial financial institutions based on a vertical labour division of financial service. For example, policy-oriented financial institutions engage in wholesale business, while commercial financial institutions provide retail services. They cooperate with each other. This method of division can be a useful alternative as it avoids the difficulty in the first way of division.

The reform of policy-oriented financial institutions should not only aim to develop effective competition in the financial system, but also try to realize sustainable development and enhance their service capability. The reform of policy-oriented financial institutions also covers policy-oriented guarantors. Efforts should be made to broaden financing channels for policy-oriented financial institutions to provide them with stable low-cost financing, and to keep improving the internal governance mechanism.

Financial regulation optimization

Optimizing financial regulation is another key aim of financial reform. The withdrawal of financial restraints means fiercer competition in the financial system. Financial regulation should be improved to maintain orderly competition and manage financial risks created by this withdrawal. On the other hand, improper financial regulation will lead to the piling up of financial risks, low financial efficiency and excessive dominance of the financial sector over a period of time. Given that, financial regulation should be optimized to prevent problems from arising as a result of the regulation itself.

Financial regulation optimization involves changes in regulation philosophy, adjustment of regulation structure, clarification of regulation responsibility, clear scope of regulation and better investor protection. The regulation philosophy should be changed, as should the extreme risk aversion of regulators. There is an urgent need to change the mindset of regulators and make them more tolerant of risks.

Higher risk tolerance has two effects. First, it promotes critical financial reform. Some financial reforms, like relaxing market access control, are accompanied by risks. Only by changing the regulation philosophy and with a certain risk tolerance can we avoid inadequately aggressive and too persistent lifting of market access control. Mindset change also helps to release risks in an orderly way and as soon as is possible. In general, the current NPL ratio seems to be too low, while the profits of banks are artificially high, which distorts resource allocation. Therefore, the NPL ratio should be identified more strictly, risks be identified and released sooner, and NPL write-off accelerated.

Optimization requires the regulation framework should be adjusted. Due to practical "regulation competition", regulation coordination is not effective. Therefore, the adjustment should focus on eliminating excessive regulation competition and enhance the effectiveness of regulation coordination. There are three options to achieve this. The first is to change the current separate sector regulation. The second is to implement the regulation coordination mechanism. The third is to apply unified basic regulation principles to similar behaviours or products falling into the jurisdiction of different regulation authorities.

Financial regulation optimization requires regulation authorities to function more effectively as regulators. China's regulation authorities are responsible for regulation and also for promoting industrial development. Unfortunately, these two functions contradict with each other sometimes, especially against the backdrop of "regulation competition". Their role as regulators gives way to the function of promoting industrial development, leading to "regulation tolerance", particularly in shadow banking or overlapped financing fields. In future financial regulation optimization, the role of regulators should be strengthened and the function of promoting industrial development should be weakened.

Financial regulation optimization requires the scope of regulation to be very clear-cut. The government-market relationship in the financial market is reflected in the scope of regulation. Regulation loopholes should be closed and regulation effectiveness be enhanced. Regulation must not sabotage the autonomy of market players. One example is the monthly control of the consensus credit scale, which erodes the decision-making independence of financial institutions. Even though consensus credit scale policy is necessary, it should be improved constantly to diverge from monthly control.

Finally, financial regulation optimization requires the financial investor protection system to be improved. At present, investor protection is excessive in some cases and insufficient in others. Overprotection is typically reflected in "rigid redemption", while insufficient protection is manifested by the fact that small and medium investors in the stock market do not receive enough protection. To solve these problems, education for investors should improve their understanding of their investment. Regulation of financial institutions should be tightened to make sure the sellers fulfill their duties.

Other reforms

First, monetary policies should be stabilized to be more predictable and prevent volatility or a "credit boom". Monetary policies should be more transparent and communication between the central bank and the market should be improved.

Second, financial infrastructure construction should be reinforced and the financial ecological environment be optimized. The rationale underlying interest rate liberalization, market access control removal and development of the multilayer capital market and non-bank financial institutions as well as other reforms is to realize "customer sinking" and reduce the financing cost under the market mechanism through fiercer competition in the financial system. However, a basic precondition is needed for the whole process: a suitable financial ecological environment should be formed, so that the market can play its part. At present, more and more financial risk is exposed and the credit environment may keep deteriorating, which will result in the banks' reluctance to provide loans or push up the risk premium. Therefore, the financial ecological environment should be improved by strengthening the credit system structure and maintaining a sound credit environment, so as to support interest rate liberalization and financial mechanism improvement.

References

Allen, F. and Gale, D. (2002). Translated by J. Wang, C. Zhu, X. Ding and Y. Hu. *Comparing Financial Systems* [M]. Beijing: China Remin University Press, June.

Chen, D. (2014a). Financial Reforms Should Effectively Address Financial Risks [N]. *Shanghai Securities News*, January 16.

The Financial Crisis Inquiry Commission (2011). *The Financial Crisis Inquiry Report* [R], January.

Ji, M. and Niu, M. (2014). Setting the Central Bank Policy Rate Expectation Anchor [J]. *China Finance*, Vol. 9, pp. 19–22.

Liu, X. (2014). A Reflection on Shrinking Bonds Issued by Private Enterprises [N]. *China Business News*, September 26.

Qian, M. and Yu, J. (2014). Losses and Gains of the Central Bank [J]. *Stock Market Trend Analysis Weekly*, Vol. 22, pp. 72–73.

Xia, B. and Chen, D. (2011). *China Financial Strategy 2020* [M]. Beijing: People's Publishing House, January.

Yi, G. and Guo, K. (2002). Thought on Opening up of China's Financial Sector [J]. *The Quarterly Journal of Economics*, Vol. 4, pp. 77–88.

Zhou, X. (2014). Deposit Rate Might be Totally Liberalized in One or Two Years [N]. *People's Daily Online*, March 11.

8 Withdrawal of the implicit guarantee
Supportive reforms in other sectors

The financial reform is most effective only as part of the whole systematic reform.
– Stabilizing an Unstable Economy by Hyman Minsky (2010, p. 277)

This chapter focuses on supportive reforms for the financial sector. Many problems in the financial system do not derive from finance; instead, they reflect problems in other areas of the economy and society. The transformation from the "extractive" to "inclusive" financial system does not only need reform in the financing system but also supportive reforms in other fields. The self-circulation of financial expansion should be broken by reforms of the land system and taxation system, the social safety net should prepare for financial restraints withdrawal and implicit guarantee should be eliminated through reforms of the fiscal system and state-owned enterprises (SOEs), to provide a level playing field for major participants in the financial market. Industrial policy adjustment, reforms of education and scientific research systems as well as other measures are needed to boost the real economy and rebalance profit distribution between finance and the real economy.

SOE reform

SOE reform is vital for effective financial reforms, given its fundamental significance for the reform of the economic system. The success of financial reform hinges on whether the implicit guarantee can be eliminated to enable financing entities to compete on a level playing field in the financial market. Successful reform also requires less soft budget constraints, reshaping of micro entities, and higher operation efficiency of financing entities to provide a stable micro foundation.

Eliminating the government's implicit guarantee

SOE reform helps to eliminate the government's implicit guarantee in two ways. The first is the reform of the state-owned assets management system focusing on capital management. Through this reform, state-owned assets and a state-owned economy will not have to be materialized as enterprises (SOEs), but be manifested by capital as a form of value (state-owned capital). The appreciation of liquid state-owned capital will replace SOEs to become the sole target of attention. The state-owned economy will not depend on the rise and fall of SOEs but on the "in and out" of state-owned capital between different industries and enterprises. Under this circumstance, the ownership label will be removed, or at least it will not be as important as it is now. Enterprises invested with state-owned capital will not be "half-government-tools" any more but become completely independent market participants; as a result, the implicit guarantee to SOEs will vanish. The form of the state-owned asset management system focusing on capital management is still widely controversial.

We think it advantageous to assign the task of managing, operating and supervising state-owned assets to different departments or institutions. Since state-owned asset management is part of the public administration function, a state-owned capital administration committee should be established in the State Council, which is in charge of national ownership policies, especially the entry and withdrawal of state-owned capital, and reports to the National People's Congress. The state-owned capital investment and operation institutions should be responsible for the market-based operation of state-owned capital. The capital administration committee should function as a firewall between the government and enterprises, and be related to invested enterprises only through equity rather than administration. Since the invested enterprise is only an asset portfolio of the investment operation institution, equity investment in this enterprise depends on whether it can appreciate in value. An independent regulation department could be established to monitor the operation compliance, assets and efficiency of state-owned capital investment institutions by auditing. An important prerequisite for this system is to significantly increase the proportion of securitized state-owned assets. To this end, SOEs should be encouraged to go public through shareholding reform.

The second way SOE reform helps to eliminate the government's implicit guarantee is to adjust the presence of the state-owned economy. While the reform of state-owned assets management system focusing on capital management continues, adjustment of the state-owned economy helps to eliminate the implicit guarantee to some degree. With the improvement of the socialist market economy system, market failure or difficulties that prevent the market from functioning are reduced. The administrative function of many SOEs has been weakened or has disappeared, and competition has been introduced in key and critical areas. It is less necessary for SOEs to stay in these areas; SOEs and non-SOEs in competitive fields, both regulated by market rules, compete on unequal terms due to ownership discrimination.

Therefore, SOEs in competitive fields should be reduced to lower the coverage of the government's implicit guarantee. The adjustment of the state-owned economy or the withdrawal of SOEs from competitive fields is closely associated with the establishment of the capital-management-focused state-owned asset management system. If this system is established and ownership discrimination is eradicated, state-owned capital will not have to withdraw from competitive fields; instead, it can be involved in competitive fields and bring returns. In that case, the nature of state-owned capital as a public good will not be reflected by its withdrawal from competitive fields but in returns sharing (Chen, 2014).

Eliminating soft budget constraints

Soft budget constraints and the implicit guarantee are interconnected and might be confused with each other, but they differ from each other significantly. First, soft budget constraint has a narrower scope for SOEs. All SOEs receive an implicit guarantee from the government, but not all of them are confronted with soft budget constraints or have such severe problems. For example, after the shareholding reform, many listed SOEs and industrial SOEs have established effective corporate governance mechanisms and no longer face soft budget constraints. At present, it is the financing platforms of local governments and many other SOEs established in recent years that have severe problems with soft budget constraints. Secondly, implicit guarantee and soft budget constraints are discussed with different objects of reference. An implicit guarantee indicates the unfairness of the competition environment, while soft budget constraints imply unqualified financing entities. Finally, although all SOEs receive an implicit guarantee from the government, they have more influence on financial resource allocation and financial stability if they have soft budget constraints.

Eliminating soft budget constraints means to promote reform or withdrawal of local government's current financing vehicles. Severe soft budget constraints for these companies are used because these companies bear too many policy burdens for stable growth. To eliminate these burdens, fiscal system reform and economic performance evaluation system reform are critical. From the perspective of SOE reform, soft budget constraints exist because the financing platforms of local government are only minimally market-based players. The government intervenes more often in enterprise and asset management than in traditional SOEs. Therefore, the reform should be deepened to establish and improve the capital-management-focused state-owned asset management system. The reform of local governments' financing platforms cannot proceed when supportive reforms, such as fiscal system reform, have not been launched.

A transitional reform scheme would comprise encouragement of financing platforms to improve internal corporate governance mechanisms, establish the modern corporate system and harden fiscal constraints.

Improving Returns on State-owned Assets

Vast financial resources are allocated to SOEs. However, the debt repayment capability of SOEs is weakening, revealing hidden risks for financing stability. SOEs deal simultaneously with the slowdown in economic growth, make difficult structural adjustments and absorb the effects of previous economic stimulus policies, and cope with industrial factors: therefore their profit margins have declined.

The performance of SOEs can be extracted from statistics of the Ministry of Finance that cover all SOEs, including enterprises regulated by the SASAC or by the Ministry of Finance and those under central departments as well as local SOEs. According to data from the Ministry of Finance, the net profit of all SOEs in 2013 was RMB1.9 trillion and the returns on equity (ROE) went down further to 5.51 percent. According to monthly data released by the Ministry of Finance in 2014, the SOEs' profit margins grew at a much lower rate than the owner's equity, indicating a further decline of the ROE of SOEs. The ROE of SOEs was 7.5 percent in 2010, 7.4 percent in 2011 and 5.9 percent in 2012.

In terms of profit structure, the top ten monopolistic SOEs made total profits of RMB970.1 billion in 2013, accounting for 58.3 percent of the total profits of central SOEs and 40.3 percent of the total profits of all SOEs. The asset-liability ratio of SOEs continued to increase from 64.46 percent in 2013 to 65.21 percent at the end of October 2014.

Financial stability should be maintained by improving the efficiency of state-owned assets. Besides the macro environment and industrial factors, government intervention is another important reason for the low efficiency of SOEs and is disliked by the SOEs. The key to efficiency improvement is to reform SOEs, including reforms for the capital-management-focused state-owned asset management system and mixed ownership. Once the ownership label is removed from SOEs, they will be exempted from government intervention and able to operate in a market-based way, although they will lose the competitive advantage brought by implicit guarantee. In this case, SOEs will not be affected by the shareholder composition and equity structure in their process of growing and expanding and selecting of industries.

The establishment of a capital-management-focused system is a long-term objective and cannot be realized in the short term; the optional reform measures are not to promote SOEs to improve the modern corporate system. The first priority is to promote reforms for mixed ownership and a joint stock system to diversify the equity. The second priority is to reinforce the core role of the board of directors and enhance the director's capability to fulfill their duties and the board's decision-making capability. The third priority is to establish a system of incentives and disincentives for managerial staff and ordinary employees, strengthen the market-based recruitment of executives, and allow employee stock ownership and equity incentives for executives.

Supportive fiscal measures

More fiscal support for financial reform

Firstly, financial reforms need direct fiscal support. For example, an important reason for policy banks to get involved in commercial business is that they have to cross-subsidize policy-related business by commercial business due to insufficient fiscal support. Therefore, the reform of policy banks needs fiscal support. Another type of policy-oriented financial institutions is the policy guarantee institution. At present, China's financing guarantee system is dominated by private guarantee companies which help make financing easier but make it more expensive. Illegal operations are frequently seen because private guarantee companies are not sustainable commercially due to regulation. According to domestic and foreign experiences, the financing guarantee system for SMEs should be dominated by a policy guarantee. Fiscal support is needed to reshape the financing guarantee system whether in the form of institutions or funds. In addition, dividends cut and accelerated risk identification need fiscal support. In 2013, the dividend yield was around 30 percent and the NPL ratio was only 1 percent for listed banks. To reduce absorption of capital and talents into the banking sector and avoid socialization of risks, it is necessary to cut dividends and identify risks sooner, which significantly affects the fiscal revenue and expenditure for the current period and needs fiscal support.

Secondly, supportive reforms need fiscal support. SOEs reform, elimination of soft budget constraints for local governments' financing platforms, and establishing the social safety net are the three major measures supporting financial reforms that need fiscal support. "Top" parent corporation restructuring is a task that we cannot avoid when promoting the capital-management-focused system reform or encouraging SOEs to improve the modern corporate system. In previous rounds of SOE reforms, top parent corporations have carried policy burdens left from the restructuring and listing of its subsidiaries, and the reform of themselves also involves lifting policy burdens imposed on them: this requires fiscal support (Chen, 2014). A precondition for eliminating the implicit guarantee for local governments' financing platforms is to remove the policy burdens on them. This can be ensured by adopting sufficiently strong fiscal policies. The country should increase spending on social security.

Advancing fiscal and taxation system reform

Fiscal and taxation system reforms can support financial reforms in two ways. Firstly, a fiscal and taxation system, under which fiscal resources match the administrative power, should be established. After the outbreak of the global financial crisis, fiscal resources controlled by local governments did not match their excessive administrative power and expenditure responsibilities. A lot of financing platforms were established to redress the mismatch. Due to severe soft budget constraints, they disturb orderly competition between financing entities at the financing market and lead to fast debt increase for local governments. To establish the fiscal and taxation system with matching fiscal resources and administrative power, the first step is to advocate the concept of broad-sensed fiscal deficit in fiscal administration, so as to avoid improper decentralization of the deficit target of the central finance to local governments.

Secondly, fiscal resources, administrative power and expenditure responsibilities should be rationally divided, and the administrative power and expenditure responsibilities of local governments should be reduced. Lastly, the transfer payment system should be further improved to enhance the proportion of general transfer payment and the efficiency of local governments' use of their fiscal power and funds.

The debt financing mechanism of local governments should be regularized. The previous round of debt governance for local governments, which was dominated by financial regulation authorities was not helpful; instead, it worsened the debt structure, led to shadow banking expansion and brought more fiscal and financial risks, rather than curbing rising debt. This was because the governance focused on restraining supply rather than on restraining demand. Local government financing platforms' financing demand generates supply, but supply cannot be restricted effectively. Therefore, local government financing platforms' financing needs should be curbed through fiscal measures. In October 2014, the State Council released the *Opinions of the State Council on Reinforcing the Administration of Local Governments' Debts*, which requires that the government financing function of these platforms be cancelled and local governments' debts be included in budget management. If effectively carried out, this regulation will mostly eliminate implicit guarantee for financial platforms. To ensure its effective implementation, the state should formulate enough supportive fiscal policies. Under the pressure of maintaining steady growth, if fiscal policies are not strong enough, financing platforms will have to keep performing the government financing function or other entities will be established to perform this function.

Promoting financialization of fiscal behaviours

Fiscal behaviours should be optimized by promoting financialization. The enhancement of financial efficiency needs proper fiscal support. An important reason for the difficulty in the financing of small and micro businesses and of technology SMEs is the market failure and mismatch in risk benefit structure between companies and financial institutions. To solve this problem, fiscal support can be embedded in transactions to improve the risk-benefit structure of loans provided by the financial sector to small and micro businesses in two ways: establishing a risk compensation fund, and introducing policy banks.

Financialization of fiscal behaviours has another advantage: optimizing industrial policies. An example is the recently established government guide fund for emerging industries with strategic importance. Investing in the guide fund will produce the best leverage effects to capitalize limited fiscal funds. Financialization of fiscal behaviours can avoid separate administration, decentralized capital and power rent-seeking, and prevent enterprises from applying to different departments for the purpose of arbitrage or from becoming specialized in subsidy application.

Industrial policy adjustment

At present, industrial policies are mostly implemented by local governments mainly through land and taxation policies. Therefore, industrial policy improvement requires three reforms.

First, the GDP should not be the sole criteria to evaluate the governments' performance in economic development. Local governments are keen to formulate industrial policies because once implemented, they can enhance the local GDP in a short period of time and help officials to get a high score in their performance appraisal. Once the GDP is not the sole criteria any more, the industrial policy impulsion of local government will be eradicated at its root.

Second, the land use system reform and market-based allocation of public resources should be encouraged to reduce the implicit subsidy to industrial land and gradually let the market play a bigger role in pricing industrial land. Land planning should be more rational and forward-looking, so as to reduce the room for arbitrage from change of land use and planning.

Third, the fiscal and taxation system should be reformed. Central government should gradually cancel preferential fiscal and taxation policies represented by various types of special funds. Local governments should not provide too many tax benefits. To be specific,

> *all laws, regulations, development planning and regional policies other than dedicated tax laws and regulations shall be drafted neither by breaking the limit of national fiscal and taxation system nor to provide tax benefits; and none preferential fiscal policies for enterprises can be formulated unless upon the approval of the State Council.*

(Lou, 2014)

Other supportive measures

First, the social safety net should be strengthened. Building a social safety net, especially improving the society security system, can play a role in two aspects. On the one hand, it helps to alleviate the concern of regulators about maintaining stability and the timely release of financial risk; on the other hand, it drives industrial transformation and upgrading by facilitating the bankruptcy and merger of companies.

Second, the education and research systems should be reformed. In educational system reform, the current employment orientation of college education towards high salaries in the finance industry should be replaced with more enlightened career guidance. The appraisal method in the research system reform should be improved to encourage cooperation among enterprises, colleges and research institutions and let enterprises play an even more dominant role.

References

Chen, Q. (2014). State-owned Asset Reform Roadmap [N]. *Caijing Magazine*, February 24.

Lou, J. (2014). Deepening Fiscal and Taxation System Reform: Three Major Urgent Tasks [N], *People's Daily*, July 6, 2014.

Minsky, H. (2010). Translated by B. Shi and H. Zhang. *Stabilizing an Unstable Economy: A Perspective From Financial Instability* [M]. Beijing: Tsinghua University Press, January.

9 Internet finance

If banks do not change themselves, we will.

– Jack Ma

Internet finance has promoted financial reforms (Borst, 2014). Booming internet finance will help to make the financial system less "extractive" and transform it to be inclusive. As far as China's current financial system is concerned, the most important functions of internet finance are to promote the withdrawal of financial restraints as a method of incremental reform, and play a role in liberalizing the interest rate, lifting market access control and providing more options for asset substitution. For China's future financial system, and those in advanced economies, its primary importance is that it can flatten and facilitate the deprofessionalization of finance by lowering the threshold for finance. It can maintain the profit margin of the financial sector within a reasonable range and avoid financial expansion compared to the development of other sectors, while promoting financialization in the financial sector.

From township enterprises to internet finance

A consensus has been reached on the great impetus provided by enterprises to economic growth and market-oriented reform on the basis of over three decades' experience of reform and opening up (Qian and Xu, 1993; Chen, Jefferson and Singh, 1992; Zhang and Yi, 1997; Li, 2008; Hua et al., 2009). Township enterprises are major players in market-oriented operations; the development of the non-state-owned sectors has expanded the field and scope of market mechanisms and catalyzed incremental reform. They receive a great deal of surplus rural labour from the agricultural sector (Wu, 2010), and thus promote fast economic growth and market-oriented reform in China.

The influence of township enterprises was not widely recognized until the end of the 1980s and they were constrained by central government when they impacted on the state-owned sector (Zhang and Yi, 1997). Township enterprises are criticized for their small size, low technical content, high consumption, severe pollution and unsustainability (Wu and Zhao, 1987; Research Group of

Experiences in the Sixth Five-Year Plan period of Chinese Academy of Social Sciences, 1986). They competed unfairly with SOEs, due to low tax burdens, for example (Xue, 1986; Su and Wang, 1989), and even caused unfair income distribution (Xia, 1988). The following typifies the governmental view:

> *Since China's non-public economy is basically small commodity economy with private ownership, and in stark construction with the state-owned economy in terms of productivity. Such productivity contrast is reverse of the household income disparity: employees in the state-owned sector with higher productivity earn lower income; while owners of small businesses with more backward productivity make more money. Such a reverse mechanism undoubtedly produces two harmful results. First, instead of promoting technical progress, it encourages and supports backward techniques. From this view, the fast development of township enterprise in recent years is abnormal and at the price of scrambling for raw material sources and markets from SOEs and replacing modernized production means with backward ones. Pervasive small private businesses have become parasites on large-scale production entities (it must be noticed, however, the root of the problem is not the development of township enterprises and private businesses but the functional disorder of SOEs).*
>
> (Wang, 1989, p. 197)

Internet finance has some features in common with township enterprises. First, internet finance is also a facilitator of incremental reform: it plays a positive role in liberalizing the interest rate, relaxes the market access control, provides more options for asset substitution and finally enhances the efficiency of the whole financial system. Internet finance helps to transform the extractive financial system into an inclusive one. Second, like township enterprises, internet finance has many deficiencies. Due to lack of regulation, there are many irregularities in the internet finance sector, especially the peer-to-peer (P2P) industry which has a low-entry threshold. Frauds and unpaid debts are frequent in P2P platforms. According to statistics of Wangdai Zhijia (literally, the Home of Online Lending), as of the end of November 2014, a total of 103 P2P platforms were suspected of being involved in fraud. Many P2P platforms are suspected of being involved in illegal fundraising. The press conference on illegal fundraising in 2014 convened by the State Inter-Ministry Joint Conference Office on Illegal Fundraising, revealed that cases have been filed about illegal fundraising by some P2P platforms and authorities regarded P2P as one of the six major ways to illegally fundraise in recent years.

Finally, creative destruction of internet finance undermines the traditional financial system and is thus controversial. For example, Yu E Bao, a financial product platform launched by Alipay, is regarded as a monetary speculation tool and is condemned as a bloodsucker and parasite bank which sabotages the financial order (Niu, 2014a, 2014b). Some people think internet finance takes advantage of unfair competition (Sheng and Zhang, 2014). This unfair competition mirrors the competition between township enterprises and SOEs which is also unfair, for example, more tax burdens are imposed on SOEs than township enterprises (Xue, 1986; Su and Wang, 1989).

Internet finance and financial incremental reform

Internet finance: a definition

There are some pervasive ideas about internet finance. First, internet finance differs from and undermines traditional finance, and its financial services use modern information technologies represented by the internet, such as big data, social media and search engines (Xie and Zou, 2012; Wu, 2013). This definition takes a technical perspective; in other words, the key criteria for internet finance is that the financial services provided are based on modern information technologies, especially the internet. The second idea further distinguishes internet finance and the financial internet. The financial internet means the financial sector extends to the internet, while internet finance indicates that internet enterprises operating as outsiders to finance begin to provide financial services (Ma, 2013). This definition is based on the nature of the provider of financial services. The decisive feature of internet finance is that the financial services should be provided by outsider internet enterprises using internet technology. In this book, by drawing on the denotative definition method, we can better understand the core connotation of internet finance by defining its major business forms.

In the light of business categories of traditional finance, we classify major business forms of internet finance into six types. The first is the monetary market fund based on the third party, represented by Yu E Bao, which challenges demand deposit services. The second is supply chain finance based on an e-commerce platform providing services to small and micro businesses, represented by the Ali micro loan. The financial services in this category are an important supplement to weak links in banks' loans to small and micro businesses. The updated form is the internet bank, such as WeBank which is operating now and the Ali Bank which is in preparation. The third category of internet finance is the third-party payment platforms, represented by Alipay and Wechat-based payment. They make up for weak links in conventional banks' payment systems. The fourth category of internet finance is peer-to-peer (P2P) lending platforms selling debt securities, presented by PPDAI and LU.com under the Ping An Insurance (Group) Company of China, Ltd. They provide additional debt financing services to small and micro businesses and individuals at the capital market. The fifth category of internet finance is crowd funding platforms represented by Dianmeng Shike (literally, Time for Dream to Come True) and Tmeng.cn. They offer complementary equity financing services to small and micro businesses. The sixth category of internet finance is internet insurance represented by Zhong'an Insurance.

The power of Yu E Bao

The internet monetary market funds, represented by Yu E Bao, are a common form of internet finance and a powerful engine to promote financial reforms.

First, Yu E Bao advances the reform and development of the fund industry. For financial reforms, or for withdrawal of financial restraints, it provides more options for asset substitution to investors. Yu E Bao is an internet monetary market fund co-launched by the Tianhong Fund Management Co Ltd and Alibaba. Under its influence, the threshold for investing in monetary funds or non-monetary funds has been lowered by a large margin; investment cost (such as purchase rates) has dropped significantly, and the liquidity of monetary market fund products is enhanced significantly. Both Yu E Bao and the monetary market fund industry as a whole embrace fast development. Yu E Bao saw its shares reach 534.893 billion with 149 million users at the end of the third quarter of 2014, and became the fourth largest monetary market fund in the world at the end of the second quarter of 2014. The whole monetary market fund industry expands rapidly. The fund shares of the monetary market totalled 1,766.403 billion at end of the third quarter of 2014, 5.81 times that at the end of the second quarter of 2013; and the total number of monetary market funds was 154, 2.08 times that at end of the second quarter of 2013 (Table 9.1).

Second, internet monetary market funds promote interest rate liberalization, and advances to end the interest margin protection for the withdrawal of financial restraints. As an important financial innovation, Yu E Bao enjoys the same liquidity and safety as demand deposits in banks and produces yields ten times those of the demand deposits in banks (Figure 9.1). High yields guide capital from banks to internet monetary market funds like Yu E Bao, and push banks to develop similar monetary market funds. Yu E Bao has the same effect on interest rate liberalization as that of monetary market funds on interest rate liberalization in the US in 1970s.

P2P lending platforms

P2P platforms represent another type of internet finance criticized more bitterly than Yu E Bao. First, they are blamed for disturbing the order of the financial market. P2P platforms expand rapidly with many irregularities because they are beyond the reach of regulation. Many have committed frauds, or have self-insurance and are suspected of being involved in cash pooling and illegal fundraising. Second, China's P2P platforms are not forms of internet finance or like P2P platforms in other countries, but China's P2P platforms provide only internet-based private lending.

Despite all the criticism, P2P platforms have provided great impetus to financial reforms. Due to lack of regulation, P2P platforms swarm into the financial market, creating a lower threshold to the market. According to statistics of Wangdai Zhijia, as of the end of November 2014, the loan balance of all 1,540 P2P platforms has been close to RMB9 billion. They also provide more options for asset substitution to investors.

Internet finance bubbles?

Since 2013, China's internet finance sector has been booming and become oversized compared with that in advanced economies. Some economists see

Table 9.1 Developments of Yu E Bao and the monetary market fund industry

	2013Q2	2013Q3	2013Q4	2014Q1	2014Q2	2014Q3
Number of Yu E Bao users	2.5156 million	13.6788 million	43.03 million	100 million	124 million	149 million
Yu E Bao fund shares (Unit: 100 million)	66.01	556.53	1853.42	5412.75	5741.6	5348.93
Monetary market fund shares (Unit: 100 million)	3,038.7	4,890.06	7,478.71	14,577.7	15,924.37	17,664.03
Proportion of Yu E Bao	2.17%	11.38%	24.78%	37.13%	36.06%	30.28%
Number of monetary market funds	73	78	94	110	131	152

Source: Asset Management Association of China, Tianhong Fund Management Co. Ltd., Alipay.

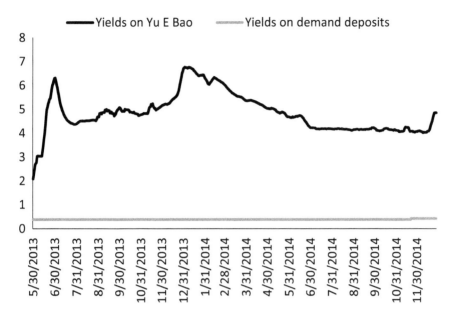

Figure 9.1 Yields on Yu E Bao and demand deposits (%)

in this boom dangerous bubbles which will eventually burst. We venture to disagree with them. China's internet finance develops on a practical foundation and its prosperity cannot be dismissed as "bubbles". First, there is a sound economic and technical foundation for the growth of internet finance. China takes the lead among major economies in the world in applying internet technology to economic development and to people's daily life. As a gauge to measure the use of the internet, the proportion of online retail sales to total retail sales of consumer goods reached 10.6 percent in 2014 and 12.7 percent in 2015 (Figure 9.2).

The share of the internet-based economic sector in the GDP of China was near the top rank in the world in 2013. According to the research of McKinsey Global Institute, this proportion reached 4.4 percent in 2013, higher than that of the US, Germany, France and many other advanced economies (Figure 9.3).

The second reason China's internet finance cannot be dismissed as containing dangerous bubbles is the strong demand. In general, competition is not fierce and efficiency is low in China's financial system, and plenty of financing and investment demands are far from being satisfied. Both internet-based monetary market funds and the P2P platforms create or satisfy corresponding financing or investment demands. The third reason is that China has a sound regulation environment. Generally speaking, Chinese financial regulation authorities are tolerant of internet finance, which is a significant difference between China and advanced economies like the US.

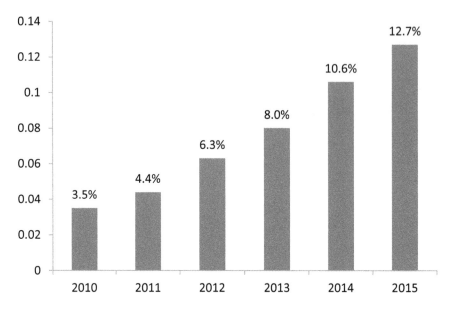

Figure 9.2 The ratio of online retail sales to total retail sales of consumer goods

Even if internet finance were to prove a bubble, its contribution to financial reform cannot be denied. Just as Jack Ma said in 2014, "even if Yu E Bao comes to an end one day when its interest rate becomes the same as banks' deposit rate, it has done its job well".

Internet finance and financialization

Financialization will keep going in China

In recent decades, almost all economies in the world, whether developed or developing ones, have undergone financialization and seen the proportion of credit in the GDP and securitization ratio increase. China has also gone through remarkable financialization after the reform and opening up campaign was launched, and China outperforms most emerging economies in terms of financial depth, but its financialization will continue.

China still lags far behind most advanced economies in terms of financialization, especially when compared with major advanced economies except Germany, indicating a large theoretical potential space for China's further financialization (Table 9.2).

Second, further financialization is strongly demanded. A key reason for increasing financialization is that the financial system provides more financing support to smaller and younger enterprise with insufficient cash flow (Philippon, 2008). At present, the difficulty in financing for small and micro businesses is a prominent

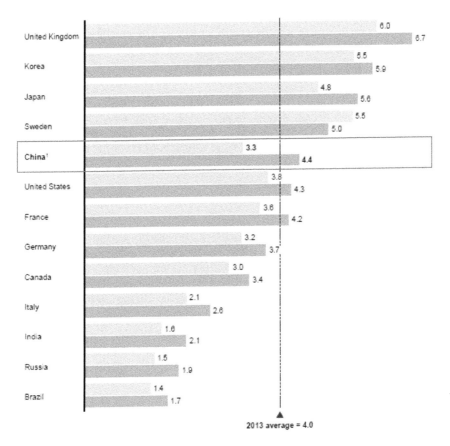

Figure 9.3 The proportion of internet-based economy in the GDP: a global comparison
Source: Woetzel et al. (2014).

problem confronting China's financial system. Among all the reasons for such difficulties, like insufficient competition in the financial system, weak financial infrastructure, the pervasive implicit guarantee (see Chapter 5 for details), insufficient aggregate is a significant one. It should be recognized that the increasing financialization and larger size of the financial sector constitute an important background for effectively solving the financing difficulties of small and micro businesses in advanced economies such as the US, Japan and Britain.

Internet finance: a way to end the ills of financialization?

As discussed previously, financialization has many deficiencies. Excessive financialization may impose excessive financial influence on the economy and enterprises and impede innovation and economic growth. How can these drawbacks be avoided while financialization keeps growing? Internet finance might be a good choice.

Table 9.2 Financialization comparison of major economies

	China	US	Japan	Germany	France	Britain
Proportion of credit from the financial sector in the GDP	191.8%	334.8%	562.50%	174.0%	233.4%	292.8%
Securitization ratio	44.9%	115.5%	61.8%	42.1%	67.9%	115.5%

Note: The proportion of credit from the financial sector in the GDP includes the proportion of domestic credit provided by the financial sector in the GDP and the proportion of central government debts in the GDP. Central government debts are not included in the proportion of domestic credit provided by the financial sector in the GDP. The proportion of central government debts in China's GDP in 2012 is estimated by authors.

Source: World Bank, calculation by authors.

Internet finance is a pattern of finance based on modern information technologies associated with the internet such as big data, social media and search engines. Compared with traditional finance, internet finance provides a possibility of deprofessionalization, or making ordinary people financers. Driven by technological progress such as big data technology, internet finance considerably lowers the entry threshold to the financial sector and realizes functional rather than sectoral financialization. It consistently satisfies the demands of the real economy.

Deprofessionalization and functional financialization have two effects. First, they reinforce competition and eliminate possible excess earnings in the financial sector, thus reducing the siphonic effect on capital, talents and other innovation factors. Second, they prevent interest groups from forming and restrain the bad effects of the financial sector on economic governance.

References

Borst, N. (2014). Internet Finance Drives China Banking Reform. *https://piie.com/blogs/china-economic-watch/internet-finance-drives-china-banking-reform*, July 2.

Chen, K., Jefferson, G. and Singh, I. (1992). Lessons From China's Economic Reform [J]. *Journal of Comparative Economics*, Vol. 6, No. 2, pp. 201–225.

Hua, S., Luo, X., Zhang, X. and Bian, Y. (2009). Real Reason of China's Miracle: A Review of the Three Decades' Reform and Opening up [J]. *China Business Magazine* (first half of the month), Vol. 1, pp. 22–25.

Li, Y. (2008). Mind Emancipation, Theoretical Innovation and Economic Reform – To Commemorate the 30th Anniversary of Reform and Opening up [J]. *Journal of Peking University on Philosophy and Social Sciences*, Vol. 9, pp. 5–9.

Ma, J. (2013). Financial Sector Needs a Spoiler [N]. *People's Daily*, June 21.

Niu, W. (2014a). Yu E Bao as a Bloodsucker [Z]. *http://blog.sina.com.cn/niuwenxin*, January 24.

Niu, W. (2014b). Yu E Bao Should be Abolished. *http://blog.sina.com.cn/niuwenxin*, February 21.

Philippon, T. (2008). *The Evolution of the US Financial Industry From 1860 to 2007: Theory and Evidence* [R]. NBER Working Paper No. 13405.

Qian, Y. and Xu, C. (1993). Why China's Economic Reforms Differ: The M-Form Hierarchy and Entry/Expansion of the Non-State Sector [J]. *The Economics of Transition*, Vol. 1, No. 2, pp. 135–170, June.

Research Group of Experiences in the Sixth Five-Year Plan Period of Chinese Academy of Social Sciences (1986). Retrospect of and Reflection on Economic Development and Reform During the Sixth Five-Year Plan Period [J]. *Social Sciences in China*, Vol. 2, pp. 3–27.

Sheng, S. and Zhang, X. (2014). Yu E Bao and Deposit Reserve Management [N]. *Chinese Financial Times*, March 19.

Su, N. and Wang, C. (1989). Establishing an Economic Mechanism for Fair Competition Among Enterprises [J]. *Reform*, Vol. 6, pp. 156–159.

Wang, Z. (1989). A Rethink of Socialist Economic Reform Pattern – An Analysis of the Fundamental Reason for Macro-Control Failure at the Current Stage in China [J]. *Studies on Marxism*, Vol. 2, pp. 195–214.

Woetzel, J., Orr, G., Lau, A., Chen, Y., Chui, M., Chang, E., Seong, J. and Qiu, A. (2014). China's Digital Transformation: The Internet's Impact on Productivity and Growth. *McKinsey Global Institute Report*, July.

Wu, J. (2010). *Course of Study on Contemporary Economic Reform of China* [M]. Shanghai: Shanghai Yuandong Press.

Wu, J. and Zhao, R. (1987). The Dual Pricing System in China's Industry. *Journal of Comparative Economics*, Vol. 11, No. 3, pp. 309–318, September.

Wu, X. (2013). Asset and Liability Management of Commercial Banks in Market-Based Financial Reform [J]. *Journal of Financial Research*, Vol. 12, pp. 1–15.

Xia, X. (1988). On Income Distribution Inequality [J]. *Shanghai Journal of Economics*, Vol. 6, pp. 53–56.

Xie, P. and Zou, C. (2012). Research of Internet Finance Model [J]. *Journal of Financial Research*, Vol. 12, pp. 11–22.

Xue, M. (1986). Retrospect and Prospect of China's Economic System Reform [J]. *China Economic System Reform*, Vol. 1, pp. 16–20.

Zhang, W. and Yi, G. (1997). China's Gradual Reform: A Historical Perspective [A]. In *China's Economic Growth and Transition* [M], edited by C.A. Tisdell and J.C. Chai. New York: Nova Science Publishers, Inc.

Index

Note: Page numbers in italic indicate a figure or table on the corresponding page.

Liu, X. 149
Liu, Y. 84–5
loan rates: calculation of 113–15, *114*; "golden rule" of 112–13
loan-to-deposit ratio regulation 91–5, *92–4*, 118–19
Lou, J. 35, 167
low-efficiency financial systems 65–7, *67*
Lucas, Robert 49–50

Ma, J. 168
Mao, Zedong 1, 108
market access for banking system 145–7
marketization: extractive-inclusive dimension and 21–2; secondary role of 16
Minsky, H. 161
monetary market fund industry 171, *172*
monetary policies: financial inefficiency and 127–8; stabilization of 159–60
Mourougane, A. 4
Mukunda, G. 5, 36, 63, 67, 69, 71, 73
multi-layer capital market 147–51
"multiplier effect", in re-allocation 54–6
Murdock, K. 78, 89, *90*
Murphy, K. 58–9, *69*

National Development and Reform Commission (NDRC) 148
net interest margin 81–3, *82*
New Palgrave Dictionary of Economics, The 20
Niu, X. 41, *42*
non-financial sector: banking system *vs.* 120–2, *121*; development of 151–3; profit proportion of 34–6, *35–6*; ROE of 39–40, *40*; in US 67–8, *68*
non-performing loan (NPL) ratio 83, *84*
Notice of the People's Bank of China on the Administration of Asset Liability Ratio of Commercial Banks released 91
not overdeveloped, overdevelopment *vs.* 27–8
not underdeveloped, underdevelopment *vs.* 27–8

one-dimensional model, of financial reform 9–11, *10*
Opinions of the State Council on Reinforcing the Administration of Local Governments' Debts 166

Oulton, Nicholas 56
ownership structure, insufficient competition and 115

Palley, T. 20
Pan, G. 81, 84–5
Pan, Y. 89
Panizza, U. 7
peer-to-peer (P2P) lending platforms 169, 171
People's Daily 3–4
per capita income: of bank *vs.* non-bank employees 44, *45*; of bank *vs.* non-bank executives 45, *46*; of financial *vs.* all employees 43–4, *43–4*
Phelps, Edmund S. 8
Philippon, T. 56, 68–9
policies, competition for 5
policy-oriented financial institution reform 156–8
predatory lending 25
Price of Wall Street Power, The (Mukunda) 69–70, 73
primary allocation 53–4, 56
profit proportion: Chinese banks in Fortune Global 500 36–9, *38*; financial institutions *vs.* all businesses 34–6, *35–7*; of financial sector 29–32; international comparison 39, *39*; listed banks *vs.* all listed companies 32–4, *33*
profits: competition for 5; financial sector 31–2
public sector, as "extractive" 8

Qian, M. 73–4
Qiang, L. 41
Question of Independence and Initiative within the United Front, The (Mao) 108

Rajan, R. 3–4
real estate sector: downside risk in 133; as "extractive" 8; implicit guarantees for 126–7
re-allocation: "multiplier effect" or "leakage effect" 54–6; overview of 53–4
reform paths, for two-dimensional model 13–17, *14*, *17*
registration system reform 150–1
rent distribution 80
research system reform 167

Taylor & Francis eBooks

Helping you to choose the right eBooks for your Library

Add Routledge titles to your library's digital collection today. Taylor and Francis ebooks contains over 50,000 titles in the Humanities, Social Sciences, Behavioural Sciences, Built Environment and Law.

Choose from a range of subject packages or create your own!

Benefits for you

» Free MARC records
» COUNTER-compliant usage statistics
» Flexible purchase and pricing options
» All titles DRM-free.

REQUEST YOUR FREE INSTITUTIONAL TRIAL TODAY

Free Trials Available
We offer free trials to qualifying academic, corporate and government customers.

Benefits for your user

» Off-site, anytime access via Athens or referring URL
» Print or copy pages or chapters
» Full content search
» Bookmark, highlight and annotate text
» Access to thousands of pages of quality research at the click of a button.

eCollections – Choose from over 30 subject eCollections, including:

Archaeology	Language Learning
Architecture	Law
Asian Studies	Literature
Business & Management	Media & Communication
Classical Studies	Middle East Studies
Construction	Music
Creative & Media Arts	Philosophy
Criminology & Criminal Justice	Planning
Economics	Politics
Education	Psychology & Mental Health
Energy	Religion
Engineering	Security
English Language & Linguistics	Social Work
Environment & Sustainability	Sociology
Geography	Sport
Health Studies	Theatre & Performance
History	Tourism, Hospitality & Events

For more information, pricing enquiries or to order a free trial, please contact your local sales team:
www.tandfebooks.com/page/sales

Routledge
Taylor & Francis Group

The home of
Routledge books

www.tandfebooks.com

For Product Safety Concerns and Information please contact our EU
representative GPSR@taylorandfrancis.com
Taylor & Francis Verlag GmbH, Kaufingerstraße 24, 80331 München, Germany